Jackson & Perkins®
ROSE
COMPANIONS

Growing Annuals, Perennials, Bulbs, Shrubs, and Vines with Roses

STEPHEN SCANNIELLO

COOL SPRINGS PRESS
A Division of Thomas Nelson Publishers
Since 1798

www.coolspringspress.net

Dedication

For Mom

Acknowledgements

With thanks to the following members of the
New Orleans Old Rose Society—Diane Wilensky, Peggy Martin,
and Leo Watermeier—and to Carolyn and Don McGavock,
Cottage Garden Nurseries, Carriere, MS, Dr. Malcolm Manners,
Florida Citrus Institute, Lakeland, FL, Gregg Lowery,
Vintage Gardens Nursery, Sebastapol, CA, Tom Carruth,
Weeks Roses, Rich and Heidi Hesselein, Pleasant Run Nursery,
Allentown, NJ, Mike Shoup, Antique Rose Emporium, Independence,
TX, Sue Feldbaum, Brooklyn, NY, Marjorie Rosen,
Dan and Esty Brodsky, all of my clients, Jenny Andrews, T.J, Kim,
Owen Korth, and my family, especially Laura and Dana.

TABLE OF CONTENTS

INTRODUCTION

THERE'S A SECRET ABOUT ROSES I'D LIKE TO SHARE WITH YOU. While they're often grown all by themselves in isolation from other plants, they make good garden plants mixed in with other shrubs, perennials, annuals, and bulbs. That's what this book is about. It's not about how to *grow* roses, but about how to create a garden *with* roses, how to use roses in the landscape, and what you can plant with them—whether your garden is the size of a container or you have several acres to spare. Breaking away from the tradition of growing roses in isolated beds, this book is about a style of growing roses that will allow you to focus less on spraying and coddling, and more on the beauty of the roses in combination with other plants.

My Grandfather's Roses

My earliest memories of roses are from my grandfather's garden in northern New Jersey. He ordered his roses each spring from Jackson & Perkins in Newark, New York. The climbers 'Golden Showers' and 'Blaze' were trained to his white clapboard fence, his prize-winning hybrid teas—'Crimson Glory', 'Eclipse', and 'Garden Party'—grew in their own bed alongside the patio. My grandmother was allowed to edge this bed with white alyssum and portuloca, but that was the extent of the other plants allowed in his rose garden. Years later, I carried on the family tradition of growing roses in this manner while I was curator of the Cranford Rose Garden at the Brooklyn Botanic Garden. Except for an occasional viola or iris seedling, which found its way in from the nearby compost heap, this classic garden contained roses and nothing else. Both of these gardens were typical of the traditional, and most popular, way to grow roses.

When I left the botanic garden and struck out on my own as a garden designer, I began learning about other plants that could be grown with roses. I still loved roses, but I had tired of growing them in the formal style. I discovered an endless bounty of plants to choose from to create combinations that show off both the roses and their companions. Now, rather than focusing on raising masses of exhibition quality blooms, my goals are to have roses worthy of the garden as well as the vase. I still grow gorgeous roses, but the gardens around them are interesting as well. I'm not turning my back on the traditional approach; there will always be a place for the formal display. However, I have found the new approach more challenging and, from this gardener's point of view, more satisfying.

This 'First Kiss' rose is even more beautiful complemented by the blue borage.

The Benefits of Rose Companions

It's not difficult to grow roses in a garden-friendly fashion. In fact, you'll find it more enjoyable. It's important to pay attention to the cultural requirements of the companions, as well as their growth habits. If planned properly, you'll discover that the sins of roses—black spot, mildew, as well as other pests that are so obvious in the traditional monoculture style of rose garden—will be less evident in the garden. Companion plants can serve as a screen to block out these ailments, and you'll discover that with proper pruning, the roses will survive and continue to thrive. When the roses are between bloom cycles or pruned to encourage new blooms, the companions become the colorful part of the garden display. An added plus is that some perennials and herbs are credited with attracting beneficial insects and repelling bad ones.

Roses grown in this fashion are now an integral part of the four-season garden. Evergreens such as boxwoods or yews add a formal touch, as well as color for the winter garden, while the rose bushes are dormant and at their least attractive. Spring bulbs, such as tulips, fritillaria, camassia, and glory-of-the-snow, add early color and, if situated properly, will complement the newly emerging foliage of the roses as they break dormancy. Grey, blue, and green foliage of herbs such as catmint, lavender, and germander work well with all colors of roses, and spiky perennials such as agastache and salvia along with summer bulbs add a wonderful fragrance to the garden while the roses are between bloom cycles. Asters and chrysanthemums can be used to hide the inevitable naked knees of the hybrid teas in autumn as they go into their final cycle of bloom.

Beauty Beyond Flowers

Roses have many pleasing attributes that contribute to the garden in all seasons. Species roses, especially North American natives, have both decorative hips and interesting cane colors. Rose hips range in color from near black to ruby red, and are of varied shapes and texture. One native species in particular, *Rosa setigera*, has a wonderful arching plum-colored cane that is especially noticeable with a snowy backdrop.

Rose foliage should not be overlooked either. The colors of new leaves range from intense plum red to bluish green depending on the types of roses grown. I underplant *Rosa glauca*, also known as the red-leaved rose, with tulips 'Shirley' (white streaked with purple) and 'Queen of the Night' (dark purple). Both of these tulips bloom as the grey-red rose foliage emerges from winter dormancy, creating a wonderful color com-

The new leaves of *Rosa glauca* make a lovely color combination with tulips 'Shirley' and 'Queen of the Night.'

bination. Tea and China roses sprout new foliage of a rich red color that can be easily complemented with perennials and shrubs.

The fragrance of a rose garden can be enhanced with other plants also. It's a magical moment during a full moon on a June evening, wandering through the garden as 'Mme. Plantier' and 'Mme. Hardy' are in peak bloom, surrounded by the airy umbels of the perennial herb *Valeriana officinalis* infusing the evening air with its fragrance of fresh baby powder.

There are even roses with fragrant foliage. *Rosa primula* and *Rosa eglanteria* (the eglantine rose) exude distinctive foliar scents. You can have fun with rose prickles as well, most notably the redwing rose, with red, nearly translucent prickles that emerge with each new cane—creating a glow like red rubies in your garden.

Roses have architectural value as well. Arching canes of ramblers and climbers loaded with hips add curves and color during the winter. A pillar smothered in 'New Dawn' rising above a bed of perennials adds a new level of sophistication to your garden, while festoons of ramblers can be created to hang with elegance across the garden bed. Walls and fences can be easily decorated with climbers and shrub roses, creating a colorful and fragrant embellishment for your home. These characteristics, as well as the variations in growth habits from rose class to class,

create varied opportunities for using roses in the garden.

Using this Book

This book will describe the habits of roses from different classes to help you decide how to use roses to enhance your garden, big or small, and show you how to use them in combination with other plants. Basic rose culture will be reviewed, but the emphasis will be on designing with roses. Perennials, annuals, spring and summer bulbs, shrubs, vines, and even trees will be discussed as companions. And finally, the book will describe in detail some of the gardens I've created that you might want to adapt to your own landscape. There will be plenty of opportunities to explore the many ways to use roses and to create wonderful gardens of your own.

My own garden continues to be both my source of inspiration and my laboratory. As I work in my garden, I often think of my grandfather and his roses. His inspiration is also there as I wander through my mixed collection of plants. I thank him for passing on his passion for gardening, and can only hope that he would understand my way of growing his favorite flower. I would like to pass this passion on to you, to take you and your roses out of the rose garden and into the mixed garden where they belong.

*Who would have thought the Queen of Flowers
would be asked to join the masses, living amongst
pansies, tulips, salvia, and phlox?*

GARDEN QUALITIES OF ROSES

Types of Roses

Designing with roses. Who would have thought the Queen of Flowers would be asked to join the masses, living amongst pansies, tulips, salvia, and phlox? Though such a life doesn't really sound so bad, does it? If you're going to take your roses out of the rose garden and bring them back into the mixed garden, it will be helpful to know your options, especially if you plan to expand your palette of roses and learn more about their unusual colors, diverse growth habits, and varied blooming times. There are many rose classes to explore, treasures to unearth in each as well as duds to avoid.

As you begin exploring the intriguing world of roses you'll soon see that while there is a rose for every garden, not *every* rose is for every garden. Each spring the nurseries and garden centers overflow gorgeous roses. Buy me, try me, plant me—as if the roses were going to simply jump from the nursery into your garden and then grow with perfection. We're all bound to learn that some roses do best if they're left at the garden centers, while others, suited for our regions and growing conditions, will give us endless joy and beauty as they bloom and blend in unison and harmony with our gardens.

Not all roses bloom at the same time during the gardening season. Some bloom only in the spring, others blossom continuously till winter. Their growth habits are diverse, ranging from miniature varieties with flowers so small that a dozen cut blooms could comfortably fit in a teacup, to rampant climbers that swallow barns, trees, and anything else in their path. Between these two extremes there are roses that will fit the design of your garden.

What are old garden roses and how do they fit your scheme? Can you combine old with new? Which roses are good for your climate? These are all important questions, and the answers provide useful information for planning a garden. Increasing your knowledge of roses to include all types will make working in your mixed garden or border even more interesting and fun.

Species roses, gallicas, hybrid teas, climbers—these are all examples of rose classes. Each has its unique personality while at the same time having the ability to complement each other and the many different plants in the garden as well. In designing a garden, it's vital to learn how different roses grow—how high they'll reach, how wide they'll spill, when they bloom, and when they bare their hips.

The most practical way to approach roses

Freed from regimentation in old-style rose gardens, roses in the mixed border mingle happily with agapanthus, campanula, and other companions.

is from a design point of view. It is easy to start by dividing roses into two major categories: those that bloom once a season, or once-blooming roses; and those that bloom continually, or ever-blooming roses. Each of these categories has many roses to enjoy and explore, with practical uses adaptable for all gardens. Three important factors to take into account when planning a new garden or putting together an order for new roses are these: Is this rose suitable for my climate? How does this rose grow? When does this rose bloom?

Once-Blooming Roses

Lilacs get away with it. So do azaleas, forsythia, camellias and other once-blooming shrubs. One burst of glory and they're done until next year. Bravo! No one seems to mind this, so why not apply the same sentiments to roses? We expect so much from roses, cultivating them to bloom from spring to winter. For years we pushed aside the once-blooming roses for the newer, bigger, better, continually blooming varieties. We gave the longer blooming roses our full attention until it was noticed that some of the once-blooming types, left on their own and neglected, seemed healthier.

So now, some (not all) of the attention has turned back to the once-blooming varieties. They make great garden plants, have interesting features, and produce beautiful roses. In fact, the once-blooming types display some of the most beautiful roses known. There's a great deal of information to discover about these beauties and how they too can be a part of your garden. So let's get reacquainted with these classics. Except for a few summertime blooming varieties, spring is their peak season. Let's start with the earliest bloomers, the original wild roses—the species roses.

Species Roses

The species class of roses is vast, full of many different types or varieties. In the world of botany, a species is defined as a plant that will produce exactly itself from a seed collected from that plant. In the gardening world, these are defined as easy-to-grow plants.

Species roses are as easy to identify on paper as they are in the garden. They're always labeled with the word *Rosa* (which is the genus name for roses), followed by a Latin name that is either descriptive of the plant or commemorates its place of origin or benefactor (which is the species name). Some names would seem to require a doctorate in plant taxonomy to pronounce, but hopefully there's a common name attached as well. Here's a good example: *Rosa pimpinellifolia* (give up yet?) is a beautiful white species rose originally found growing wild in central Asia. The species name means the foliage resembles another plant, *Pimpinella*, which can be confusing if you've never seen this other plant. But I love the rose and its common name, Scotch rose. There's absolutely no good taxonomic reason for the common name since the original plant is not native to Scotland, but Scotch rose is so much easier to say.

Another example of a species rose is *Rosa setigera,* a native species with tiny hairs on the leaves. The Latin name is descriptive of the leaves. The problem is with the common name. Depending on whom you ask, *Rosa setigera* is the prairie rose, the Detroit rose, or the Michigan rose. Common names can be problematic, changing over time or from region to region, causing confusion between gardeners. So, try to learn the Latin names, they are usually more consistent.

There is a great variety of species roses to choose from, of different colors, growth habits, and temperature hardiness. Species roses occur naturally in the wild throughout the northern hemisphere north of the tropics in all types of situations: hot, dry, cool, wet, and even up into the arctic zone. Within this vast group of roses, there's one common characteristic—the flowers are simple. This means that the petal count is either four or five to eight maximum. The colors range from pure white to blood red, flower sizes are various, many are extremely fragrant, while some fragrances are not very pleasant. Many species roses also produce showy hips, the fruit-like capsule that encloses the seeds of the rose. The hips attract birds to the garden as well as having ornamental value.

There's a wide range of growth habits

among species roses. Tall arching shrubs, long-caned climbers, and compact upright shapes are found among these wild roses. In general they make good garden plants, however there are a few with a tendency to grow out of bounds through root suckering and self-seeding.

Some examples of those with a shrubby habit of short to medium height, ideal for the middle of garden borders and blooming at the beginning of the season, include many of our North American native roses. *Rosa carolina, Rosa arkansana, Rosa virginiana,* and *Rosa californica* are some of the pink-flowering native species. Many foreign species have been in our gardens for a very long time. Included are some of the most beautiful spring blooming bush types ideal for the middle of the border: *Rosa pimpinellifolia* 'Altaica' (white), *Rosa davurica* (pink), *Rosa hugonis,* or Father Hugo's rose (yellow), and *Rosa foetida bicolor,* the Austrian copper rose (yellow and orange, plus the fragrance of linseed oil or dirty socks). Ideal for the rear of the border and tall enough to be trained onto a wall or fence are *Rosa roxburghii normalis,* burr rose (pink), *Rosa glauca,* red leaf rose (pink), *Rosa moyesii* 'Geranium' (blood red), *Rosa primula,* incense rose; and *Rosa eglanteria,* sweetbriar rose.

And finally those with growth habits to be reckoned with, best if let loose (and left alone) to grow up through trees or over fences, to cover stone walls, or to spill down embankments: *Rosa moschata nepalensis,* Himalayan musk rose (white), *Rosa banksiae,* Lady Banks rose (yellow), *Rosa setigera,* prairie rose (pink), *Rosa bracteata,* Macartney rose

(white, also known as the fried egg rose in Bermuda), *Rosa wichurana,* memorial rose (white), and *Rosa sempervirens,* evergreen rose (white, evergreen in warm climates).

Species roses are generally the first roses to come into bloom in the garden. In the warmest climates, *Rosa banksiae* is the first to bloom, in some parts of our country as early as February. Up north, during my tenure as curator of roses in the Cranford Rose Garden in Brooklyn, *Rosa carolina* signaled the beginning of the rose season on May first, every year. In my southern New Jersey garden, the first to bloom is *Rosa primula.* Of the once-blooming species, there are two that are late in the season: *Rosa wichurana* and *Rosa setigera,* both aggressive growers and rambling types that bloom about a month after the modern roses have peaked.

European Old Garden Roses

This large group of once-blooming roses is known, among rose collectors, as European old garden roses. They all have their origins in Europe, Asia, Northern Africa, and the Middle East. Nearly all of the varieties grow best if they are exposed annually to a cold winter. The following rose classes make up this group: gallica, damask, alba, centifolia, moss, hybrid China, and hybrid Bourbon.

Within these classes are many exceptional rose varieties that look best within the informality of a mixed border. The combination of foliage textures, pastel flower colors, and delectable fragrances allow these historical roses to be mated with just about any perennial, herb, annual, or shrub.

Gallica

When I think of gallica roses, I think of sprawling plants, dark crinkly green foliage, and freely suckering growth habits. An old gravesite I came across in southern New Jersey is completely covered with the medieval variety *Rosa gallica oficianalis*, the apothecary's rose, sprouting from the roots of the original plant of nearly a century ago. This growth style is typical of the many varieties of this class, especially when they are grown on their own roots.. The majority of the gallicas are medium height shrubs excellent for the middle of borders. 'Complicata', with its cerise pink five-petaled blooms, is a favorite of mine for training onto pillars. This variety creates a second display in the autumn, with pumpkin-orange hips that hold on through the winter. The burgundian rose, *Rosa burgundica*, is a very short-growing shrub with miniature-sized blooms of pinkish-purple. This rose was a popular miniature rose in many American colonial gardens.

The gallica class contains many useful and beautiful varieties, all excellent garden roses for the colder zones of our country. I've seen them growing in southern California and southeast Texas, but they look so sad in that heat. Gallica roses do much better as garden plants in regions where the winters are cold and spring is wet.

The roses produced by the varieties of the gallica class are wonderfully fragrant. Their petal counts range from single roses to densely packed blossoms. The blooming period is near the beginning of the rose season and, depending on how quickly the temperatures warm up, can last as long as two months.

Damask Roses

Inhale the fragrance of a damask rose, and you'll know what a rose should smell like.

COMPANIONS FOR GALLICA ROSES

As the gallica roses flop and sprawl from the weight of their large flowers, strong companions should be there to catch them. Silver, chartreuse, and lavender are beautiful colors to consider when searching for suitable companions, each highlighting the colors of these old roses while making a statement of its own.

For chartreuse, there are several low-growing plants from which to choose. *Euphorbia amygdaloides robbiae*, or 'Robb's Spurge', is stunning under the red-purple, very fragrant rose 'Charles de Mills'. *Alchemilla mollis*, or lady's mantle and *Lysimachia nummularia* 'Aurea', or creeping jenny, are both superb ground covers that will light up the garden when planted as companions for the rich pink and magenta tones of these old-fashioned roses.

Lavender 'Hidcote', with its intense violet-lavender flowers and gray-green foliage, offers a perfect blend for gallicas, especially the two-toned pink 'Empress Josephine', a sprawling variety that creates a close encounter of fragrance and color when grown in a bed edged with 'Hidcote'.

Heady fragrances from these old fashioned roses stir memories of old fashioned perfume. Still used today as a major ingredient in rose oil production, these fragrant roses are produced on long arching branches that tend to fall over from the weight of the large flowers.

'Kazanlik', the variety grown in Bulgaria for attar production, is a more upright variety, growing tall and wide—ideal for the rear of the border. 'La Ville de Bruxelles' is a good middle border shrub, with nice smooth canes. 'Leda', also known as the painted damask rose, is a lax shrub for the middle border with red rose buds that open to nearly pure white roses.

Certain varieties of damask roses could be coaxed to climb with a bit of persuasion. 'Mme. Hardy', a popular garden hybrid usually planted in the middle of the border, looks especially beautiful when her bristly lax canes covered in green-eyed blooms are tied around a pillar.

Damask roses tolerate drier conditions, but appreciate a colder climate with ample spring rain. They begin blooming as the species roses are peaking and continue through the peak bloom of the hybrid tea roses. The color range of these fragrant roses is from pure white to rich pink, with a few stripes and mottled variations in between. One oddity of this class is the repeat blooming, and very old, 'Autumn Damask'.

Alba Roses

Albas are rugged looking roses, easily identified by their rough blue-green foliage and baby powder fragrance, which is quite a contrast. Some of the tallest shrub roses are found in the alba rose class. The oldest of this class, 'Alba Maxima' and 'Alba Semi-Plena', both pure white, become huge arching shrubs if left to grow on their own. 'Félicité Parmentier', a blush hybrid from the mid-eighteenth century, is a beautiful full shrub, balanced enough to be grown on its own to show off its shape. 'Mme. Legras de St. Germain' (white) and 'Königin von Dänemark' (pink) are two French hybrids with lax canes, giving them versatility as either middle of the border shrubs or excellent choices for pillars.

Like most of the European old garden roses, the albas grow better in cooler climates, preferably those allowing good winter dormancy and plenty of spring rain. The French hybrids begin to bloom as the tulips and narcissus are fading and last until the summer heat has set in. The blooms of the alba class range in size from the large blushing white roses of 'Great Maiden's Blush' to the small clusters of 'Pompon Blanc Parfait'. All alba roses are wonderfully fragrant.

Centifolia Roses

These roses are so densely packed with petals that they are deserving of their nickname cabbage roses. The plants are upright, medium-sized shrubs until they bloom, when the weight of the fragrant roses causes them to sprawl. The prototype for this group, often seen in the paintings of the Dutch Masters, is 'Cabbage Rose', one that I continually find growing abandoned in old cemeteries and around farm houses in the hills of northern New Jersey. A truly unique variety in this class is 'Cristata', also known as 'Chapeau de

Napoleon'. This name is descriptive of the closed flower bud with extended frilly sepals resembling the feathers on the little general's hat. There are several dwarf varieties in the centifolia class as well. 'Spong', 'Rose de Meaux', and 'Petite de Hollande' produce the smallest flowers of this group. 'Petite de Hollande' is not necessarily a miniature plant, and it tends to sprawl, so don't grow this one too close to the edge of the garden bed.

Centifolias are most attractive when grown in cool climates so they are good choices for the coldest zones. Due to the thick petals and dense blooms, cabbage roses tend to rot on the stem if the air is too humid, if your garden is close to the sea, or if they are exposed to continual fog and mist. The color ranges are from pure white to purple-reds, including some striped cultivars as well. Depending on how long the cool spring days last, the centifolias can remain in bloom for about a month, usually starting soon after the species roses have peaked.

Moss Roses

My niece came to me one day, totally frustrated because her roses were completely covered in aphids. She had spent the morning, to no avail, trying to scrape them off. What she thought was an insect infestation turned out to be the identifying characteristic of the moss rose class—soft, sticky, and fragrant aphid-like fuzz. Each and every flower bud and pedicle is completely covered in this moss-like coating. Planted where the sun catches the glow of this resinous growth, the newly emerging flower buds sparkle like jewels in the garden.

Moss roses are known to have existed in North American gardens since the colonial era, and in Europe much earlier. The origins of this unique group are not clear, except that the oldest known varieties were naturally occurring sports of two different rose types—centifolia and damask roses. Moss roses with origins from the centifolia roses have a soft green moss, while those from the damask roses tend to have a more bristly and darker shaded moss.

The oldest existing cultivar, 'Communis', also known as the common pink moss—is still available today and an excellent shrub to use in the middle of the perennial border. 'Communis' has a nice upright growth, typical of most moss roses, with an arching habit caused by the weight of the flowers as they grow and open.

There are many varieties of moss roses to choose from today, and there are a handful that are short and suitable for the front of the border, most of which are repeat blooming types (see "Moss Roses" under "Ever-Blooming Roses" below). There are some that will grow very tall, lending themselves to training on a pillar or against a wall. Since they're very prickly, this will be a painful procedure. I often use 'William Lobb', a purple hybrid, as a pillar plant, or I'll allow it to scramble into evergreen hedges.

Moss roses don't grow well in the combination of excessive heat and humidity. Like the centifolias, they have a problem with blooms rotting on the stems in areas of high humidity. They do well in northern California, away from the coast, and throughout the upper Midwest and northeast.

The moss-like coating on the buds and stems of the moss rose add texture and visual interest to the garden.

Hybrid China and Hybrid Bourbon Roses

These two classes of roses have long been overlooked and misunderstood. During the nineteenth century they were the hottest commodities in the rose world. Originating as the first generation of seedlings that resulted from crossing China and Bourbon roses with damask, gallica, centifolia, and alba roses, these hybrids were the rage of the Victorian era. The goal of plant breeders at that time was to create a new race of large-flowered, ever-blooming roses. Well, that eventually happened, but this first generation—very vigorous shrubs with a once-blooming habit and fragrance—were loved by all gardeners and florists of that time. As the twentieth century neared, these lanky hybrids were pushed aside for new ever-blooming varieties.

Both hybrid China and hybrid Bourbon are important classes that contain some excellent garden varieties for all climates, providing great colors, fragrances, textures, and growth habits. Both groups are similar in habit—vigorous shrub roses with long canes suitable for the rear of the border, for training onto fences, or wrapping around pillars.

'Fantin-Latour' is a popular variety, a large shrub with delicate pink roses. Another, a favorite of mine, is 'Paul Ricault', a large flowered crimson-carmine rose from 1845.

This makes a wonderful fountain of blooms when trained to a pillar. 'Mme. Plantier' is pure white and lights up my evening garden during the full moon in June. For the middle border, I would recommend two hybrid Chinas: 'Shailer's Provence'—an old favorite with crepe-like pink petals; and 'The Bishop' (recently re-named 'Velours Episcopal'), a crimson rose that fades to purple.

Miniature Roses

The oldest known miniature rose is the burgundian rose, *Rosa burgundica*, a member of the gallica class. Also known as 'Pompon de Bourgogne', this once-blooming rose produces tiny purple-pink blossoms on a freely suckering plant that may attain a height of two feet. This rose has been dated back as far as the seventeenth century. Not as old, but still old, are two other once-blooming miniatures. 'Rose de Meaux', small pink button flowers on a four-foot plant, and 'Spong', also pink and of dwarf habit, are both cold- loving centifolia roses not requiring too much space. Prune in the same manner you would a larger centifolia. Each summer remove old wood if the plant is crowded, and keep the shrubs free of clutter.

Ramblers

Climbing roses are among the most versatile of all the rose groups. A pillar smothered with roses, nestled in a bed of perennials, or a wall covered with a tangle of roses and clematis raises the gardens to new heights. Climbing roses are not true vines, but instead reach higher places in the garden by scrambling and clambering over structures and other plants.

There are no tendrils or twining canes to keep the roses in place. The prickles do assist them, but it's necessary to tie the canes to keep the rose permanently climbing. The most famous of all the ramblers is the rose that launched Jackson & Perkins, 'Dorothy Perkins', the ubiquitous, small-flowered, large-clustered, pink rambling rose.

Ramblers grow many long canes annually from the base of the plant as well as from points along the older canes. Most of the blooms are produced from wood that grew the previous season. Well adapted to most climates, ramblers are found in the coldest zones as well as the warmest. Ramblers start blooming early in the season and continue until about midway through the summer.

Ever-Blooming Roses

In June, throughout the northeast, they're everywhere. Hybrid teas are on display, climbing roses are spilling off of porches, and shrub roses are scenting the air with their new and exotic fragrances. There is nothing more alluring than a garden overflowing with roses at the peak of bloom. At that point the focus is on the flowers. For most people, the first encounter with any rose begins with the sighting of a captivating multi-petaled blossom, and no sooner do we ascertain the presence of a rose than the encounter progresses to burying one's nose in the soft fragrant petals—from one ever-blooming rose to the next. After a long hot summer, the roses lure you back to the garden and you do it again—glorying in the fragrance. Only, this time they have richer color, as if to say thank

This rambling rose adds beauty and fragrance to the porch railing.

you for bringing back the cool weather.

I could never give up ever-blooming roses. Everyone loves plants that bloom over and over again in their gardens, especially roses. I love them as much as I love my simple *Rosa primula*, or the loosely petaled apothecary's rose. They're all distant memories as I inhale the fragrance of the musk rose outside my office window or watch as 'Neptune', a new and exciting lavender hybrid tea, shows off

amidst a mass of red and purple annual *Cuphea* 'Bat-face'.

This ever-blooming trait is not so old with garden roses. It was just a little over two hundred years ago that the arrival of ever-blooming China roses shook the sanctity of the rose world with their monthly blooming habit—including the coldest months of winter. Until that time, there were only a handful of roses that bloomed seemingly non-stop.

There are more rose classes to learn about, most of them stemming from the results of rose hybridizers creating new and exciting varieties by crossing the once-blooming roses with those new arrivals from the Orient. Within all of these classes are some good varieties, worthy of being included in a garden design. There are three varieties from the species group worth mentioning, so let's start there.

Ever-Blooming Species Roses

There are two true species roses with a continuous bloom cycle—*Rosa moschata,* the musk rose, and *Rosa rugosa,* the beach rose. Both of these species have been in gardens since ancient times and continue to be a fragrant part of our landscapes today. *Rosa rugosa* is known to have been cultivated in Chinese gardens since 1100 AD but wasn't introduced to western culture until the 19th century. The musk rose has been documented in western gardens since at least the sixteenth century. Both are prized for their fragrance, unique blooms, and interesting growth habits.

In the garden, *Rosa rugosa* has an upright, slightly spreading habit of medium height, with a tendency to sucker freely. There are numerous hybrids of *Rosa rugosa* worthy of consideration. Many are popular garden plants, some are quite rare and worth the hunt. Their growth habits range from short and suckering, perfect for the middle border, to tall arching shrubs excellent for the rear of the border; they can be trained as pillar roses, or espaliered against walls and fences. The training requires a good deal of work and bloodletting—the stiff canes of these hybrids are viciously armed with prickles. 'Frau Dagmar Hastrup' (silvery-pink, simple blooms) and 'Purple Pavement' (purple flowers, part of what is known as the Pavement Series) are two hybrids ideal for the front of the border.

There are many excellent hybrids for the middle of the border. One of my favorites for delicacy in blooms as well as fragrance is 'Mme. Georges Bruant', rarely seen in gardens today. The crepe-like semi-double blooms of white are tinted with hints of pink and lavender. 'Thérèse Bugnet' (often pronounced "bug-net" by the little old ladies of the rose world), with her crimson-pink roses and plum colored pedicels is a shrub tolerant of many adverse conditions. 'Rose à Parfum de l'Häy' is one of the most fragrant roses ever created.

Of the tall hybrids, I strongly recommend growing 'Sarah Van Fleet' with her intensely fragrant pink roses, 'Nova Zembla', a rare and beautiful hybrid with full blush pink roses great for cutting, and finally 'Dr. Eckner', pink infused with sunrise colors and a wonderful fruity fragrance.

In general, *Rosa rugosa* and the hybrids grow best if they can have winter dormancy. The species are very good for the coldest climates.

Rosa moschata, the musk rose, is a tall growing, at times arching, shrub that could be espaliered or trained to a fence. As a freestanding shrub, it is a fragrant masterpiece best placed near the back of the border, or near an open window.

As the other roses come into their first flush of bloom in the garden, the musk rose is just beginning to show hints of bloom. Mine doesn't start blooming until at least the beginning of July—and it still doesn't become noticeable until the autumn. It's reliably hardy from Zone 7 and south, but severe winter weather and spring freezes will kill back some of the last season's growth. In Zone 7, plant it in a protected site to ensure the best performance. I grow *Rosa moschata plena* (double white flowers) in the bed immediately outside my office window, in a southern exposure. Not only is this a sheltered spot in my garden, I can enjoy the wonderful perfume from its clusters of small white roses from July through November—sometimes as late as December. This is definitely the last rose of summer for me.

I've seen this rose growing in gardens on the east coast from Washington, D.C. to Florida, and in northern California. In Florida, at the rose gardens of Florida Southern Citrus Institute, the musk rose and its found varieties (recently discovered, thought to be extinct varieties of this species) are all planted together. Here they bloom monthly through the entire year, planted as a rose hedge.

One final rose I've included in the ever-blooming species section is not a species at all. Instead, 'Stanwell Perpetual' is a hybrid species of unknown origin. The foliage and habit are very similar to the species *Rosa pimpinellifolia*, with lacy, fern-like leaves on bristly canes. However, the flowers are large and full, more like a damask rose. This ever-blooming species hybrid has a spreading, medium height growth habit making it perfect for the middle of the border. The plant seems to be cold hardy at least to zone 6, and does very well in temperate climates as well. The flowers are blush pink, very double with a fragrance that remind some of old-fashioned perfumed soap.

China Roses

The rose world was turned upside down at the end of the 18th century, when the first ever-blooming roses from China, 'Slater's Crimson China' and 'Old Blush', were brought to the western world. With the exception of the musk rose, 'Autumn Damask', and 'Stanwell Perpetual' all other roses grown at this time in Western gardens were once-blooming roses. Called China roses due to their origins (or provenance), these new roses were capable of producing blooms twelve months of the year. It didn't take long before new ever-blooming seedlings began flooding the market. The immediate result of this was the creation of a new class of roses known simply as China roses.

The growth habits of this group vary from short and scrappy to robust and scrappy. I find their architecture very twiggy and not as defined as the growth habits of the once-blooming old garden roses. However, they bloom and grow from every part of the plant and are capable of sending up long shoots ending in a cluster of blooms at any time of the season. They provide constant color for the border in climates where winters are mild, generally warmer than Zone 7. The most vigorous and hardiest China rose for this zone is 'Mutabilis'. Two other good choices would be 'Old Blush' and 'Viridiflora'. Otherwise, China roses grow best in warm climates, especially warm and dry.

Nearly all shades of pink, red, white, and green are covered in the China class. Most common is the velvety red found in so many of the varieties such as 'Cramoisi Superieur', 'Slater's Crimson China', and 'Louis Phillipe'. 'Mutabilis' will show all colors—cream, yellow, scarlet, and pink—during its floriferous display, often at the same time on one bush. The other oddity of the China class is, perhaps, the most unusual rose ever introduced, 'Viridiflora'—also known as the green rose. All of the petals have reverted to sepals, the protective green layers of a rose flower. Sometimes peppered with a burgundy hue, this green-flowered variety can go nearly unnoticed in a border. It deserves to be singled out and planted with a companion that will emphasize its unique green flowers.

Tea Roses

Nodding flowers are the signature characteristic of tea roses. These are gorgeous roses; some are simple with loose petals, and others have a fuller look. The colors range from velvety red to amazing shades of pink, yellow, apricot, cream, and white. The oldest varieties have a scent reminiscent of green tea, hence they earned the name tea roses. The first tea roses came to Western gardens along with the first China roses, and together these two classes forever changed the way gardeners look at roses. 'Safrano' is one of the oldest tea cultivars and perhaps the first time that the color apricot was ever seen in an ever-blooming rose. It was quite fashionable during Victorian times to have a bloom of this rose on display in a single bud vase during the winter.

Tea roses have a similar habit to China roses, but are more robust in warmer areas. In my Zone 7 garden, tea roses are very small plants—pruned hard each year by winter. In climates where the winter is mild or non-existent, these are the roses to grow. In New Orleans and northern California they're in full bloom nearly twelve months of the year and are capable of growing into shrubs six feet wide by eight feet tall. For gardeners in these regions I would recommend using tea roses as middle of the border and rear border plants. There are also climbing tea roses, as well, which are wonderful for smothering the pergolas and walls of the warm climate garden.

Noisette

During midsummer it's easy to spot the Noisette roses in my garden, that being the time they begin producing massive clusters of small roses. 'Princesse de Nassau', by the beginning of August, can have over a hundred small rose buds in each cluster. This clustering is a trait inherited from *Rosa moschata*, one of the parents of the first Noisette rose.

Climbers and vigorous shrubs, all with clusters of roses, are characteristic of this group of roses. Best in warm climate gardens, Noisettes have a long bloom period. There are many hybrids that were created using tea roses as one of the parents. These are exceptional climbing roses in Zone 8 or warmer. Up in Zone 7, 'Mme. Alfred Carrière' does reasonably well as a climbing plant. With winter protection, 'Princess de Nassau' and 'Belle Vichysoise' are taller plants for the rear of the border in Zone 7.

COMPANIONS FOR TEA AND CHINA ROSES

Tea and China roses are perfect landscape roses for the warmest climates, especially if there is an occasional drought. These roses have enjoyed many years of carefree existence throughout the South, California, and Bermuda, continually blooming month after month.

Of the two groups, tea roses have the bulkiest growth habit; in some regions they are excellent for creating hedges as a backdrop for a perennial garden or as a strong source of color in the middle border. China roses can have an irregular habit, with stronger red colors. Tea roses generally have easier colors, usually soft pastels, to mix into the garden.

Choose plants that are adaptable to drier conditions as companions for these roses. In California, favorites to grow with tea and China roses are many varieties from the succulent family echeveria, rosemary, agapanthus, kangaroo paw, and agaves. Among the colorful herbaceous perennials that work well are salvias, penstemons, gaura, erigeron, and pelargoniums. A popular groundcover is the silver-leaved licorice plant, *Helichrysum petiolare*.

Bourbon Roses

Bourbon roses were first introduced into commerce from France in the early nineteenth century. The growth habits of Bourbon roses include climbing, arching, and compact. The most popular of the climbing varieties is 'Zepherine Drouhin', an extremely fragrant brilliant pink rose with canes completely free of prickles. Her sports—'Kathleen Harrop', soft pink, and 'Martha', salmon-pink, are equally as pleasant to work with. 'Louise Odier', 'Mme. Ernest Calvat', and 'Mme. Isaac Pereire' are versatile cultivars that lend themselves to being grown either as freestanding shrubs with elegant arching habits—excellent for the middle to the rear of the border—or trained to grow on a fence or pillar. Or they can be pegged to the ground to create a carpet-like display.

One of the most popular of all the Bourbon roses is 'Souvenir de la Malmaison'. This compact blush pink shrub rose has a growth habit and delectable fragrance that make it an ideal candidate for the front of the border. One drawback of this beauty—the flowers fail to open in gardens in areas of high humidity or ocean mist. A possible substitute, and equally as beautiful, is 'Souvenir de St. Anne's', a sport of 'Souvenir de la Malmaison' with blush pink flowers with six to eight petals.

Bourbons are most vigorous when they are grown in warm climates. They can tolerate cold as well, but their growth is not as vigorous. There are several varieties capable of surviving at least Zone 6, even colder if given extra winter protection.

I include Bourbon roses in my garden designs for their fragrance, despite the fact that they have a propensity for foliage diseases. By August their stems are usually naked, but I hide the bare canes with the foliage of other garden plants. Their colors—from vivid scarlet to various shades of pink and white, are very adaptable to just about any perennial, herb, or annual combination. And their fragrance is wonderful.

Portland Roses

The Portlands continue to be a class of mystery to many rosarians—so much so that some nurseries drop this class entirely and scatter the varieties under other groups. But Portlands deserve to be singled out. Their origins are not quite clear, but many of them do seem to resemble continual blooming damask roses—perhaps with a bit of restraint in their growth habit. Longstanding arguments over names and classes of old garden roses always make rose society meetings interesting, and many such arguments are in reference to this rose class.

Needless to say, there is a place for these shrubby, ever-blooming shrub roses in your garden, not only for their rich colors, beauty and fragrance, but for their historical significance as well. The oldest hybrid of this class is 'Rose du Roi' which dates to the earliest part of the nineteenth century when it was an integral part of the evolving cottage garden. The crimson blooms set off by the grayish green damask foliage reappear in the

The bourbon rose 'Louise Odier' is a natural companion for catmint.

heat of the summer. 'Rose de Rescht', a magenta-red, is another popular variety of this group. Both belong in perennial gardens where they look wonderful underplanted with gray foliage plants, such as *Artemisia* 'Powis Castle', and partnered with blue delphiniums. One cut bloom from these or any of the other Portland varieties will fill a room with old rose perfume.

Also sold as "damask perpetual" roses, these Victorian hybrids are, for the most part, upright shrubs. Their growth habit is short to medium height, ideal for the front to the middle of the border. The colors range from white, pink, and striped to shades of crimson. All of the varieties are extremely fragrant, a trait passed on from their damask ancestors.

Moss Roses

There are a handful of repeat-blooming moss roses still available today. The growth habits range from short to medium height, good for the front and middle of the border. Like the once-blooming moss roses, these varieties do best when they have a cold dormant period. They make a curious and welcome addition to the summer and autumn perennial border.

Hybrid Perpetual Roses

When hybrid perpetuals were introduced to the world, the way of growing roses changed forever. This was during the reign of Queen Victoria. In fact one of the very first hybrids was called 'La Reine' in honor of the Queen. These new roses from France were large, fragrant, and colorful. The plants weren't necessarily attractive garden plants nor were they truly perpetual bloomers, but the roses were winning the top prizes at local flower shows and everyone wanted them.

Hybrid perpetuals grow in nearly all habits, except as dwarf front-of-border plants. The

COMPANIONS FOR NOISETTE ROSES

With growth habits ranging from shrubs to vigorous climbers, and colors from pure white to the glorious colors of a sunset, Noisettes offer many possible combinations and uses from zone 6 to the warmest regions.

In temperate zones, 'Blush Noisette' creates a formidable hedge and a beautiful backdrop for a perennial border. 'Maréchal Niel', underplanted with lavender and trained to a lattice, creates a beautiful wall with purple clematis twining among its soft yellow nodding roses.

Joe pye weed, *Eupatorium maculatum* 'Gateway', has been a companion for the noisette 'Belle Vichysoise' in my zone 7 gardens for many seasons. The arching canes of this pink Noisette become entangled and hidden by the new growth of this tall herbaceous perennial each season. During mid-summer the two plants bloom simultaneously. Just as 'Gateway' begins displaying small pink flower buds, clusters of pale pink roses suddenly appear, emerging through the textured foliage of the Joe pye weed.

plants are medium upright to very tall with a lanky habit. Some of them can be trained as climbing plants for pillars or fences. Hybrid perpetuals seem to grow best in climates that permit winter dormancy and have cool wet springs. The hotter and drier the climate, the fewer repeat blooms there will be.

Hybrid Tea Roses

When most people think of roses, it's likely the hybrid teas they have in mind. These are long-stemmed roses on upright plants, and they come in a huge range of colors, with fragrance ranging from none to very strong. They are the roses typically seen in traditional rose gardens where roses are grown in isolation.

Hybrid tea roses date back to 1867, when 'La France', a seedling of the hybrid perpetual rose, was discovered. The hybrid teas are the oldest of the modern roses—generally, rosarians classify any rose bred prior to 1867 as an "old" rose, while any from after that date are considered "modern" roses.

Although hybrid teas typically have had only one bloom per long, strong stem, they are evolving to have many blooms per cluster, which sometimes makes them difficult to distinguish from other classes of roses discussed below. The plants themselves still have an upright, rather stiff habit, and I find them best used as middle border plants.

Hybrid teas need a winter dormancy period, whether brought on by weather or by pruning. Their preferred climate is cool with plenty of spring rain and without baking heat in the summer. Prolonged periods of heat will slow the growth of the hybrid teas and stunt the size of the flowers, although with fall's cooler temperatures, they'll usually bounce back.

Many hybrid teas are susceptible to a wide range of disease and fungus, including blackspot, mildew, and rust, so they either need to be sprayed regularly or carefully placed in the border so their neighbors will disguise their blemishes. For a great many gardeners, hybrid teas are more than worth the trouble for their color, form, and beauty in the vase.

Some of the most popular hybrid teas are 'Diana, Princess of Wales', a cream-pink-yellow blend, 'Midas Touch', yellow, 'Gemini', blushing pink, 'First Prize', deep rose pink, 'Veterans' Honor', red with huge flowers, 'Ronald Reagan', a very distinct rose red with white reverse on the petals. 'Aromatherapy', said to be intensely fragrant, is being introduced in 2005, and 'Tahitian Sunset' and 'Spellbound' are both 2006 award winners worth exploring for your garden. Jackson & Perkins calls its own-root roses "New Generation," which includes some hybrid teas.

Grandiflora Roses

The grandifloras are the result of breeding floribundas to hybrid teas, and the plants show characteristics of both parents—they flower in clusters, and they're quite tall, ranging from three to six feet. They're good for background bedding in borders and also make nice hedges and specimens. They have large, full blooms on strong stems, so they're good for cutting, and they're pretty well constantly in bloom throughout the growing season, which will please gardeners who want an abundance of flowers. The best-known grandiflora is the pink 'Queen Elizabeth', which was introduced in 1954, the year Elizabeth ascended the English throne. It is still a very popular rose, and she is still a very popular queen. 'Cherry Parfait' is a new cream and red grandiflora that was a 2003 AARS award winner, and 'Melody Parfumée' is a plum-lavender beauty with a very strong scent.

Floribunda Roses

The floribundas have mixed parentage involving a great many roses, but the modern floribundas resulted from crosses between hybrid tea roses and polyanthas, which are discussed in the section below on "Miniature Flowered Roses." Floribundas bear their flowers in clusters, and the plants typically are quite shrubby in form, usually wider than they are tall. They were originally developed in an effort to breed roses hardier than the hybrid teas, though that didn't work out to be true in many cases. A good bit of fragrance was lost in the effort, but floribundas are somewhat more disease resistant than many hybrid teas. In recent years, floribundas and hybrid teas have been so interbred that it's difficult to make a visual distinction.

Generally, floribundas make good hedges and are excellent in mixed borders. There are some short-growing floribundas ideal for the front of the border; one that comes to mind is , and the pink-orange blend 'Disneyland'. The majority of the newer floribunda hybrids belong in the mid-border area. Some good ones to consider are the orange 'Tuscan Sun', and 'Grand Prize', with pinkish-apricot buds that open into creamy flowers. Also

notable for those of you who like yellow is the 2004 floribunda of the year 'Honey Perfume', with abundant apricot-yellow flowers and a strong fragrance.

Shrub Roses

The shrub rose category tends to be used for every sort of rose that doesn't fit into some other classification, but it includes some of the most beautiful and useful modern roses for our gardens. Sometimes referred to as landscape roses because of their suitability for mixed plantings, shrub roses come in a wide range of sizes and forms, and they generally require much lower maintenance than many other rose types. They tend to be more disease- and insect-resistant and require less pruning than traditional rose types. Some even drop their flower petals cleanly, so no dead-heading is required to keep the blooms coming. And some breeders are now offering these on their own roots, rather than grafted, meaning that if the above-ground portion dies, the plant will come back true to type.

Shrub roses can be medium or large upright shrubs, lower, mounding shrubs that ramble about, or even lower-growing "groundcovers," although no rose is truly a groundcover, and some described this way are as tall as 2-1/2 feet. The English roses also tend to be tall shrubs and have proven among the most popular recent rose introductions. David Austin of England, the "father" of English roses, began his breeding program about 20 years ago, crossing old and modern roses to produce shrubs with modern disease resistance but the fragrance and flower shapes

COMPANIONS FOR HYBRID TEA AND ENGLISH SHRUB ROSES

Among the ever-blooming roses, hybrid teas, floribundas, and shrub roses are the most popular. Shrub roses have growth habits ranging from short to tall enough to be used as climbers. Hybrid teas and floribundas have a rigid, upright habit, just begging to be dressed up with companions.

These roses offer a seemingly unlimited choice of companion plants. Make your decisions based on the habits of the individual roses. Include companions that create color during the times the roses are not in bloom as well as those that will complement the glorious rose colors. It's important not to crowd modern roses as they tend to be prone to foliar diseases. Better yet, choose roses that are more disease resistant.

Blue- and pink-flowered companions, such as salvia, nepeta, and delphiniums, are popular choices. Phormiums, iris, and acidanthera add interesting colors as well as foliage textures. Lavender, artemisia, and arctotis add a soft touch of silver to the otherwise rigid-looking roses.

of antique roses.

Other breeders followed suit, so in addition to English shrub roses, there are renaissance roses originating in Denmark, and generosa roses from France. Many of the English roses tend to be tall and wide growing plants, best as rear of the border plants or climbers. Be warned that if grown in zone 7 and further south, the English roses attain a height and spread unknown in England, so the size information provided on the tag and in books needs to be interpreted for your climate. 'Golden Zest' is an English style shrub rose with an old-fashioned look and a compact habit. 'Fragrant Wave' is a lovely 3- to 4-foot floribunda, often classed as a landscape rose, that has been described as a fragrant and healthier 'Iceberg'. And 'Pure Perfume', another Austin type, grows 4 to 5 feet tall with

old-fashioned looking white blooms and a strong, citrus scent some say is a dead ringer for Ruby Red grapefruit! Hybrid musk roses are wonderful shrub roses with a spreading and arching habit. These could be used as middle border plants, rear border plants, and even climbers.

The low-growing types of shrub roses are best used in the front of the border, although some are tall enough for mid-border. The Knock Out™ series is taking the gardening world by storm, with a rose-red and a pink variety already available, and white on its way. It grows to about 2-1/2 feet and needs virtually no maintenance, reblooming well even without either deadheading or fertilization. 'Sea Foam' is a very popular older white groundcover rose. 'Snow Cone' is a new upright compact groundcover that works well in mixed gardens. 'Yellow Ribbons' and 'Red Ribbons' are excellent groundcover types, and 'Electric Blanket' is a very hardy, disease-resistant, coral pink.

With truly ever-blooming habits, a range of sizes, good disease-resistance, and relatively undemanding natures in terms of pruning and feeding, shrub roses are the best bet for many gardeners, especially those wishing to mix roses into the border and into other parts of their landscape. It is a group with something for everyone.

Miniature Flowered Roses

There are three classes of ever-blooming roses represented in this group: China roses, miniature roses, and polyantha roses. Each class contains roses with exquisite miniature blooms. The oldest ever-blooming small flowered roses are the miniature China roses. 'Pompon de Paris' and 'Rouletii' have been known since the earliest part of the nineteenth century as miniature roses. There is a debate raging right now in the rose world as to whether these two miniature roses are indeed the same plant, for they do look very similar. They both display one-inch pink button roses and when grown in warm climates can reach a height of three feet. Because of their dwarf size, they tend to be hardier than other China roses so they can be grown in colder areas as well, if a warm spot is found for them. There is also a climbing form of both varieties. It's suspected that these China roses are responsible for spawning the earliest modern miniature roses.

The fascination for small flowered roses increased over the years as conservatories and greenhouses became a part of the private landscape during the nineteenth century. The cut-flower industry also saw the demand rise for small flowered roses as cut blooms or potted plants. This brought on the next generation of small flowered roses, the polyantha roses—also known as sweetheart roses.

Polyantha roses created a niche during the Victorian era as buttonhole roses. They are wonderful garden plants as well. Many of them produce perfect little rose buds on medium sized plants that are best if used in the middle of the border. One of the oldest and most miniature in flower is 'Mlle. Cécile Brunner'. Her perfect little pink rose buds still stop me in the garden when she is in full bloom. There is a vigorous, once-blooming, climbing version of this rose as well.

These are short upright shrubs, most of the varieties reaching around three to four feet in height and width, making them ideal for the middle of the border. There are climbing sports of these roses also.

The smallest ever-blooming roses, as well as some of the hardiest roses ever created, are modern day miniature roses. These plants are best in the front of the border, in containers, or as bedding plants. Occasionally some sprout long sprays of blooms, but for the most part they average from six inches to eighteen inches in height. 'Sun Sprinkles' is a very bright yellow prize winner, and 'Party Lights' is a healthy, rounded mini with large bright coral-pink blooms. It's not uncommon for 'Cinderella', a white miniature with pinkie-nail sized blooms, to send a stalk straight up topped with blooms like a large lollipop. I've

The climbing rose 'New Dawn' (right), combined with 'Bubble Bath' and 'Royal Sunset', makes an ordinary garden shed a focal point in the garden.

seen talented rosarians train these foot tall growths into miniature standards. There are some climbing cultivars as well. 'Climbing Jackie' and 'Hi Ho' can grown to six or eight feet, ideal for training on lattice. 'Jeanne Lajoie', a rose-pink miniature climbing rose, easily grows to fifteen or twenty feet when given the space. Even though these roses may reach great heights, the blooms, foliage, and prickles remain miniature. While some of the polyanthas and China roses may need some protection in zones colder than 6, the majority of these miniature roses are cold hardy and heat tolerant, as well.

Large-Flowered Climbing Roses

Ever-blooming climbers are stiff woody plants that produce large flowers along long canes. The flowers are produced from laterals (side shoots from the main canes) as well as from the ends of the longest canes. If left as freestanding shrubs, they have a mounding habit of six to eight feet high. Trained to a sturdy structure, some varieties easily cover fifteen to twenty feet.

There is a climbing rose for every climate. The most versatile is 'New Dawn', the blush-colored rose that set the standard for ever-blooming climbing roses back in 1931. 'Mermaid', a vigorous house-eating climber in the South, has a manageable habit in Zone 7.

ROSE COMPANIONS WITH DECORATIVE FRUIT AND SEEDS

This summer, large umbels of seedpods on my agapanthus made a distinctive display beginning in July. This is one of several bulbs that I allow to go to seed, adding color as well as texture to the garden. Starting as early as spring, you can include fruit and seeds from bulbs as part of your display. Many of the species tulips set seed with interesting seedpods; two I recommend are *Tulipa turkestanica* and 'Ice Stick'. Quite often the globular blooms of alliums last through summer, sometimes even into autumn, as ghost-like structures. As their flowering season comes to an end, many lilies develop seedpods, the most notable being Formosa lily.

Of other summer-flowering bulbs, the fiery blooms of crocosmia evolve into small green ball-like fruits on their wands, and belamcanda, the blackberry lily, leaves a fruit that cracks open to reveal shiny black seeds that look very much like blackberries. In the autumn, *Iris foetidissima* splits open its seedpods to reveal brilliant orange seeds.

'Blaze of Glory' is a heavy-blooming bright orange climber, and 'Scent from Above' is a fragrant yellow climber. Ever-blooming climbers have their peak bloom around the same time as the hybrid teas and continue blooming through the season, some better than others, until there is a freeze or drought.

Flower Colors and Forms

Color continues to be a driving force behind the creation of new roses. Since the earliest times of gardening, there have been new hybrids introduced regularly with a wide palette of colors from pure white to the possibility of blue. As I sit here today, there's once again talk of a blue rose for the garden. Blue, black, and brown are the three colors that have never been found naturally in roses, and there seems to be a determination to bring these colors into the rose world. In the case of the blue rose, it may actually happen as a result of cancer and Alzheimer's research going on in Nashville, Tennessee. It just so happens that a liver enzyme used in this research has the ability to turn things blue. As an independent project, the scientists involved want to try this on roses—to echo the sentiments of the majority of the rose world, here we go again!

The original colors of roses were white, red, pink, yellow, and orange, all found among the oldest known roses—the species roses. The most unusual colors have been red, not known until the China rose 'Slater's Crimson China' appeared on the scene in the early eighteenth century; yellow—it's debatable but probably the oldest yellow species is *Rosa foetida*, also known as the Austrian yellow rose; orange, discovered as the Austrian yellow sported into a bicolor form, orange with a yellow reverse, known as the Austrian copper rose, or *Rosa foetida bicolor*. Unfortunately both of these roses are black spot magnets. Early rose breeders, to create the first yellow hybrids used. However, along with the yellow color, they introduced foliar diseases.

Today, red remains the most popular rose color. From the older China roses to modern hybrid teas, there are great red roses to pick from. One of the newest red roses, and most fragrant, is 'Lasting Love'. 'Mr. Lincoln' is a popular tall hybrid tea with a strong fragrance, and down south, 'Louis Phillipe', an old China rose, continues to dot the landscape as a truly hardy ever-blooming red rose. Red is a good color to combine with blue flowers, silver foliage, and green hedging.

Orange is not far behind in popularity. Russet and apricot colored roses have evolved from orange and are causing quite a stir, with some interesting disease resistant as well as fragrant hybrids for today's gardens. This is a great color to work into the border as well. Among the best of these are 'About Face', a grandiflora rose; 'Fragrant Cloud', a hybrid tea; and 'Tuscan Sun', the 2005 floribunda rose of the year. Apricot also makes a state-ment in the tea and Noisette group: 'Safrano', a tea that pales from rich apricot to nearly white; 'Crépuscule', a vigorous Noisette with delightful sunset colors; and a favorite among my clients, 'Gloire de Dijon', a Noisette with soft amber blending to pink.

Softer colors are abundant in both modern and old garden roses. There are three beautiful tea roses with exquisite blends of pink, salmon, and cream that are wonderful in a warm climate mixed border— 'Marie van Houtte', 'Mme. Joseph Schwartz', and 'Mrs. B.R. Cant'.

Damasks, albas, and centifolias generally have roses of soft shades of pink, blush, and pure white. The mosses, gallicas, hybrid Chinas, and hybrid Bourbons have these colors as well as strong purples, reds, and stripes.

Striped roses are not new. Early hybrids such as 'Perle des Panachées' (gallica, pink/white), 'Variegata di Bologna' (hybrid Bourbon, crimson/blush), and 'Rosa Mundi' (red/white) are among the most popular striped old roses. There has been a flurry of activity in modern times to create a good striped hybrid; among the successful ones are 'Scentimental' (red/white, hybrid tea), 'Tigress' (purple/white, grandiflora), and 'Fourth of July' (red/white, climber). 'Viridiflora', a China rose of the nineteenth century, is the only rose that is truly green. This is not a green-hued rose, but instead all of the petals have reverted to sepals (the outer green cover of a rose bud).

Flower forms of roses range from simple to complex. Species roses, such as *Rosa carolina* and *Rosa setigera*, are examples of simple, or single, flowered roses. There are five petals with clearly visible stamens (male part of the flower, yellow or golden orange) and pistils (female part of the flower). *Rosa sericea pteracantha*, also known as the red wing rose or wingthorn rose, due to its red glowing prickles, is the only species with four petals. Up to eight petals are still considered single flowers.

Single flowers aren't limited to species roses. Some wonderful single modern hybrids are 'Dainty Bess' (pink, hybrid tea), 'Mermaid' (yellow, climber), and 'Mutabilis' (multi-colored, China). Besides the delicate butterfly effect these single roses add to the garden, they often have a dramatic stamen display, adding color to the border even after the petals of the flower have fallen. Noted roses with colorful and noteworthy stamens displays are 'Dainty Bess' (maroon stamens), 'Bolero' (cream, climber with dark colored stamens), and 'Mermaid' (whose yellow stamens are prominently displayed long after the petals have fallen).

Semi-double roses are lovely loose-petaled flowers, still exposing the stamens and pistils. As with the single-flowered roses, the colors of the flower center become an important color contribution to the border.

Double-flowered roses are the most complex. The petals are tightly packed, rarely opening up fully to display the centers. The shapes of double flowered roses can be flat, rounded, or high centered. Classic hybrid teas are good examples of high centered roses—this is a prize-winning form. When viewed in profile, the highest part of the flower is the center, and dramatically pointed. Many of the shrub roses and old garden roses are rounded or flat. Some display a quartered look, as if you could divide the flower into four equal pie pieces.

The sizes of flowers range from very tiny (miniatures) to enormous peony-like blooms of shrub roses—some of these can be over six inches in width. The manner that flowers are clustered on the bush is known as the inflorescence. The shapes of the inflores-cences are varied as well. Common among the hybrid teas and certain shrubs and climbers is a solitary or single stemmed display. Otherwise, the displays tend to be in groupings called corymbs.

More than Just Blooms

We all have our favorite memories of roses. I have many—the roses on my grandfather's fence, the glorious display of six thousand roses all in full bloom on Rose Day at the Brooklyn Botanic Garden, and especially the lone tea rose I came upon in a cemetery in Mississippi in full bloom despite years of neglect. At first, the blooms seduce you, not the stem texture, prickles, or hips. Unless of course your first close encounter with a rose was becoming tangled in a mass of the prickly hips of the burr rose as you attempted to get a close-up look at the peeling bark, or a bloody rendezvous with the prickles of the wingthorn rose as you slipped while gazing into the large and mesmerizing ruby-red winged prickles. Those attributes are worthy of rose memories, too.

Roses are sought, cultivated, and sold on the merits of their flowers and the powerful seduction of their scent, as evident from the glossy pages of nursery catalogues replete with image after image of luscious rose blooms and their descriptions, attempting to capture the subtleties of a hundred indescribable fragrances. Let's face it, this is the *why* we grow roses, for their fragrance and the beauty of the flowers.

From a gardener's point of view, however, there's a good deal more to roses than mere flower or fragrance. Roses have many other distinctive features that contribute to the garden in all seasons. Rose hips, rose canes, growth habits, prickles, and foliage are all important non-flowering traits of roses, each with their distinctive characteristics worthy of our attention. These are key ingredients providing color, fragrance, contrast, and texture—necessary elements for a successful mixed border. If you are familiar with these botanical traits, you can put them to good use in the garden.

Rose Foliage

A good place to start when discussing other characteristics of roses is with the foliage. More often than not discussions of rose leaves are limited to diseases. Unfortunately, many roses do have a propensity for fungal and bacterial blights. And to make matters worse, many insects find the leaves and flowers tasty. When these problems strike, that's when we usually pay attention to the foliage. But there's more to rose foliage then black spot, mildew, and Japanese beetles. The leaves of a rose serve as a foil for the flowers and other blooms in the border as well, framing the masterpiece while creating a backdrop for the beautiful display. Leaves herald the beginning of life in a garden, the beginning of a new season, and the continuation of color. There are numerous roses to choose from and their foliar aspects are various as well.

Rose foliage offers many opportunities to create interesting combinations in a mixed border. There are unique colors and fragrances to enjoy, and textures that will make you question whether these plants are truly roses. Take the time you need to stop and smell the roses. But, while your nose is ravaging the blooms, consider the foliage as well. Leaves are more than green. They can be gray, red, pink, and even have highlights of silver.

Foliage Color

Color in the rose garden really begins in spring as the leaf buds break dormancy, long before the first rose bud opens. The first noticeable color is green, and among the earliest sources of this verdure are the species roses.

Green is the basic color of a garden. While I was the curator of roses at the Brooklyn Botanic Garden, I spent my spring mornings in the quiet rose garden, months before the roses were in bloom, watching green appear. When the species awake, the garden comes to life with wands of inchworm green delightfully catching the rays of the early season sun. I felt the excitement of the coming rose season, as the soft light of the early spring sun would catch the color of the emerging leaves of the species roses. The leaf buds of the species roses cracked open their protective layers, displaying a refreshing spring green color—the first sign of renewal of life in the rose garden.

At first, in early April there were just a few to see, but each day, as the sun rose higher in the sky, there were more and more leaves stirring from their winter dormancy. By late April, the garden beds with the species roses were full of green leaves carefully protecting their May roses. But until then, the foliage would be the attraction.

It is amazing to me just how many variations of green there are. There's emerald green, inchworm green, chartreuse, and a green so dark it appears nearly black. This is the quiet moment of the garden, a unique chance to study the foliage; this is the green time of the rose garden.

Among my favorites that I would

recommend for interesting foliage are *Rosa pimpinellifolia* 'Altaica', a shrub of around three to four feet in height, with leaves of a near-black green; *Rosa davurica*, a rare species, and seldom seen outside botanical gardens, standing erect about six feet tall and presenting delicate pale green leaves with hints of gray; *Rosa hugonis* spilling over onto the walk, the canes weighted down from the weight of soft green foliage; and *Rosa primula*, freely arching canes as high as eight feet, displaying an emerald green color. The canes of these roses reach out and catch the spring rain and morning dew on the foliage, glistening in the early sun. *Rosa primula* is the first rose to show signs of life in my garden. When it does, the border is suddenly alive.

Blue Atlas cedar, lavender, and *Artemisia* 'Powis Castle' are among the plants I use to introduce one of my favorite garden colors—blue-gray. *Rosa glauca* offers this same color with the added feature of a strong pink hue especially noticeable on the petioles (leaf stems). As the earliest foliage of *Rosa glauca* unfurls, it tends to have a dark, near-red coloring, earning this rose the name red leaf rose. But as the species settles in for the season, the foliage tends to actually look more blue-gray than red, with subtle hints of green and pink throughout the season.

Rosa glauca is a European species that has become rooted firmly into American gardens over the course of several centuries. Perhaps the best known of all the species roses, *Rosa glauca* is a popular commodity in perennial nurseries as well as rose nurseries. This rose has crossed garden lines and is often used by gardeners who otherwise turn up their noses

at roses. Unlike others of its genus, the foliage of *Rosa glauca* does not change to green. Instead it keeps its reddish-gray-blue hues through most of the summer. Humid evenings will cause the foliage to drop.

One of the last species to break dormancy is *Rosa moschata*, the musk rose. This ancient species is slow to start, not showing its pale, slightly gray, foliage until late in the spring. In fact, just when I think it may have died from the winter and I'm ready to dig it up, small leaf buds begin to break. The foliage of the musk rose remains a soft pale green throughout the entire season. I have mine entangled with *Buddleia × weyeriana* 'Honeycomb', and at a quick glance it's difficult to tell them apart, both having similar gray-green foliage. The buddleia fills in the space nicely. The musk rose deserves a spot where you can observe the delicate foliage and later on, enjoy the wonderfully fragrant flowers.

While species roses are the harbingers of the rose season with their fresh spring foliage display, many provide autumn color as well. Some of the best for this purpose are natives of North America. *Rosa setigera,* found growing wild throughout the cooler regions of the east coast and Midwest, turns to a blaze of orange-yellow in the autumn. Other natives, including *Rosa carolina, Rosa virginiana,* and *Rosa arkansana* display traditional autumn colors. The leaves of *Rosa rugosa,* a species introduced from Japan, generally turn a brilliant yellow before they drop in the late autumn. This is true of most hybrid rugosas as well.

The variations in green are particularly

interesting among the old garden roses, especially within the classes of the European old garden roses. Gallica roses have the darkest green foliage of all roses, a perfect foil for brightly colored perennials. The richness of the gallica foliage color persists throughout the season with very little change in color. One of my favorite varieties of the gallica class is 'Charles de Mills'. The dark foliage beautifully sets off its purple-red blooms with tightly packed petals. Mix this with the chartreuse blooms of lady's mantle, and you have an incredible spring display. The colors of the flowers may vary but the leaves of the gallica roses are consistently a wonderful dark green.

Alba roses are another old garden class that is distinguishable from others by its foliage. The subtle blue tones are not as obvious when the roses are planted as individual plants. Mix them with other garden plants and different roses and you'll notice the infusion of blue. Unlike the pink tinctured foliage of *Rosa glauca*, the alba roses have a range of dark greenish-blue to a soft gray-green. Two of the oldest alba varieties, 'Great Maiden's Blush' and 'Alba Semi-Plena' are bluer than green. 'Mme. Legras de St. Germain' and 'Königin von Dänemark' are two hybrids that tend to produce a paler foliage with more hints of gray, persisting that way throughout the entire season. Their foliage is especially noticeable when paired with the darker green of evergreen shrubs such as boxwood or holly.

One summer evening I received an urgent phone message from one of my clients. "You've got to come out here immediately,

we've got poison ivy!" The description was right—glossy red leaves, branches entwined throughout the lattice. But this wasn't poison ivy at all—instead, it was the beautiful fresh growth on the client's large-flowered climbing rose 'Royal Sunset'. My client had noticed the most dramatic color of rose foliage—red.

While gardeners up north are preparing to make the first pruning cut of the season, warm climate gardeners are already experiencing a lush red foliar growth on their rose bushes, indicative of the next flush of blooms. China and tea roses show this color throughout the season as new leaves begin to grow. So do Bourbons, Noisettes, and countless other varieties and classes that can link their heritage to Chinas and teas, including hybrid tea roses. As roses begin to grow up north, they fill our gardens as well with the new red leaves.

This foliar character seems to have originated with the China and tea roses. The red growth grows from all parts of these roses—from the base, from dormant buds on the canes, and even from immediately behind fading blooms, often year-round if the weather is agreeable. This is not a pure red but instead tinted with hues of green and bronze (very much like poison ivy), at times so dark it's best described as sanguine, maroon, or even chocolate. It's an agreeable color for any border, creating a common thread that often works to pull everything together visually. This foliage color is not permanent and it eventually matures to a bronze-hued green.

As a result of breeding new roses from tea and China roses, roses today display this telltale red of their ancestors at some point during the growing season. In addition to modern hybrids, there are countless varieties of old garden roses with this noteworthy color characteristic. These too are all descendants of China roses. Hybrid Chinas, Portlands, Noisettes, and Bourbon roses all have varieties with this distinctive red foliage cycle.

Foliage Fragrance

Imagine the scent of green apples and Russian leather all in your garden, and all coming from roses. That's right, Russian leather. This is the fragrance description given to one of the most fragrant roses in our gardens today, not a flower fragrance, but a leaf fragrance. The plant is the yellow-flowered species *Rosa primula*. My *Rosa primula* is about eight feet tall, and arching in every direction to around four feet wide of heavily scented foliage. I smell the fragrance while walking through the garden on damp spring mornings and again in the autumn when there is a burst of new growth. I've never smelled Russian leather before, so I can't vouch for the accuracy of the description. But it is definitely fragrant, and not one of my favorite fragrances, either. It's especially strong after a rainstorm and on humid days. Grab any of the fresh leaves, crush them in your fingers and you'll release the heady scent.

Rosa roxburghii has so many leaflets it almost looks like a fern.

Also known as the incense rose, this species rose was first discovered around 1910 in central Asia—the color and fragrance were the enticements for collecting this rose. At that time, seeds were sent to the Arnold Arboretum in Boston where it was initially labeled as *Rosa ecae*. Ernest Wilson, the famed plant collector for the Arnold, praised this rose and recommended it for the fragrance of its foliage. After many bouts of botanical squabbling, the name *Rosa primula* was finally agreed upon. My specimen is a seedling from the original plant of the Arnold Arboretum.

For me, green apples have a much more pleasing fragrance. This is why I grow the sweet brier rose, *Rosa eglanteria*. Also known as the eglantine rose, the new foliage of this species is rich with oils scented like green apples, though the flower has very little fragrance. An extremely old European species, known to have been in our landscape since the colonial era, the eglantine rose is a tall growing shrub that can be trained to cover a wall or fall over an archway. Imagine walking through an arch or past a garden wall scented of green apples! Crushing the leaves also releases the fragrance, and regular pruning during the summer promotes an abundance of fresh new fragrant foliage.

Foliage Texture

Variations in texture make a garden border much more interesting. The shiny leaves of camellias, the rough foliage of Joe-Pye weed, and the downy pubescence of lavender all draw your eye across the garden. There are different levels of texture to be achieved in a garden by using foliage. Roses can be an important source of this texture.

Rose foliage varies from surfaces that are smooth and glossy to rough and pubescent. Foliage texture not only includes the appearance of the leaf surface, but also the arrangement of the leaves on the plant, which is a visual texture. The most interesting are the fern-like leaves of the species roses, adding a new layer to the texture of the garden. Study the roses with striking foliar textures that make them worth considering when creating a garden.

All roses have compound leaves. This means that each leaf is composed of smaller leaves known as leaflets. The leaflets are displayed in arrangements of three per leaf up to as many as fifteen per leaf. Hybrid teas, modern rose hybrids, and most of the old garden roses average around seven leaflets per leaf. The species roses and their hybrids annually captivate my interest with their small foliage composed of intricately arranged compound leaves. From a distance you notice the light catching these small leaves. Up close, the patterns, swirls, and variations of green are very much like fronds of ferns.

The roses with interesting leaf textures I find most interesting and suitable for creating living garden architecture are species roses. There are many with leaves that are intricately made up of smaller, more delicate leaves, best described as "fern-like." You may not even notice that these are roses, until you take a closer look. These are the roses I consider to be a vital ingredient to any border for creating living architecture.

Rosa pimpinellifolia roses (if that isn't tongue twisting enough, they're also known as

Rosa spinosissima roses), or Scotch roses, are the class with the most varieties to choose from with small leaves. The original species of this class, *Rosa pimpinellifolia* , typically has nine leaflets per leaf—a trait passed on to most of its hybrids. I have three favorites from this group: *Rosa spinosissima* 'Altaica', a beautiful creamy white single flowered rose from Central Asia with fragrant foliage and blooms; 'Stanwell Perpetual' with nine leaflets and blush pink, fragrant blooms; and 'Harison's Yellow', a large shrubby hybrid perfect for the rear of the border.

'Harison's Yellow' is not the only yellow rose with small leaflets worth considering for the garden. *Rosa hugonis* and 'Canary Bird' both have eleven leaflets; *Rosa primula* has a leaflet count of thirteen to fifteen; and the champion among the yellows is the one with the longest name, *Rosa sericea pteracantha*, the wingthorn rose, with a leaflet count of seventeen. The rose with the most leaflets, and other interesting attributes as well, is *Rosa roxburghii*. Loaded with up to nineteen leaflets per leaf, this rose is truly amazing in many respects.

Rosa rugosa is aptly named since "rugosa" means "wrinkled"—the foliage is wrinkled and a beautiful green. It's a rough and tough rose, suitable for many different locations in the garden. This species and its many hybrids make up the group of roses with the roughest textured leaf, puckered from the day they emerge from their tight buds to the day they fall to the ground. These leaves are durable and provide a distinctive characteristic that is an outstanding feature for any border.

Rosa wichurana is just the opposite of *Rosa rugosa*, as far as the foliage is concerned. With its small leaves, smooth, and highly glossy, this rambling species caught the eye of many rose breeders when it was introduced from China in 1868. Not necessarily a great garden plant itself, instead this rose became a parent of many great garden roses. All have the characteristic glossy foliage and strong disease resistance, the two best traits of this rose. Many of the wichurana hybrids are rambling roses and climbers. From France we have 'François Juranville', 'Albéric Barbier', 'Jactte', and 'Leontine Gervais'. From America, 'American Pillar', 'Silver Moon', and the most famous hybrid, 'Dr. W Van Fleet', which later sported to 'New Dawn'. All of these have distinctively glossy foliage.

Other notable roses with shiny foliage not related to *Rosa wichurana* are *Rosa virginiana, Rosa primula,* and *Rosa sempervirens*, the evergreen rose. New hybrids with glossy foliage continue to be introduced every season. Besides adding a glimmer of texture through the garden, these cultivars are more disease resistant. The glossy foliage has a great deal to do with this.

Rose Hips

Rose hips are the berry-like remains of a rose. This is not a fruit, but instead a receptacle for the fruit and seeds. The fruit of a rose is actually the hairy coating that surrounds each seed, inside the hip. As soon as a rose is pollinated rose hips begin to develop. By the time the petals have fallen, there is usually a noticeable rose hip forming, left on the bush to mature and ripen. Most roses are capable of producing hips and some of them are

Rosa moyesii has distinctively shaped, bright red hips that add color and texture to the garden after its blooms have faded.

extremely decorative. With ever-blooming roses it's advisable to remove faded flowers during the growing season to prevent the formation of hips since hip production can slow down flower production. However, there are some roses that should be grown for their hips as an added feature to the garden.

The colors of rose hips range from green to blackish-purple to vermillion to bright cherry red. The sizes and shapes of rose hips are various too—from egg shaped to elegant fluted forms. Some are smooth and shiny while others are dull and bristly. Rose hips begin forming as soon as the flower is fading, some will ripen by midsummer, and others will not make a noticeable display until the autumn.

One of the most bristly and foreboding is the hip of *Rosa roxhburghii*. This hip is covered with small bristles, earning the rose the nicknames of burr rose and chestnut rose. It does resemble the casing of a chestnut, but smaller. The hips of *Rosa roxburghii* begin to develop in early summer (this rose blooms before the peak of hybrid teas) and stay on the bush until midsummer. When these hips fall they're still green, with the remains of the sepals firmly attached. The mature hip is ovoid in shape, measuring an inch wide by a half-inch high.

One of the many nicknames for *Rosa rugosa* is tomato rose because the hips of this rose resemble little tomatoes. And, if you pick them at the right moment, they're very tasty. Many hips need a season to ripen but these hips ripen fairly quickly, and the signal is the tomato-red coloring. *Rosa × microgosa*, a hybrid between *Rosa rugosa* and *Rosa roxburghii,* is a tall spring blooming shrub with large pale pink single flowers. Its hips have the look of the chestnut rose with the red color of *Rosa rugosa.*

Some other species with notable hip displays are *Rosa arkansana* (red, pear-shaped, shiny), *Rosa virginiana* (red, shiny, half-inch wide, free of sepals), *Rosa villosa*, also known as the "apple bearing rose" (dark red, bristly,

pear shaped, very tasty), *Rosa canina* (egg shaped, bright red), *Rosa bracteata* (round, orange-red, bristly), *Rosa spinosissima* 'Altaica' (black, round, shiny), *Rosa sericea pteracantha* 'Redwing' (scarlet, shiny, small and globular), and *Rosa setigera* (small, orange-red, round).

Cane Color and Texture

At first you may think that all roses have green canes. This is not true. Many do have green canes, but there are several species and varieties that should be grown for their interesting cane colors and textures. This is especially important if you are planning a

The peeling bark of **Rosa roxburghii** is a striking addition to the winter garden.

Rosa complicata has an abundance of showy, round orange hips.

four-season garden.

Several varieties of roses have a distinctive plum-colored cane. During my days at the Brooklyn Botanic Garden, the arching canes of *Rosa setigera* filled the snow-covered winter garden with color. This native rose tends to have an arching habit. Loaded with fire-colored rose hips, the combination of colors was very impressive. The canes of *Rosa glauca* are carmine, obvious in the summer garden as well as in the winter. This color is best on the newer growth; as the canes age the carmine fades to silver-gray. 'Thérèse Bugnet' is a hybrid of *Rosa rugosa* with distinctive plum-colored canes. In combination with the magenta-pink blooms and bronzy-green foliage, this is a wonderful rose for all gardens.

Perhaps the most unusual cane display of any rose is *Rosa roxburghii*, the chestnut rose. My non-rose-loving friends (yes, I do keep a few of those around) are always in awe of the peeling bark of this species. The older it gets, the more dramatic the peeling. The older canes are tree-like and have that same textural feel of other peeling bark plants such as crape myrtle, paperbark maple, and river birch. My specimen of *Rosa roxburghii* is nearing eight feet high and I intend to prune it this winter to expose more of the base for a better display of the exfoliating bark.

Roses such as the redwing rose add beauty to the garden with their foliage and even their prickles.

Prickles

Technically roses don't have thorns—they have prickles. Prickles come in many shapes and sizes. Most modern roses have slightly hooked prickles while many of the older types have anything from bristles to severely hooked armatures. There is one rose that has a truly unique prickle, *Rosa sericea pteracantha*, or the redwing rose. This name is well earned. As the prickles of this Asian species emerge they are translucent red. As the sun catches them through the day, they glow like little rubies in the garden. However, they don't stay small for long. In a season's growth period these prickles can easily have a base of two to two and a half inches. As they age, the prickles turn gray, but they last on the canes for a very long time. Continual pruning of this shrub will encourage new growth with fresh red prickles for the entire season.

Good news for those of you who don't want to share your blood with the roses—roses without prickles do exist. Only a few, in my opinion, are worth growing. The best variety is 'Zépherine Drouhin', a fragrant pink Bourbon hardy in Zone 7 and warmer. This old garden rose has been a part of garden landscapes since the mid-nineteenth century. If grown in the warmest and sunniest spot in the garden, 'Zépherine Drouhin' is an ever-blooming rose. 'Mrs. Dudley Cross' is a twentieth century tea rose, nearly free of prickles. She'd be a safe rose to have near a doorway in a warm climate garden. In 1906 a "thornless" rambler was introduced to the rose world from Germany. 'Tausendschön', also known as 'Thousand Beauties', is a once-blooming rambler with trusses of roses in various shades of pink and white. 'Roserie', a sport of this rambler with consistently pink roses, is also a prickle-free rose. Both are easily grown from Zone 5 to the warmest climates.

Close up, the prickles of the redwing rose, *Rosa sericea pteracantha*, glow like little rubies.

KNOWING YOUR LOCATION

IN THIS CHAPTER:

- **Working with Nature**
- **Know Your Climate**
- **Evaluating a Site**
- **Extreme Heat and Cold**

Working with Nature

Location, location, it's all about location. When my clients return from trips abroad, I get very nervous. Long lists of roses and perennials suddenly appear in my e-mail notes. I then have the responsibility of delivering the bad news—"too tender," "won't grow here," or "can't find *that* in our country." I hate to crush the enthusiasm, but I also hate to waste anyone's money.

I understand their reaction, though. I'm always inspired after a visit to the rose gardens of Bagatelle in Paris—the roses are so big and lush and full of fragrance. Double festoons of climbing roses swing along the gravel paths, rustic arbors drip with blooms. Tree roses cascade canes of pink roses down to the same rose in bush form planted below. Then there's the enchanting wall of roses and clematis in the cottage garden—the yellow roses of 'Maréchal Niel' entangled with a purple clematis, lavender poking out from the foot of a Noisette rose. Absolute heaven. I take notes, and when I'm home I wonder where to start recreating my favorite part of the trip.

Traditional European-style rose gardens are beautiful but not very practical for most gardeners.

If you live in the nation's warmest zones, you'll be able to combine roses with tropical plants to gorgeous effect.

I plant my four-inch liner plant of 'Maréchal Niel', and then winter arrives and doesn't leave for three months. This is a reality check; I garden in New Jersey, not Paris. It gets very cold here, sometimes with lots of snow, but always with long periods of freezing temperatures. Paris has mild winters in comparison. When spring arrives, I pull back the mulch and say "*au revoir*, Maréchal" as I pull out the dead rose. It's back to growing 'Golden Showers'.

The moral of the story is to know your location. Being aware of temperature ranges and other weather phenomena in the part of the country where you have a garden, or plan to start one, will make your gardening experience more satisfying and enjoyable. An understanding of the forces of Mother Nature that control and guide a garden through the change of seasons is important. How cold does it get? How hot are the summers, and for how long? Does it rain? Does it snow? Or, even more basic, which way is east?

But there's still more to understand—you also need to find out what's unique about your specific site before you start breaking ground or bringing home plants, especially when combining plants with different needs and characteristics in one garden. The following sections cover basic principles of regional gardening and some practical guidelines for site selection.

Understanding Your Region

It's important to understand your region's weather and any climatic peculiarities unique to the area where you wish to garden. I've gardened in many different zones, from Maine to Texas. Each area was very different and each was a challenging learning experience. Differences in climate have a strong influence on how plants grow. Some plants thrive where the summers are hot and the winters are mild, others wither away in the heat. Some plants will die when the ground freezes, others need a cold winter to survive. There are variations like this among all plant groups, including roses.

Walls and fences help create microclimates that are warmer than other spots in the garden and may permit plants to flourish that really belong in a warmer zone.

To better understand how plants grow in your region's climate, learn about the factors unique to your region that may affect the garden. Are you near the sea? If so, you need to understand the effects of the ocean on your climate. If you garden in the mountains, do you know from which direction the coldest winds will blow? How cold will it get during the winter, how hot during the summer? These are important questions to answer.

Our country has many different gardening regions, each defined by variations in climate, weather patterns, geography, rainfall, and soil type. These parameters will guide the way you garden in your region and which plants you should choose. Before detailing region information, let's look at the important basics used to define the different horticultural regions of the United States.

Cold Hardiness

Plant hardiness, a term found in all gardening books and plant catalogues, is determined by two things: the plant's ability to survive cold and heat. The lowest temperature a plant can endure determines the cold hardiness of that plant. Many years ago, the United States Department of Agriculture created a cold hardiness map using the average coldest temperatures recorded within the different areas of our country as its criteria. At that time eleven zones were designated, Zone 1 being the coldest with an average minimum temperature of –50F and Zone 11 the warmest with an average minimum temperature of 40F. Over the years, this information has been updated with Zones 2 through 10 subdivided into "a" and "b" levels, creating a total of twenty different cold hardiness zones. This map still serves as the guide used when discussing the zone hardiness of a plant. The USDA and the American Horticultural Society are in the process of updating the hardiness zone map and expect to produce a map with 15 zones rather than the current 11, so keep an eye out for the new version.

These hardiness zones should be taken as reference points only and you should be aware of variations within each zone. Fluctuations in temperatures can make a significant difference in the survival of a plant. How quickly the cold weather happens and whether or not it remains consistently cold makes a difference. Winter thaws can be critical in determining whether or not a plant is going to survive the winter.

The colder a zone, the shorter the growing season. My experience is that in areas with shorter seasons, the plants seem to grow faster and more vigorously as if to get as much out of their limited time as possible. In cold zones, gardeners tend to do most of their planting in the spring after the danger of a freeze has passed. However, if you have at least a month of autumn, I would recommend planting in the autumn. The soil is still warm, there's usually plenty of rain, and the plants are

Even during winter dormancy, roses add interest to the landscape.

EXTREME WEATHER

Be aware of the nature of your climate and make sure the plants you wish to grow can survive the extremes. Winter is the season most people associate with extreme weather. Snow is Mother Nature's mulch, protecting plants from destructive cycles of freezing and thawing. Ice and cold winds can be a garden's worst enemy. Cold winters are beneficial for many old garden roses such as albas, damasks, and gallicas. Many perennials, spring-flowering bulbs, and shrubs also thrive in this environment. Mulching is essential in winter to help keep the ground around the plants frozen during premature thaws.

The catmint planted underneath the rose 'Lavender Lassie' acts as a living mulch.

Heat is also an extreme that does damage. Many plants slow down or go completely dormant during long periods of hot weather. If this is the kind of a climate you garden in, you should be growing tea, China, and Noisette roses with heat-tolerant perennials and annuals. Mulching is essential during summer to keep roots cool and to prevent the soil from drying out.

always marked at a discount! It is advisable to mulch the plants after the first hard freeze to keep them consistently cold during the winter.

Many plants have the natural ability to go dormant as protection during the winter. Those with this ability are categorized as cold hardy plants. Deciduous shrubs and trees lose their leaves and essentially shut down their systems. All roses except for teas and Chinas have this natural ability to go dormant. Perennials can do two things: either store their food in the roots and die to ground level each autumn, or drop their foliage and spend the winter in the garden as a dormant "skeleton." Annuals complete their life cycles each season, and scatter their seeds for next season. Some plants, like daffodils, tulips, and lilies, store everything they need for growth in a bulb deep in the ground during winter.

Heat Hardiness

Until recently, the ill effects of heat on plants had been ignored. Failure of plants in the garden due to heat and confusion caused by the zone system of the cold hardiness map inspired the creation of the American Horticultural Society's heat zone map. In a design similar to the cold hardiness map, the heat zone map is divided into twelve zones. The zones are determined by the average number of days a region may experience temperatures over 86F, the temperature when plants start to display significant signs of heat stress. These are referred to as heat days and Zone 1, the coldest, has an average of one heat day (the highest peaks of the Rockies, for example) while Zone 12, the hottest, could average at least 210 heat days (the lower

southwest corner of Florida and Texas). This information is especially helpful for gardeners in the South and the Southwest, the two hottest regions of our country.

Gardeners in the South appreciate the long autumn season after their typically hot summers. This is the ideal time to plant trees, perennials and shrubs, especially roses. Often, spring doesn't stick around very long, and as soon as the heat of summer arrives, many spring-planted plants aren't ready and can suffer. Roses and others planted in the autumn stand a better chance of establishing strong roots that will help sustain them through both the winter and the following hot summer.

Humidity

Humidity is the amount of moisture in the air, and the higher the level of humidity, the more moisture and the more oppressive the temperature. Prolonged periods of high humidity combined with heat may cause some plants to rot and die. This is especially true of hairy leaved plants such as lambs ears and common garden sage. Black spot and powdery mildew, two major foliage diseases that affect roses, are spread when the humidity levels are high.

Precipitation

Precipitation varies across the country in amount, frequency, and type. Eastern coastal regions are prone to rain year-round, the east coast having more storms during the spring and summer. Winter storms leave a protective layer of snow in our gardens and throughout the Midwest and mountainous areas as well.

EXPOSURE TO THE ELEMENTS

Gardening on rooftops and terraces offers every challenge a gardener could imagine. There's a price to pay for that view. Never mind the facts that you have to lug everything up and down flights of stairs, pay off numerous doormen, and continually worry about leaky roofs and whiny neighbors below; it's the strong wind and heat that continually test the endurance of your plants. Not only are the tops exposed, the root zones are suddenly vulnerable as well since you're gardening in containers, not in the earth. Way up in the sky, plant zone references are hardly valid. Spring comes and goes, and comes again —often in the middle of winter. It's a challenge, but not impossible, to find the right combination of plants to survive this extreme exposure to the elements.

Choose wind-tolerant shrubs and perennials. Densely-petaled roses that fail to open in humid ground-level gardens usually open to perfection in a roof garden. Blackspot and spider mites rarely exist on rooftops. Tasty culinary herbs such as thyme and oregano love this environment, and so does lavender. With proper adjustments in watering and mulching, wise plant selections, and chutzpah you can make a beautiful garden up in the sky.

With well-chosen plants, roof gardens can be just as lovely as their ground-level counterparts.

Southern California has a rainy season during the winter and early spring. Fog is a common form of precipitation in many parts of the country, especially along the northern west coast. The Gulf coast is known for its monsoon-like summer storms. In the center of the country, the summers can vary from drenching storms to hot and dry conditions, depending on the dip of the jet stream or the push of Gulf moisture from the south.

Water is very important for plants, especially roses and any of their suitable companions. Lack of natural precipitation will need to be compensated for with additional irrigation by hand or from an irrigation system.

Altitude

Gardening in a higher altitude not only brings you into a colder zone, but also increases the possibility of exposing your garden to severe weather. Fluctuations in temperatures and strong winds are situations you could encounter when gardening in higher altitudes. Wind and drought tolerance are characteristics to look for in plants in this situation. Gardening seasons in the mountains can be shorter than those only a few miles away at sea level. A key to plant survival in the mountains is to be aware of your bearings. Know where north is, since the coldest winds of the winter will blow from this direction. Mountains can also influence temperature and rainfall for surrounding areas. Coastal ranges can prevent moisture and cooler ocean temperatures from reaching areas on the inland sides of the mountains.

Soil Makeup and pH

Soil across the country is divided into several types based on mineral content, organic content, and fertility. Below are the major soil types.

- *Clay Soil:* made up of extremely fine particles with a high retention of water, heat, and cold; tends to be difficult to dig; very fertile
- *Silty Soil:* from old river bottoms, a fine particle soil with good water retention and moderate fertility
- *Sandy Soil:* a very fast draining soil, composed of larger particles than clay or silt, less likely to compact; since nutrients drain out quickly this type of soil is the least fertile
- *Loam Soil:* a well balanced mix of clay, sand, and silt; good drainage and water retention, very fertile
- *Chalky Soil:* shallow, free draining, moderately fertile, highly alkaline
- *Organic Soil:* derived from decaying plant material, high in mineral content, high in fertility, acidic

The pH is a measurement of the acidity in the soil. The pH of soil is measured on the scale of 0 to 14 with a pH of 7 as neutral. A pH with a higher number than 7 is alkaline, a pH with a number lower than 7 is acidic. Most plants, including roses, do best in a slightly acidic pH range of 5.5 to 6.5.

Evaluating Your Site

At this time, I garden in three regions, all in cold hardiness zone 7 and similar in many aspects, yet different at the same time. A great many factors other than just heat and cold zones affect a garden site. Many of the gardens I tend to are located in a unique area of eastern Long Island, about one hundred miles east of New York City. They are all situated within a mile of the Atlantic Ocean and ten miles from Long Island Sound. This area is definitely affected by water. Temperatures in winter are a little bit warmer than further inland and the summer temperatures are a little bit cooler as well. Wind plays a huge part in the life of a garden; bitter winter winds can damage exposed evergreens and salty summer winds can burn foliage. Mist and fog are regular events as well.

My Brooklyn clients are in a slightly warmer zone, partially due to the higher amount of concrete, enclosed garden spaces, and shelter from the extreme elements. Very close to water, these gardens are all a bit warmer in winter than those further west or north and hotter in the summer due to the number of buildings and less green space. Some of the completely enclosed gardens have plants in bloom nearly twelve months of the year, and Southern magnolias and *Camellia japonica* varieties are capable of wintering over without much difficulty.

My personal garden is in southern New Jersey, about one mile from a large bay and six miles from the ocean. On latitude just south of Philadelphia, I'm practically a Southerner! The garden is protected from the winds off the water by huge old trees. We enjoy a slightly longer season with plants in bloom year-round. Winter ocean storms can drop up to three feet of snow, as late as March, and as early as December. All sorts of camellias bloom in my garden, again, as well behaved plants, and Lady Banks' rose makes an honest effort to bloom on a three-foot plant. The soil is very sandy, and not a rock in sight.

Plants thrive in the gardens in all three regions, as long as we are careful to select plants that will accept the prevailing conditions. The best site for a garden is one that will provide everything the plants need to perform their best—enough sunlight, good fertile soil, and adequate moisture. The site can be flat, have some elevation changes, have a stream, a pond, an ocean nearby, or even be twenty floors high on a terrace in the middle of a city. Your garden will become

both a part of the natural landscape and a part of your home. It should be sited so it is visible from important vantage points both indoors and out.

Light

Locate the sunniest spot in the garden. This is where roses and their companions will grow best. Ever-blooming roses require at least six hours of sunlight each day to grow strong and healthy. They will grow in less light, but they'll bloom less and be more prone to foliage diseases. Once-blooming old garden roses such as the gallicas, damasks, albas, and species will do fine in four to five hours of sunshine. The companions you choose for your roses should suit these sunlight requirements. Some of the plants can be used as underplantings, so they could be types that will grow with less than full sun. But then there will be those that will need as much sun as possible to be worthy of sharing a bed with your roses.

Pay attention to how the sunlight changes through the seasons as the sun moves higher and lower in the sky. When I first planted my garden in Barnegat, I had to replant because I hadn't planned on the massive tulip tree on my property casting as much shade by summer as it does. After planting with great enthusiasm in the early spring, I discovered the site I had initially designated as my rose garden was practically in full shade by summer as the sun rose higher in the sky and the canopy of leaves thickened. I relocated the roses to a site with full sun during the morning and afternoon, and a bit of dappled shade from a neighbor's tree during the middle of the afternoon. This afternoon shade cuts down a bit on the summer heat in the garden. During the winter, as the trees defoliate, my garden is in full sun—good for viewing the evergreens I planted for winter color.

Soil

Get to know your soil. Take a spading fork and push it as far as you can into the ground. If you can get it in at least halfway, then your soil has possibilities. If you can't penetrate the site or the handle breaks, then pick another spot for your garden or create a raised bed on this site—or move to southern New Jersey! In any case, you will need to amend the soil with organic matter.

Get on your hands and knees, grab a handful of soil and smell it, squeeze it—how does it appear to you? It should smell good. Check out the particle sizes. Are they very tiny, like silt, or do you have a very granular soil? Does it smell rancid or pleasantly earthlike? These tactile tests are very important to help you decide what sort of soil you are going to be dealing with. They will also impress your neighbors, who will, no doubt, be watching from behind lace curtains.

There's a simple test to see how well your soil drains or holds water. Clear away a small surface and expose enough soil to dig about eighteen inches deep. In this hole, place an empty coffee can with the top and bottom lids removed. On the same site, dig another hole deep enough to push an empty coffee can sleeve two inches into the soil. Fill both cans to their tops with water, and record how long it takes the water level in each can to drop an

inch. An ideal draining time is about one inch per hour, which occurs in sandy-loam soil. Sandy soil should drain much faster, while clay soil can take as along as 0.02 inches per minute.

To improve either the water retention or the drainage of your soil, add organic materials such as compost or manure. Cow manure (two months out of the cow) increases the water retention of sandy soils; horse manure (a week out of the horse) along with the stable "fixins'" improves the drainage of clay soil. Or, if you are having difficulty locating stables, try garden compost, leaf mold, or fine bark chips—all good for improving both types of soil. Finally, send off a soil sample to your extension agent to find out what's in it. County Extension services will run a complete soil profile for a nominal fee to determine if your soil lacks nutrients or if you have an overabundance of any particular element.

Moisture

To get an idea of the amount of moisture available for your garden, first determine how much rain your area receives. Also, check to see if there are any underground roots that may steal moisture and nutrients from the site. I had a serious problem in the Cranford Rose Garden with invasive roots from nearby Norway maples. None of my newly planted roses would survive the competition of these large established trees. My solution was to plant new roses in 20-gallon nursery pots (21 inches across and 17 inches deep). That was not a fun experience.

Flower gardens do best if they receive an

inch of water weekly. If there isn't that much rain, you'll need to supplement with an irrigation system. If at all possible, install a drip system, which directs water to the base of the plants, preventing the spread of foliar diseases and the knocking over of plants from strong sprinkler jets. Putting down a layer of mulch is an excellent way to maintain moisture around the roots of your plants. I prefer garden compost and manure as mulches. Whatever you decide to use for mulch, it should look good and eventually break down to become a part of the soil. I don't care what they tell you on the local television garden show, do not use pre-colored mulches. They're ugly.

Are you near a significant body of water, such as an ocean, a bay, or a large lake? These bodies of water could be a source of moisture that's not as obvious to you as rain. In some areas, like the northern coast of California, there could be a significant amount of moisture added to the garden by way of fog.

Views

There are some views you want, some you don't. I was faced with the challenge of making my neighbor's hideous above-ground swimming pool disappear. Puncturing its side to cause leaks would have removed me from the annual Pig Roast invitation list. What was I to do? Huge, blue, loud, and ugly—this pool

If you have a neighboring view that's unpleasant, try screening it with a border of roses along the top of the fence.

In my own garden, I "borrow" my neighbor's wisteria from the other side of the fence while it's in bloom to combine with my own yellow climbing rose.

was in the sight-line of the full sun area of my garden. The problem was solved when the neighbors offered to build me a beautiful fence, blocking my view of the pool, and adding a structure to train more roses onto. Of course it didn't happen overnight; it took a great deal of plant sharing to convince the neighbors that the fence was for their benefit as well.

If you have neighbors in close proximity, consider the view you can borrow from them. Are there trees and shrubs in their landscape that create a decent backdrop for your garden? I firmly believe in the "borrowed landscape" approach. On one side of my property are two beautiful red-leaved Japanese maples, in the neighbor's yard. I get the benefit of the backdrop of this beautiful foliar display. (They get the benefits of the exercise from raking the leaves each fall.) On the other side of my property, the neighbors have a wisteria vine that spills into the rambling roses along our shared fence. When the wisteria is in full bloom, I pull the blooms over onto my side of the fence. When they are finished, I give the vines back.

Needs

What does your site need to work as a garden?

■ *Sunlight:* Increase the sunlight by

removing or thinning tall shrubs, carefully pruning tree branches, or removing a tree entirely. On sites where the heat zone days are plentiful, create some midday shade to protect the plants from the hottest time of the day.

- *Soil:* Amend the soil as directed above, or build a raised bed if the soil is too thick with roots or rocks, or too wet. Use stones, wood, or even a wattle design low fence to raise the soil level so you can plant 18 inches deep. In areas such as New Orleans and southeast Texas, it's sometimes very difficult to make anything grow in the native "gumbo" soil—a silt-loam thick with organic material and silt with poor drainage. Raised beds have been good solutions for gardeners in such regions.

- *Water:* In arid climates, choose your plants carefully. The coastal regions of California have a Mediterranean climate—winter and spring rains followed by long periods of dry and warm weather. Tea and China roses work well here. There are many companion plants that adapt well to this cycle of moisture, too. In all arid areas, it pays to mulch the gardens and use a drip watering system to conserve water.

- *Protection from Frost:* Avoid planting in frost pockets. These are depressions in the landscape and are also found at the base of slopes. Frost arrives first in low spots, so you'll be setting yourself up for an early dormancy as well as a late spring start in a situation like this.

- *Shelter from Wind:* If you're near the ocean or a large body of water, no doubt you'll experience strong wind off the water. The same can be said for a site on a hillside—the view is great, but oh, the wind! Figure out some way to create shelter from the wind year-round. Summer winds can dry out plants and soil; winter winds can cause severe burn from desiccation. Structures and hedging would be wise investments in a situation like this. In winter, it's best to wrap evergreens to prevent them from drying out.

I've managed over the years to test the limits of my zone and have had great success in adding plants supposedly not hardy in my area. But I try not to get too attached to some of them, since there's always the chance that and old-fashioned cold winter will come roaring back, and it always does. Meanwhile, 'Mermaid' has made it through some of the hardest winters of the last ten years. This yellow climbing rose covers a south-facing wall on my house. Nearby is a fairly large specimen of *Camellia japonica* 'Professor Sargeant'. He doesn't always bloom, since some winters kill the flower buds, but I still have a beautiful foliage display. I located my "hot" spots—areas of my garden that allow me to play and experiment with less hardy plants—and that's what gardening is all about. Now, if I could only figure out a way to get 'Maréchal Niel' to grow, maybe buy the property behind me to build an orangerie, maybe, maybe, maybe. . .

DESIGNING YOUR GARDEN

IN THIS CHAPTER:

Garden Styles

A client once turned to me and asked, "What does it take to make a great garden?" "Patience," was my reply. Maybe you're starting with a bare patch of land, or you've inherited an older garden, or you've just lugged a pot and soil up to your terrace. These are all beginnings of the opportunity to make a garden of your very own. Perhaps you want a collection of fragrant plants, a garden of pink flowers, a private hideaway, or maybe you're a "rose rustler," and you need to show off your prized "loot." These are all good reasons for having a garden. But making a beautiful garden takes more than sticking plants in the ground—it requires planning, creativity, lots of elbow grease, but most of all, patience.

To make your garden interesting, combine different types of plants and allow them to grow together. Turn a collection of flowers, rare roses, shrubs, or fragrant plants into a fun

This formal rose garden combines hedges, a pergola, and symmetrical plantings to create a strong sense of order.

Another formal garden with repeated rose-covered arches and symmetrical repeated plantings underneath.

garden. Create a space that will display them to their best, show off their most attractive features, and most importantly, provide you with a place to go where you're surrounded by plants you love. These should be your goals. And the best way to achieve those goals is to develop a clear vision of the style of garden you want, then spend some time thinking through the design of that garden before you ever begin digging or planting.

I look forward to winter. This is when I can once again see the bones of my garden—the patterns of boxwood hedges, wooden columns, lattice panels, and rusty towers. These forms are all covered or blocked from view with green growth and flowers during the spring and summer. By the end of

autumn, I look forward to the opportunity to be reacquainted with my garden's design.

My garden is small but very complex. It is partially a sweeping border with hints of a cottage garden, the bones of a traditional style, and the flair of a collector's garden. You really can't get more schizophrenic than that. And at every sunny opportunity I include roses.

There are many styles of gardens. In traditional formal gardens, symmetrical geometric shapes such as squares, circles, and rectangles are typical. In a cottage garden, the shape is informal, defined by the boundaries of the space allotted for the garden. In an expansive border design, a gentle curve invites you in, giving you the feeling of walking into the garden without leaving the lawn or path.

Traditional Rose Garden

Traditional rose gardens have a formal design with strong elements of repetition and symmetry. Inspired by French and Dutch gardens, repeated plantings of a low growing small-leaved evergreen, usually boxwood or Japanese holly (*Ilex crenata*), define the edges of beds containing roses. Hedges are used to create continuous lines and a backdrop to the garden. A parterre design (symmetrical arrangement of square, rectangular, or curved beds) is an example of a formal garden design. The shrubs used for the parterre usually are the only source of color other than the roses. A whimsical variation is to create a knot garden of intertwining hedges by combining different colored foliage or using variegated forms in combination with solid green types.

Tightly clipped shrubs, shaped into balls or cones, are often added to give balance and symmetry in this style of gardening. It's not uncommon to use shrubs of contrasting foliage color, such as *Buxus sempervirens*, common boxwood, with the variegated boxwood, *Buxus sempervirens* 'Elegantissima'.

Simplicity is key with a formal design, and repetition of shapes is essential. A wooden structure or iron pillar centered in the beds to display a climbing rose adds a vertical element to the garden. Columnar evergreens such as boxwood 'Graham Blandy', *Taxus baccata* 'Fastigiata', or *Cupressus sempervirens* 'Swane's Golden Italian Cypress' are excellent choices of plants to add a strong vertical element.

In this informal garden, roses mingle in seeming abandon with yarrow, violas, dianthus, and other companions.

Cottage Garden

An American cottage garden has its roots in the colonial era. Colonial gardeners didn't have the means to create large elaborate gardens; instead the gardens were smaller and near the fronts of houses with an eclectic mix of plants: roses, perennials, herbs, annuals, and shrubs. During the colonial era, gardens were more for survival than for ornamental purposes, since people had to produce not only much of their own food, but their own medicines, as well. Roses were included as medicinal plants and as sources of fragrance and rose water. Today, this type of gardening is still with us but has evolved into a popular ornamental style, especially good for smaller spaces, on roof tops, as an entrance garden to a house, surrounding a deck, or for smaller plantings near a swimming pool.

A cottage garden is of a manageable size and relies heavily on harmony and contrast among flowers, foliage, and growth habits. Evergreens, planted in groups of three, can create a sense of unity and act as the anchor to hold everything together. One columnar evergreen could work as well, if space is a limiting factor. Hedges can help neatly define this garden style; evergreen perennials such as liriope or common kitchen sage can be used to create a loose textured hedge. Dwarf boxwood can add interesting evergreen hedge texture as well. 'Child's Play', a delightful miniature rose, would make a colorful deciduous alternative.

Roses, delphiniums, foxgloves, and hollyhocks are classic ingredients in a cottage garden. Hollyhocks with their large leaves are good as background plants. Use roses as a centerpiece, flanked by the spires of delphiniums and foxgloves. One hybrid tea or ever-blooming shrub rose and three of the tall perennials would create a charming combination. Fill in the front and sides of the garden with lower growing perennials, annuals, and herbs. I generally plant perennials and annuals in odd-numbered groups of at least three, which gives a graceful, informal appearance. Salvia, artemisia, and spring and summer bulbs offer many possibilities in color and fragrance.

Natural Border

A large sweeping border is a naturalistic style of garden when compared to the traditional formal parterre garden. Bigger than a cottage garden, a natural border gives you an opportunity to do basically whatever you want to do. However, the most beautiful of these gardens are well thought out. Understanding the growth habits and blooming cycles of plants is crucial to creating a sense of balance. There is ample space to add structures and ornaments and even the opportunity to create a range of elevations. With a garden of this size it's especially important to plan for winter color and to create a succession of bloom

Roses, even on ornate arches, fit beautifully into the most naturalistic borders.

Repeated groupings of fuchsia-colored perennial geraniums and pale pink rose 'Penelope' down the length of this border establish a strong sense of unity.

boxwood-edged squares ranged on either side of a central path divided by cross-paths, each boxwood square containing a tree rose in the middle, surrounding by lower-growing shrubs. That is a perfectly balanced, symmetrical composition, and most people will feel very comfortable in its midst.

Balance can also be achieved, however, in informal compositions. A flowering tree of moderate size—say, a dogwood—on one side of a central path may be balanced by a grouping of three lower shrubs massed together on the other side of the path. Though the effect is very different than a symmetrical arrangement, the visual weight of the shrubs balances the visual weight of the tree, and the composition is a comfortable one.

Unity and Repetition

Unity is the sense a well-designed garden gives of being a coherent, meaningful whole rather than just a collection of disparate plants and other objects. One of the easiest ways to achieve a sense of unity is by repetition in different parts of the garden of one or more aspects of it, whether plants, colors, materials, or shapes. We noted above that cottage gardens, which can easily suffer from shapelessness if care isn't used in their design, can benefit from repeated groupings of evergreens in the same rounded or upright shapes to act as anchors. Formal gardens almost always contain repeated elements, contributing greatly to their air of coherence or oneness.

Repeating groupings of the same plants—say, roses or delphiniums—several times in a long border lends a sense of unity, as does selecting and sticking to a color scheme rather than mixing flowers of all colors together. Repeated use of foliage shapes creates a nice rhythm in the garden. I use potted tropicals such as blood-leaf banana, elephant's ear, and canna lilies for this effect. Repetition of sword-like foliage from irises and daylilies brings curves and lines into the border that change as the garden matures. Other ways to contribute a unified feel to a garden are to use the same materials for containers—terra cotta, perhaps—or hard-surfacing—brick or stone, maybe—throughout the entire garden.

Harmony and Contrast

Just as in life or music, harmony in the garden means every aspect works together to produce a peaceful, soothing result. But also just as in life or music, too much harmony can get a little boring, so we add occasional jolts of contrast to liven things up and at the same time underscore the pleasures of harmony. A garden composed entirely of spiky, upright plant forms would not feel very harmonious to most people, but an occasional spiky accent against a background of more rounded forms draws attention to the smoothness of the round shapes and jolts the eye into appreciating them. Similarly, a perennial garden composed entirely of plants with large,

The contrast of the spiky shape of the delphinium with the rounded rose shows off both blossoms to their best advantage.

rough leaves or of plants with small, refined leaves would quickly dull the eye and the mind. However, the fine, feathery leaves of a fern offset by the broad flat surface of a hosta leaf draws attention and appreciation to both.

Contrast and harmony among plantings makes a garden interesting to explore. As soon as you combine any rose with any perennial, annual, or shrub, you have a contrast of some sort. I use a weeping Japanese larch, *Larix kaempferi* 'Pendula', as a fine-needled focal point in one bed. The delicate needles cascade down in delightful contrast to the larger leaved perennials and roses, creating a softening effect in this part of the garden. A classic example of contrast is to use small-

The upright evergreen boxwood 'Graham Blandy' gives a terrific vertical accent to a garden, especially in winter.

leaved shrubs such as boxwood and Japanese holly to create a dense backdrop for the larger leaved roses. In my curb planting there are repeated groups of *Sedum spectabile* 'Brilliant' interplanted with the pink single hybrid tea 'Our Lady of Guadalupe' and *Caryopteris* 'Longwood Blue'—an interesting contrast of foliage and flower types.

Form

Form refers to shape. Silhouettes of plants and structures in the winter, twining stems, arching growth habits, sweeping curves, square beds, winding paths, straight allées, peaked arches, fluted pottery, solitary pillars—these are among the many forms that make up a garden. Swirls of petals, panicles of blooms, spiked inflorescences, single stems, quilled petals, opposite leaves, square stems—these are the details of flower and plant shapes. Forms in the garden come from both structural architectural features and from plants.

Structural elements are permanent features, introducing patterns and shapes to the garden as well as serving a functional purpose. Structures anchor the design in place with their permanence and provide a place for plants to grow. They define the spaces, create rooms in a garden, and expand the garden from a mere collection of plants to a true garden.

While structural architectural features give a sense of permanence, plant forms contribute greatly to a garden as an important ever-changing design element. Generally speaking, roses such as hybrid teas, floribundas, and any others that are continually pruned to produce blooms don't contribute much beauty in terms of plant shape. Species roses have the most natural beauty; a minimal amount of pruning will improve them year after year. Old garden roses, shrub roses, and climbers have interesting architecture, especially if assisted by skillful use of a pair of pruning shears.

There are many trees and shrubs that can be relied on to provide shapes of permanent beauty in the garden. Columnar—tall, straight, and narrow—is my favorite plant form to use in a garden. It's especially good for small gardens and tight spaces. The plants I use to provide this shape are *Ilex crenata* 'Sky Pencil', Irish yews, and 'Graham Blandy' boxwoods. These evergreens are naturally upright and vertical, so they need no pruning to remain that way. Balls, pyramids, cones, mushrooms, rectangles, and squares are all forms you can introduce into the garden with evergreen shrubs. Keeping these shapes will involve regular shearing and clipping—small leaved and fine-needled evergreens such as boxwood, ilex, and yews are the best plants for this.

Defining Boundaries

Boundaries give the overall garden a shape or form that distinguishes it from the surrounding landscape. To create your garden space, you'll want to frame it or otherwise define its boundaries. Enclose the garden within a solid wall, a fence, a hedge, or an allée of trees—these are lines you create to determine where the garden begins and ends. Within the garden you can further define beds and spaces and at the same time create shapes by adding edging, pathways, and structures. You can even create rooms within your garden just as you have rooms in your house.

Fences, Walls, and Gates. Fences and walls have their practical uses. They enclose a garden and give you privacy. They offer protection from the elements and can even increase the hardiness level in your garden by a zone or so. They keep deer out, pets under control, people out, or people in. They also offer more space to grow plants. Walls and fences can be constructed of wood, stone, or metal.

Walls don't have to create a complete enclosure to be effective. They can be used as partitions to divide a garden into rooms, create private spaces within a garden, and perhaps even add a bit of mystery. A lattice fence used to separate one garden area from another allows a partial view into the next room, without giving the entire garden away in one glance. Fruit trees can be espaliered to create an interesting living fence as a backdrop for roses or as a freestanding fence to separate areas in the garden. Heights of partitions can vary, from very short to very tall, depending on the scale of your garden and your design.

At some point in your fence or wall, you'll need one or more gates. A gate covered in roses says welcome. A solid gate that is shut says stay away. Either one creates an access point or an exit for the garden. Passing through a gate brings you from one world to another. The gate should reflect the character of the garden. It should frame the garden, setting the mood for what lies ahead.

GOOD TALL HEDGES

Some recommended evergreen shrubs for a background or tall hedge are

- *Chamaecyparis obtusa* (Hinoki False cypress)
- *Cryptomeria japonica* 'Yoshino' (Yoshino Japanese Cedar)
- *Osmanthus fragrans* (Tea Olive)
- *Prunus laurocerasus* (Cherry Laurel)
- *Taxus × media* 'Hatfieldii' (Yew)
- *Thuja occidentalis* 'Emerald' (Arborvitae)

Evergreen hedges define this garden room, which is furnished with the eglantine rose, the Bourbon rose 'Louise Odier', catmint, santolina, and gorgeous old containers.

Paths can be made of many surfaces, including green grass, which shows off surrounding plants to perfection.

Hedges. A tall hedge can serve the same function as a wall or fence. An evergreen hedge offers the most privacy along with interesting color possibilities, while a deciduous hedge brings a marked change in the character of the garden as the seasons change. Hedges obviously take longer to become effective than do constructed walls or fences, and they will compete for water and nutrients with the other plants in the garden.

Like walls, hedges can be of varying heights and serve different purposes. I prefer to use evergreens in my gardens. As tall hedges they create a frame or background, and as low hedges they define garden beds and create patterns within the garden. Most important of all, they create color for the winter garden.

A hedge can be used to divide a garden into individual rooms and also to add a colorful pattern through a bed. 'Simplicity' is a great larger shrub rose, particularly useful for hedges, and available in pink, red, white and yellow. One garden I maintain has an elaborate boxwood knot garden, featuring two types of roses—'Cherries 'N Cream', a purple moss rose, and 'Pure Perfume', a white

GOOD SHRUBS FOR LOW HEDGES

Some recommended evergreen shrubs for low hedges are

- *Buxus* species (Boxwood)
- *Chamaecyparis obtusa* 'Nana' (Dwarf Hinoki False cypress)
- *Ilex crenata* (Japanese Holly)
- *Lonicera nitida* (Box-Leaf Honeysuckle)
- *Taxus* × *media* 'Hicksii' (Hicks Yew)

Bourbon rose with pink-kissed flower buds. The roses are planted within the knots of boxwood, an outstanding combination of foliar textures and color contrasts.

Paths. Paths through the garden create lines and shapes that invite you in and lead you through the garden. A garden path can be straight or curved, long or short, made of brick, stone, gravel, wood, or grass, or just a few stepping-stones into a bed. My lawn has become the garden pathway, a gentle sweeping curve of green. Stone is ideal in heavy traffic areas to prevent trampling and establishes a stronger line through the garden. Steps can be added to a path to lead you from one level to the next.

Edging. The purpose of an edge is to define a garden. Sometimes a manicured look, other times a whimsical feature, both outline the shape of a bed and at the same time bring form to the garden. An edge can be as simple as a small trench between the garden and the lawn. Stone and brick are traditional edging materials. Antique iron hoops, tile, wood— these are all perfectly good materials to use as well. An edge can also be a repeated planting. Some edging plants commonly used with roses are lavender, boxwood, holly, germander, and even miniature roses.

Installing edging provides an opportunity to make new patterns in the garden, a chance to create something whimsical. It is also an opportunity to bring in patterns, details, and a sense of individuality, as well as ornamentation.

Evergreen edging immediately makes your garden a four-season garden. Dwarf, small-leaved evergreens create the tidiest and most

For a non-living edging, try brick or stone rather than plastic or metal. Here, violas combine prettily with an edging of concrete pavers.

PERENNIAL EDGING

Here's a short list of perennials to use as a living edge

- Liriope
- Hellebore
- Rosemary
- Dwarf Iris
- Dwarf Agapanthus
- Sage
- Society Garlic
- Garlic Chives

An informal edging of roses and dusty miller spills out onto this brick path, giving informal charm to a formal path.

formal living edge. The most popular choice is *Buxus sempervirens* 'Suffruticosa', a slow-growing boxwood great for making straight lines or curves. There are also several cultivars of *Buxus microphylla* var. *japonica*, known as the little-leaf boxwood, that are good edging plants, especially in the warmer regions of the South. One highly recommended cultivar is the dark green 'Morris Dwarf'. At times the fragrance of boxwood can be a bit over-powering. A good alternative, but still with a tidy formal look, is *Ilex crenata*, otherwise known as Japanese holly. There are many varieties of this small leaved holly that produce the same look of a boxwood hedge without the fragrance.

Evergreen doesn't always mean clipped and shaped. There are other choices with a less rigid look. One of my favorites for small intimate spaces is sweet box, or *Sarcococca hookeriana*, a low-growing evergreen shrub with loosely arranged leaves. This plant has the added bonus of a delightful spring fragrance from small white flowers hidden

from view by the glossy foliage.

Evergreen perennials can also be used for a garden edge. I frequently use *Liriope muscari* 'Big Blue', a grass-like member of the lily family. With clumps spaced twelve inches apart, I have a delightful edge of violet spikes during the month of August emerging from the dark green foliage bordering a bluestone path. Some years the foliage is damaged by snow or severe cold. To remedy this, I simply cut out the damaged foliage or shear the plant close to the ground. Each spring, leaves emerge from the center of the plant. Otherwise, I do absolutely nothing to maintain an edge of 'Big Blue'.

Plants aren't the only option available for a good edge. The easiest edge, but perhaps requiring the most maintenance, is to simply cut a separation between the garden bed and the lawn with either a spade or a half-moon edger, a tool specifically created for this purpose. One of my favorite chores each year in the Cranford Rose Garden was to cut the edge of each bed with a half-moon edger guided by a line of string pulled taut to mark the edge. This always gave me the cleanest cut and great satisfaction when I looked back to see the sharp division between the lawn and the rose bed. I would cut my edges twice a season. How often you do this chore will depend on how fast the lawn encroaches on the bed.

I don't recommend plastic or steel edging since there will still be a need to trim the grass that grows over the edging material. If you garden in a zone where the soil freezes and thaws, there's the strong possibility that the edging material will pop up. And that's very annoying! Try something creative and decorative such as bricks, stone, antique tiles, or iron curves. There's no reason you can't have fun with this—make your garden distinctive by starting with a unique edge. I use several different materials as edging in my garden. Near the house I use old brick, the same that was used for the foundation of the house. This ties the garden directly to the architecture of the house. I simply lay the bricks flat, end to end. The height of this edge is the width of one brick.

I'm creating a new bed in front of an espalier of apple trees. The design of the espalier is medieval, called a Belgian fence, with the apples trained into diamond patterns. In this bed, I've added several old roses including the single-flowered version of the musk rose, 'Carefree Delight' (Bourbon), and 'Fairy Queen' (Portland). In keeping with the old theme, I decided a wattle, or woven, fence would be appropriate. The materials I used were willow branches woven between 1/2-inch bamboo stakes. I spaced the bamboo

stakes 6 inches apart to accentuate the curves of the willows as I wove them through the bamboo stakes. The height of this edging is 9 inches. A variation on this theme is a raised garden I created for a client using wattle as a 9-inch high wall holding the soil in place. The sod

I cut to make the rectangular beds lines the inside of the wattle to keep soil from leaking through.

Edging my bed containing the shrub roses 'Knockout' and 'Topaz Jewell' is a variation on antique iron hoops but using branches of forsythia instead. I don't have a preferred cultivar, any long, pencil-thick forsythia branch will do. Insert one end of a cut branch firmly into the soil at the edge of the bed. Insert the other end at a point that allows the curve you're creating to be about a foot high. Insert the next branch in the same manner, but start this one directly under the highest point of the previous curve. Repeat this for the distance of your edge. Eventually you'll have a series of overlapping branch hoops running the length of the bed. During the winter, I see a whimsical series of brown curves. In spring, the hoops bloom and grow. As they grow, either insert the new growth to lengthen the edge, or trim it away.

Garden Structures

Structures bring an important design element, so often missing from gardens, into the garden—a vertical form. Arches and pergolas can transform tedious expanses of plants into interesting and seductive above-ground gardens. A pillar or tower engulfed in roses, rising up from a garden of perennials,

BUILDING PILLARS AND TOWERS

Pillars and towers offer simple ways to display roses above the garden. A rustic look for pillars is the easiest, least expensive, and often the most beautiful. I prefer rough cedar posts with a diameter of four to six inches and at least eight feet in height, allowing for two feet to be sunk into the ground. If rustic doesn't work in your garden, iron or aluminum posts with decorative finials offer a more refined style. Whether you've chosen a rustic or refined design, plant two roses per pillar. For an interesting effect, combine a once-blooming variety with an ever-blooming cultivar to extend your season of bloom. One of my favorite once-blooming roses for a pillar is the purple moss rose 'Cherries 'N Cream'. Another interesting rose to use on a pillar is 'Hansa' or 'John Cabot' or 'William Baffin', a very old gallica that produces a beautiful hip display for winter.

Lean three or four posts together and you have a tower. Or, if you desire a more formal design there are many styles of towers to choose from: open sides, enclosed with lattice, pointed tops, columnar, or even circular. It's important that the base of the tower measure at least 2 to $2^1/_2$ feet from corner to corner or in diameter. Depending on the scale of your garden, a height from 6 to 10 feet creates a dramatic display. One four-cornered tower could accommodate up to four rose bushes; a triangular tower could be planted with three. Again, as with the pillars, mix ever-blooming and once-blooming roses for a longer blooming season.

For towers and pillars, it's important to train the rose canes in a wrapping style. Spiral them around in parallel patterns. Not only does this make the canes send out side shoots, but this shape also adds to the beauty of the design. The side shoots that grow as a result of the wrapping will produce the best roses—from the bottom of the structure all the way to the top.

improves the aesthetics of the garden. In a practical sense, structures provide more space for roses and other plants to grow. Roses can be displayed up and over the beds and walkways, creating rooms and ultimately a more intimate feeling within the garden.

Pillars and Towers. Pillars and towers are structures that can be used as solitary ornaments in the garden or placed in series, strengthening the sense of visual perspective.

Pillars can be decorative, rustic, or plain iron rods. Connecting pillars with chains or ropes and training roses across them to create festoons adds more opportunities to display roses as well as providing an elegant addition to the garden.

Arches. Every garden needs at least one arch. An arch is the ideal frame for supporting climbing roses. Arches can be curved, peaked, flat, or as embellished as your budget will

Pillars, towers, and obelisks such as this one establish strong vertical patterns in a garden while providing support for climbing roses. Note how clever this design is with the obelisk echoing the shape of the conical evergreens further in the background.

allow. Besides adding new shapes to the garden, these structures become links from one border to the next, giving perspective to the garden, and creating entrances to new areas of the garden.

Pergolas. Pergolas are essentially a series of arches connected together to make one unit. Pergolas offer shelter in the garden, provide more space for plants to grow and be displayed, and add an additional vertical

element of interesting architectural value. It's especially nice if you can build seats into your pergola.

Seats. You need a place to sit and view the garden. A garden seat always adds a romantic touch. I have two old Adirondack chairs that are now completely engulfed in Virginia creeper and rotting from below. Hey, but they look great! I obviously no longer use these seats for sitting; instead they've become garden ornaments. Soon they'll be mulch. More functional seats offer a place to rest and view the garden, and also serve as focal points within the design.

Pots and Planters. Planters play a key part in a garden design. These have functional as well as decorative uses. I have a combination of styles—a wooden planter on my curb, home to my white polyantha rose 'Crystal Fairy' or 'Sea Foam'; time-worn antique concrete urns showcasing annuals and miniature boxwoods for colorful accents; modern large concrete pots to display annuals, cannas, and brugmansia in strategic locations; and terracotta pots with tender tropical plants that are moved onto the porch as winter approaches. In some instances I use pottery to mark an important intersection of pathways. I use other containers to add instant color and texture to a bed. Containers also offer the opportunity to move plants around the garden to show them off to best advantage.

FESTOONS OF ROSES

Rose festoons will add a whimsical flair to your garden. There's nothing more beautiful than a boa of roses hanging low over a garden bed. One method of creating a festoon is to drape a chain (preferably a 1-inch, heavy gauge iron) or thick rope between poles or towers. If the structures are about 12 feet high, you could make a double garland. The swag, or swags, should hang gracefully over the garden bed—as close as 5 feet from the ground at the lowest point of the curve. A single festoon could run across the middle of a bed, or you could use it as a backdrop to the garden. A double festoon would look much nicer as a backdrop. Plant one or two roses at the base of each support, and train them to meet at the midpoint of the chain or rope.

Another style of festoon is to have the swag hang low, about a foot from garden level at its lowest point. Plant the rose at this spot, and let it run up the swag in either direction, and have other roses coming down from the supports. I've seen this style used very effectively in European gardens both as a backdrop and as a mid-border design. Unfortunately the best roses to use for swags are usually those with the fiercest prickles. Select a vigorous variety with pliable canes—ramblers such as 'Wild Spice' or 'America' or 'Joseph's Coat' are perfect for this style. Ramblers are the easiest to work with, but they only bloom once each season. Try ever-blooming large-flowered climbing roses such as 'New Dawn' or 'Lace Cascade' in combination with the vigorous ramblers for a continuous display.

You'll need at least two growing seasons for the roses to meet on the chains. In the meantime, you'll have to prune regularly to keep the festoon looking neat. As the plants grow, wrap their canes around the chain or rope. Limit the design to three or four canes tightly twisted around the chain, and remove all other growth. The amount of time it takes for the roses to cover the swag will depend on the distance, growing conditions, and the roses you select.

Color combinations in the garden should suit your taste—here the red nicotiana and the golden English rose are vibrant and striking.

Water in the Garden. Water is a very relaxing element to introduce to the garden. It can be as simple as a birdbath or as complex as an elaborate fountain or a stream and pond fully stocked with plants and fish. Fountains and birdbaths offer opportunities to add a sculptural vertical element to the garden. And these fanciful focal points bring birds into the garden. Ponds add light and texture to the garden as they reflect the sky and trees above. Ponds and pools also offer an opportunity to bring aquatic plants into the garden. Tall stands of papyrus provide an airy, yet substantial green vertical element. Water sounds are soothing. Even when just the sprinklers are running, I go into a trance.

Color and Fragrance

Color and fragrance are two design elements that make big contributions to the overall mood of a garden and to its impact on human visitors. Hot colors—reds, oranges, and yellows—tend to make viewers feel energetic, even restless. Cooler colors—pinks, blues, lavenders—are restful and calming. Fragrance from flowers and foliage is appealing and evocative, often rousing memories of other gardens in other places.

Garden Color

Color is a key element we need to consider for every season in the garden, not just during the growing season. Color is everywhere. It creates interest, draws us into a space, and pleases the eye. Although when we think of color, we typically think of flowers, the reality is that the dominant color in any garden is green from the plant foliage. There are many, many shades of green, ranging from bluish to yellowish to pinkish, and of course, the foliage of some plants is variegated, combining another color with green. Although at any given time, blossoms may add their sparkle and brilliance to a garden, the real color workhorse in the garden is plant foliage.

Your garden is an extension of your home, so you should think of it as another room. When it's cold or unpleasant to be outside, you may not spend as much time in the garden, but it's there to enjoy during those sunny moments or warm spells in winter. The off-season needs color as much as the peak seasons, and you need to plan for those times when color will be scarce, as well as for times of peak bloom. Off-season color may seem a bit more challenging, but the possibilities are many: evergreen trees and shrubs, with various shades of green and variegated patterns; colorful stems; fruits and berries; bark; and of course, any winter-blooming shrubs, perennials, bulbs, and annuals you can find! I'm always adding pansies and other cool weather annuals to my garden; even if they only give me an extra month of color, they are worth the effort.

Don't overlook the value of structures, both ornamental and functional, as a source of year-round color. Pottery, posts, pillars, towers, or any other garden treasures that appeal to you contribute their share of color.

Garden Fragrance

It's a humid August morning, nearing the end of a month of hot and humid days. Most of my roses have gone into a dormant phase; there are very few with blooms to enjoy. Recently, as is typical of late August, the evenings have been cooler. As if it were a signal, the garden is starting to show renewed signs of life. One indication of this is that while I sit at my desk a wonderful fragrance is wafting through my office. It's coming from the bed immediately outside the window where I've created a shrub garden of fragrance—what I consider one of the most important elements of garden design. The source of the perfume I've detected is the centerpiece of this bed, 'Pure Perfume', the double-flowered musk rose—responding to the cool evenings by producing a seemingly endless supply of fresh and fragrant roses. That's exactly why I planted this old rose in that spot.

Fragrance is a key component in any garden, especially a garden with roses. Fragrance and roses have been connected to gardening all through history; roses have been an important source of fragrance as long as there have been gardens. Ancient civilizations dropped perfumed petals of damask and gallica roses from the ceilings at climactic moments of their revels. Colonial innkeepers scattered damask and centifolia petals across the floors of bedchambers to mask the smells of beer and perspiration. I create gardens of intoxicating fragrances to perfume the night air.

Some of the more fragrant roses to choose from are in the old garden rose group.

Damask and alba roses head this list for climates with cold winters. Temperate zones have the added luxury of growing tea roses, noisettes, and the musk rose. There has been a significant resurgence in fragrance with modern roses, most notably the cultivars of shrub roses being produced in England under the group name of "English" roses. The English are no longer alone in the renewed love affair with rose fragrance; there are many new fragrant hybrid tea roses, climbers, and other shrub types introduced each season from American breeders as well.

Unfortunately not all roses are fragrant, and there will also be periods during the season when there may not be roses in bloom. That's when you have to rely on companion plants to do their part in the design by contributing fragrance to the garden, as well as complementing the perfumes of your most fragrant roses.

Some plants have a noticeable fragrance during the day, some only at night, while some are capable of producing fragrance all the time. Often the fragrant oils are locked in the leaves of plants, only released when the foliage is crushed or brushed against. When designing a garden, keep this in mind as you decide on placement of your plants in the garden.

There are many varieties of annuals, perennials, and herbs with fragrant flowers and many with fragrant foliage, as well. Many culinary herbs such as sage, basil, thyme, and oregano with their strong foliage fragrances have a place in the ornamental garden, especially as companions to roses. There are also many non-invasive members of the mint family with fragrant foliage—varieties of agastache, calamintha, and many beautiful salvias. The tall growing garden heliotrope, *Valerian officinalis*, is a source of floral fragrance as are many of the summer lilies, acidanthera, and nicotiana. These are just a sample of the many choices you'll come across when searching for flower perfume.

Fragrance in the garden is a four-season element. Southern gardens and other warm climate areas have the unfair advantage of being able to grow fragrant winter shrubs. Wintersweet and tea olive fill the air of the South during February. Some sheltered gardens in Zone 7 can also enjoy these as well. Winter honeysuckle is another favorite, while witch-hazel extends the possibility of winter fragrance further north. *Daphne* × *transatlantica* 'Jim's Pride' produces a fragrance in my garden whenever it's in bloom—that's usually every month of the year. I use *Sarcococca hookeriana*, sweet box, as edging in my gardens. This low-growing evergreen shrub produces a sweet early spring fragrance. Spring-flowering bulbs also offer lots of opportunities for early season fragrance.

Texture

Your garden is composed of layers, each layer absorbing light and reflecting it back to you in different ways. Patterns are created by the way light plays with these textures. As a breeze blows through a garden, the textures change as the foliage and branches move. The weave of a garden is complex. Texture, like color and fragrance, is a key four-season element of a garden. The main sources for texture are

The pink blossoms of 'The Fairy' rose make a smashing combination with the purple foliage of the 'Silver Miles' barberry.

foliage and flowers, inviting the eye and beckoning you to touch. But stems and fruit also contribute to the elaborate pattern.

Foliage Texture

Everyone likes to touch plants. It's hard to resist the sticky glands of a moss rose, the silver-gray fuzzy leaves of lamb's ears, or the ever-so-soft leaves of scented geraniums. An encounter with these textures is a memorable and sensual experience. Use them in the garden, growing them where you can easily reach and touch them. Plant them near benches, at the edge of raised beds, or in pots so you can move them around the garden.

Foliage texture creates subtle layers of density. You may not realize it at first, but foliage patterns are often what really draw your attention in the garden. As the breeze moves through or as the light shifts, you suddenly notice the shadows and shapes. That's the beauty of texture in the garden. A number of plants contribute delicacy: ferny-leaved species roses *Rosa hugonis* and *Rosa primula*, thread-like foliage of coreopsis, feathery leaves of bronze fennel, fine cut-leaf patterns of *Centurea gymnocarpa* 'Colchester White'. Then there are the bold textures of cannas, elephant's ears, and even bananas, which can be used to create dramatic focal points and contrast with finer textures. But texture also has to do with surfaces. Downy lavender leaves, glossy camellia foliage, and the shiny hybrid tea foliage all catch light in different ways and at different levels of the garden. These become beacons of the border.

Combining plants with foliage of different sizes and types will make your border more interesting. Try the fern-like species roses with broader leaved perennials such as *Eupatorium rugosum* 'Chocolate' or the annual strobilanthes. Not only do the leaf sizes differ, but the foliage color creates an interesting contrast as well. The lacy patterns of the species rose plays off the denser leaves of the other two plants. In my garden, the larger leaves of the large-flowered climber 'Autumn Sunset' combine with the fine needles of the blue atlas cedar as the rose climbs further up and into this tree. This creates a stunning combination of textures and color.

Flower Texture

In most gardens, the leaves are the backdrops for the flowers. In a way, I feel flowers contribute as much to the texture of a garden as they do to its color. Single-petaled roses are especially valuable this way. The tightly packed flower buds of *Rosa primula* and other species are dainty treasures that cling closely to the arching canes. In the summer-blooming roses, the wavy petals and prominent stamens of 'Betty Prior', the ethereal blooms of 'Mutabilis' hovering like colorful butterflies over the garden, the wide face of 'Mermaid', with her soft butter-yellow petals and golden stamens, opening from long tapered flower buds—all add an intriguing lightness to the border.

The summer sun catches the convoluted texture of 'Knockout' and 'Topaz Jewell' as they and other semi-double roses tease you with glimpses of golden centers. The soft texture of the pink petals of 'Mary Rose', the quilted layers of the petals of 'Mme. Hardy', and the bold stripes of 'Perle des Panachees' are just a sampling of the diverse patterns of blooms shrub roses and old garden roses bring to the garden. And of course, the hybrid teas with their trophies displayed on long stems, held high with honor, are bursting with texture. The curves and points of the soft petals; the long tapered buds, some with exaggerated sepals; the concentric arrangements as the petals unfurl, the quilted cushions and the high-centered beauties—all add to the intricate patterns of texture that make up a beautiful garden.

But what about that inevitable period of time when the roses aren't in bloom? Not to worry, there are unlimited sources of flower textures. Peonies with their globular masses of beauty, the quill-like petals of dahlias, spiked inflorescences of salvia, and umbels of fennel and Queen Anne's lace are just a few of the possibilities.

The English rose 'Katherine Morley' looks especially lovely when mingling with the needles of the common rosemary. And imagine the fragrance as you brush by!

Texture from Fruits and Seeds

Often, we're too quick to deadhead faded flowers and don't get the opportunity to enjoy the fruits and seeds of their labor. Many roses produce hips of various colors, shapes, and textures. If you live in a northern climate, it's best to stop deadheading repeat-blooming roses by the end of summer to help them harden off for the winter. One way they do this is by setting fruit and seed—rose hips. Put the pruning shears away and enjoy one of the autumnal features of these roses as they display hips of all shapes and sizes. By fall, many of the species and old garden roses may have already dropped their hips, while others are just starting to show them off. High in the upper branches of my blue atlas cedar are fat orange hips of 'Autumn Sunset'. Scattered about the ground is a mulch of spiny hips from *Rosa roxburghii,* discarded but still beautiful.

Besides rose hips, there's a plethora of fruits and seeds waiting for you in the garden—shiny apples, fuzzy peaches, firm grapes, the angular spikes of crunchy seeds on the chaste tree, *Vitex agnus-castus,* a favorite feeding stop for birds, particularly cardinals and goldfinches, the shiny red fruits of the dogwood tree, and the long, fuzzy seed pods of wisteria. Many of these, including rose hips, will last the entire winter as holiday and winter ornaments for the garden.

Bark Texture

Winter is the season *Rosa roxburghii,* with its brown exfoliating bark, becomes the focal point of my garden. Proper pruning further enhances the beauty of this shrub and makes the texture more visible and a part of the garden during the growing season as well. Trunks of all sorts of trees, shrubs, and vines contribute to the year-round textural beauty of the garden. There are numerous varieties with peeling bark, mottled patterns, and vivid color displays to consider. *Stewartia koreana* and *Stewartia pseudocamellia* are both beautiful examples of trees that are not too imposing in the garden and offer a wonderful palette of bark. *Stewartia pseudocamellia,* Japanese stewartia, develops a striated muscle-like texture with peeling bark; *Stewartia koreana,* Korean stewartia, offers a range of colors from green, to gray, to cinnamon as the bark flakes away. My crape myrtle 'Natchez' is starting to shed from the oldest trunks, revealing smooth trunks of a delicious butterscotch-swirled cinnamon color.

I inherited an old deutzia with my garden. I've kept this shrub for two reasons—the shower of white flowers each spring and the exfoliating bark display in the winter. Aging stems of climbing hydrangea, clematis, and even grapes all offer a range of textures and colors for decorating the walls, fences, and pergolas of the garden.

Texture from Ornaments

Sources of texture are not limited to plants. Wood, stone, iron, and various other materials introduce textures in the guise of ornamental features or functional structures. Cedar posts, with flaking and peeling bark still intact, create a rustic texture and a perfect vehicle for displaying pillar roses and annual vines.

Wooden tubs and cedar planters add a softer touch to a container garden. Fine finished wood, natural or stained, enhances the aesthetic value of the garden. Leave structures natural or paint them with colors to complement the landscape, whether to blend in or to jump out and make a bold statement.

Posts of aluminum or iron, painted or rusting, add elegance and character to a garden. Black painted structures disappear

The bark of trees, such as this eucalyptus, adds great texture to the garden and provides a good foil for rose blossoms in companionable colors.

into the background to let the roses have the show in summer, then take center stage in winter. Rusted iron adds a color that is very compatible in the garden, and the patina of copper is stunning as a background color for roses. Latticework is an easy and instant way to add texture to any garden—the smaller the openings, the finer the weave. Lattice can be left to weather naturally or it can be painted as a source of color in the garden as well.

Stone belongs in every garden. Sometimes you don't have a choice—every time a spade goes in the ground, another boulder is born. Where I garden, near the coast of New Jersey, rocks are rare and highly sought-after commodities. There's an indigenous stone of this region known locally as "bog iron." A rusty brown conglomerate loaded with sand, iron, and lots of textured surfaces, these beautiful rocks come out of the ground ready for the garden. We've used them for edging, for the foundation of our fountain, to create the waterfall for our sunken pond, or just as a place for moss to grow, adding character to the beds.

Pottery, brick edging, pathways, flagstones, stepping stones, boulders, columns of stone, and stone walls—all of these are non-living garden components that add texture to the garden.

Design Examples

The following two examples of gardens I designed illustrate the design principles discussed above. While the gardens are quite different, they are both beautiful and fragrant four seasons of the year.

A Walled Garden

Located in Zone 7, seven-foot stucco walls on three sides and the wall of the house enclose the rectangular space outside the clients' bedroom that I have been asked to convert into a garden. The only way into this garden is through a gate or the master bedroom. It's a very private space. The only pre-existing plant material is the lawn filling the entire space. The goal is to make this a fragrant garden of pink and white flowers with enough room for two lawn chairs, a small table, and an outdoor shower.

The first step is to create a planting space without taking away too much of the sitting area. We did this by digging out a two-foot wide bed around the perimeter of the space, leaving the center lawn to define the sitting area and to serve as a path to each of the doors and gate. Within this perimeter bed I created a fragrant four-season garden.

Winter

As a vertical element, without taking up too much space, eight-foot specimens of *Ilex crenata* 'Sky Pencil' are planted in repetition along the two longest walls, framing the doors and creating symmetry within the space. Centered on these walls, opposite each other, are three-tiered fruit tree espaliers—a Bartlett pear and an Asian pear. Dormant vines and roses are trained to cover the walls, adding interesting patterns and textures. The beds are edged with *Sarcococca hookeriana humilis*, and a cold hardy camellia, 'Long Island Pink', grows in the three shaded corners. With these textured evergreens, the garden beds are established, a sitting area is created, and the walls are now a part of the garden. For winter

Good garden design can take a beautiful home and make it even more stunning. This is the porch before the garden was created...

fragrance, 'Wintersweet' (*Chimonanthus praecox* 'Lutea') is tucked into a corner. Eventually this will be trained on the wall as it sends out long arching canes. The spicy fragrance permeates the cold February air in the garden.

Spring
Fragrance begins again in mid-March as the hidden blooms of the sweet box, *Sarcococca*, fill the air with their perfume. For a spring bulb display, the beds are planted with fragrant bloomers, all naturalizing types: a cluster-flowering species tulip, *Tulipa turkestanica,* several double-flowered narcissus 'Bridal Crown', 'Cheerfulness', 'Abba', and 'Albus Plenus Odoratus', and lily-of-the-valley. The sweet box hides the bulbs' foliage

as it fades.

The roses begin growing in early April. They're trained to cover the walls. 'Paul's Himalayan Musk Rambler', a blush-colored climbing rose with a vigorous climbing habit, produces long canes that fill the wall with a textured pattern as well as fragrant spring roses. 'Zépherine Drouhin' provides fragrance, continual bloom, and foliage color. Since this variety has no prickles, I felt comfortable planting it near the doorways as well as on the lattice partition of the outdoor shower. In each of the two sunniest corners I've planted fragrant roses—'Whisper', a pure white climber and 'Abraham Darby', a shrub rose with peachy-pink blooms.

For an extra touch of texture and fragrance, I also planted the walls with

and this is the porch afterward, brimming with roses, iris, peonies, yarrow, lamb's ears, and other rose companions.

climbing hydrangea and *Akebia quinata*, the chocolate vine, which produce curious foliage and floral displays with the roses. Akebia blooms in early spring; its small chocolate-colored flowers giving off a delectable fruity fragrance. The hydrangea blooms in early summer.

Summer

As summer begins, the roses come into bloom and fill the garden with their fragrance, day and night. Within arm's reach of the chairs, planted at the base of each of the espaliered fruit trees, is a large specimen of white lavender—the cultivar is unknown but it's very fragrant. During the summer, *Acidanthera murieliae,* heliotrope 'Alba', *Nicotiana sylvestris,* and night-blooming jasmine are added for texture and evening fragrance. Apple-blossom pink, double-flowered impatiens tucked in behind the sweet box give the appearance of miniature roses throughout the border.

Autumn

Foliage and fragrance continue to be the focus as the roses, akebia, and climbing hydrangea cover the walls. 'Zépherine Drouhin', 'Whisper', and 'Abraham Darby' are still producing roses, and will continue until frost arrives. Orange-red hips are forming on 'Casa Blanca', adding another color and texture to the garden.

A Garden of Shapes

This is a Zone 7 garden where the request was

to create a formal garden with pink and white roses. When I took on the project, the outline of the garden was in place—four elongated rectangular beds in pairs, perpendicular to the house, and flanking a wide lawn. The outside edges of the paired beds were defined with a 2-foot boxwood hedge and a 6-foot wide channel of lawn separated each pair of beds. At the far ends of each paired bed were four symmetrical square beds, all edged with boxwood. Beyond this was a wide expanse of lawn.

Winter
Creating a forced perspective, 8-foot tall arborvitae, each sculpted to a tight pyramidal shape, are planted in the lawn along the outer edges of the paired beds. Eight-foot pyramidal lattice towers are placed in the beds, repeating the shape of the arborvitae and adding a vertical element to each bed. This pyramidal shape is repeated once more at the corners of each bed with a $2^{1}/_{2}$-foot pyramidal *Buxus sempervirens*.

To completely define the shape, the inner edges of each paired bed are edged with miniature boxwood. Extending from this dwarf edging is a zigzag pattern of miniature boxwood dissecting each bed and creating symmetrical triangular planting spaces for roses and perennials. Softening the edges is a gray haze from the faded foliage of lavender 'Provence'. One hardly notices the stick-like shapes of the hybrid teas, planted within the triangular beds.

Spring
During early spring, the roses are pruned and begin to grow. Climbers and ramblers

decorate the towers with fresh green and red foliage. Small spring bulbs—chionodoxa, puschkinia, muscari, and camassia—fill the triangular spaces within the beds with early color and fragrance. The four square beds at the far end are in full bloom with the white trumpet daffodil 'Mt. Hood'.

As the days become longer and warmer, herbaceous perennials planted with the roses throughout the triangular spaces begin to re-appear and send out new spring growth, filling in the empty spaces around the roses with green and gray. The lavender is pruned as the new leaf buds begin to break open.

Summer
The boxwood and arborvitae frame the display of roses and perennials planted throughout the garden. The roses, a mix of hybrid teas and shrub roses in the beds and ever-blooming climbers on the towers, are the dominant color display. They gradually give way in late summer to garden phlox and lavender. The four beds at the end are in bloom with the pink rose 'Sarah Van Fleet' amid the foliage of its later-blooming companion, *Hydrangea paniculata* 'Limelight'.

Autumn
The hybrid tea roses reappear for their second flush and rose hips decorate the towers. The garden phlox, 'Shortwood' and 'David', are still blooming. The four square beds are now in full bloom with 'Limelight' and a smattering of the rose 'Sarah Van Fleet'. This display continues until a hard frost, usually in mid-November. At that time, the evergreen boxwood and arborvitae are once again the focus.

CHOOSING AND GROWING ROSES AND THEIR COMPANIONS

IN THIS CHAPTER:

- Types of Companion Plants
- Perennials for Your Purpose
- The basics of Growing and Care
- Think Seasonally

Growing Roses

There is an enormous array of choices available as you begin to fill in your garden design with actual plants. We've already looked at the wide variety of rose types available, and of course there are exponentially more possible companions for the roses. Whatever specific plants you choose, it's important that each fills the function you have designated and that all of the plants have the proper growing conditions so they are healthy and beautiful.

Sun and good drainage are both essential for roses, and many companion plants appreciate the same conditions.

Roses come in so many shapes and sizes that there's a rose for almost every garden purpose from ground cover to climber.

Roses have needs that can't be overlooked, especially when they are grown in the company of other plants. Full sun is essential. Don't plant a companion too near a rose bush if it takes away valuable sunlight. Make sure your roses receive at least six hours of sun each day.

Good air circulation is helpful in keeping diseases to a minimum. Make sure that taller companions with dense foliage keep their distance from the roses. This is especially important with modern hybrid shrub-type roses—hybrid teas, floribundas, grandifloras, and shrub roses.

Roses need regular watering to bloom well. Along with this, a well-drained soil is crucial to their survival. Roses do not grow well if their roots remain wet for any period of time. Roses will bloom best if they receive at least an inch of water each week. The water should be applied to the root area, not the foliage. Many rose companions would appreciate this as well, so it may be worthwhile considering a drip irrigation system for the garden. A light layer of mulch is recommended, as well, to prevent the soil from drying out too quickly.

The soil should be rich in organic

materials such as compost, manure, and fishmeal. These are all beneficial to companions, as well as to the roses. Apply a fresh layer of compost or composted manure in the spring, after pruning, and in the autumn, as the garden is going into its dormant phase. Supplemental fertilizer is beneficial for roses, but not necessary if the soil is well enriched. If you use granular fertilizer for your roses, apply it carefully and avoid fertilizing the companion plants. Too much fertilizer on some companions could cause growth that will crowd the roses. Roses can be also be fed using foliar fertilizers.

Pay attention to how roses grow in your area. Climates with milder winters generally have larger growing plants; the winters of cold climates limit the sizes of bushes, and let you plant more per bed. A hybrid tea in New Jersey will not grow as large as one in California. Tea roses down south have the potential to grow into huge shrubs while in cooler climates they remain considerably smaller.

With a little extra work, a rose tier can be created against a wall, making a striking focal point.

Roses need room to grow. Be generous with their spacing when planting with other roses or shrub-like companions—the larger the plants, the farther apart they should be. Hybrid teas should be given at least two feet, while larger shrub roses (including old garden roses) should be separated by at least three feet. Smaller roses, such as miniatures and the smallest polyanthas, could be as close as a foot, and climbers and ramblers need six feet between them.

Using Roses in the Garden

Roses have many potential garden uses in addition to planting them in a mixed or shrub border or training them on an arbor. They can fill a number of functions if you are imaginative in your design.

Roses on the Wall

A blank wall offers numerous opportunities to be creative with roses, especially climbing roses. The key to getting the most blooms from a climber is to spiral the branches around a support, or to bend and curve the canes on the wall or fence. This causes side shoots to grow from the main branch, and these side shoots produce the best blooms. A traditional way to attach a rose to a wall is by installing a lattice panel or stringing wire along the walls to support the rose canes. In some cases, the design of the house doesn't allow for a lattice support or visible wires.

Instead, you can use lead anchors and cable wire clips to secure the rose canes to the wall.

For a different approach to a pillar rose, try creating a column of roses, a pseudo-espalier, to decorate a sunny wall. Here's how I accomplish that with 'Paul's Himalayan Musk Rambler', an aggressive growing, spring-blooming rambler.

Plant a bare-rooted specimen of 'Paul's Himalayan Musk Rambler' in the autumn or spring with a sturdy 1-inch thick bamboo stake, 8 feet long, inserted 2 feet into the soil. I recommend bamboo because it's strong and blends in with the rose. The support structure needs to be less obvious since the rose is the starring vertical element.

During the first season, there won't be many blooms, but that's okay. What's needed during that first year is new growth to train onto the bamboo pole. As the rose grows, spiral up to three or four canes around the bamboo, tying them securely to the stake. Remove all other canes or shorten them to

The climbing red rose, 'Red Fountain', and a pyracantha make a beautiful display when planted on adjacent walls.

various lengths from 3 to 6 inches. Top off all growth that goes higher than the bamboo.

The second spring after planting, the rambler will bloom as a neat and tidy pillar of roses trained against the wall. Keep trimming new growth while the rambler is in bloom. However, once it has bloomed, you may want to train the new growth to cover the entire wall. To keep the pillar look, you will need to annually remove older wood from the rose to make room for new. 'Paul's Himalayan Musk Rambler' will require lots of pruning to maintain this form. You could achieve the same results with ever-blooming climbing roses such as 'White Cap', 'Sombreuil', or 'Blaze of Glory', which don't have as aggressive a growth habit. As a companion to this design, I use the upright growing *Ilex crenata* 'Sky Pencil' for a permanent evergreen pillar.

A more traditional approach to growing roses on walls is to allow as much growth as possible to cover the walls. All climbing roses and vigorous shrub roses are excellent choices for training on walls. Often, the limiting factor is the size of the wall. I often mix ever-blooming roses with once-blooming varieties, or large-flowered roses with small-flowered varieties. A combination I've used frequently is the small-flowered 'Trier', a white hybrid musk, with 'Whisper', a large, white-flowered climbing rose. During the first season 'Trier' is the aggressive grower and has pliable canes that I immediately train into shapes on the wall. I train the slower growing 'Casa Blanca' into the circle of 'Trier'. As the roses come into bloom, rising up from behind a dark green hedge of *Taxus × media* 'Hicksii' (Hicks Yew), they are quite an ever-blooming sight.

ESPALIERS AND ROSES

Shrubs and roses grown together can be a colorful way of decorating and softening a sunny corner of a house. Try a combination of 'Stairway To Heaven', an everblooming red climbing rose, with pyracantha, a white-flowering evergreen shrub. 'Stairway To Heaven' is a good climber for training into smaller spaces, since it can be trained to grow within the space of a lattice panel 2' × 6'. The fragrant roses are produced from spring through autumn with very little maintenance involved. Pyracantha can be trained to a lattice panel in a similar fashion to 'Stairway To Heaven'. When planted on perpendicular walls in the same corner, the contrast of the white flowers of pyracantha with the red roses makes a spectacular display. Long after the rose becomes dormant, pyracantha will decorate the wall with green leaves and orange-red fruits for most of the winter.

Fragrant Fences

A split rail fence covered in roses is a tradition as American as apple pie and Miss America. My grandfather grew 'Scent From Above', a yellow climber, trained to his split rail fence, and the fragrant yellow roses spilled over the textured wood year after year.

As properties got bigger, the fences got higher. Roses can still rise to the challenge of making an ugly chain link fence beautiful. Many of my clients use roses to make their tennis game look and smell better by

Roses are great at softening and disguising less than attractive fences.

completely enclosing their courts in roses. By weaving and arching the canes of roses like 'New Dawn', 'Inspiration', 'Sombreuil', and 'Moonlight' through the openings, the roses eventually make their way to the tops of these fences creating a panoramic view of hundreds of fragrant roses.

Hedges

Left to grow without support, a climbing rose becomes an arching shrub producing mounds of color. Like other deciduous shrubs, roses can be planted in lines to create a colorful, and impermeable, barrier. Roses with larger growth habits make the most attractive hedges. Planting the rose bushes four feet apart will guarantee a fast-growing hedge. There are hedge choices from every rose class, even miniatures could work as a rose hedge. Some varieties such as the pink shrub rose 'Carefree Delight' or our native species *Rosa setigera* leave a long lasting display of hips that are as impressive as the hedge in flower.

Tree Roses

Roses grown in standard form, or "tree roses", have a unique decorative style. Any type of

This hedge uses the rose 'Simplicity' in a very effective manner.

rose, from miniatures to climbers, can be grown in this manner. The top part of the standard is a different rose budded onto tall stems of 'Dr. Huey' rootstock. Currently you will find tree roses from 18 inches to 5 feet tall. These make good vertical accents in any sunny garden.

Roses in Containers

My first garden as an adult was a square box I rescued from the curb on trash day in Brooklyn. Measuring 1 foot square by 10 inches deep, it was large enough to hold one rose, 'Katherina Zeimet', a white polyantha with a miniature habit. She grew at the top of

Standard, or "tree," roses make a real statement in the garden. This one is 'Iceberg' and is partnered with lavender to good effect.

This rose 'Nozomi' has been trained into fountain form, and it serves the same design purpose as a small tree.

the stoop, chained to the railing (that's how you garden in Brooklyn) outside my apartment. In the summer, I added the annual moonflower vine, *Ipomea alba*, which grew up to my kitchen window directly above the front door, on the second floor. I had the best of both worlds—fragrance by day as I passed the container on the way to work, and fragrance at night as I sat near the window in the evenings having dinner. I softened the edge of the container with blue torenia, an excellent

cascading annual that grows well when planted at the base of roses. I did have one small boxwood in this planter for winter color, but it was stolen the first winter. This container has traveled with me to my house in New Jersey, and now, nearly ten years later, proudly displays white roses all summer in the curb garden, basking in the sun and still blooming after all these years.

Growing roses in pots and wooden planters on rooftops and terraces is the norm for New York and other urban settings. As far as companion plants are concerned, you have unlimited choices as long as there is space in the container. For shrub-type roses and climbers, the container should have at least a 15-inch diameter and depth. Wooden and fiberglass planters are best since there is less water loss through evaporation and the roots are more insulated during winter. When you grow plants in a container, the roots of the plants are exposed to wind, heat, and cold from the sides because they don't have the protection of the earth. Stone planters, as beautiful as they are, offer less protection from the heat and cold, since they hold cold and heat much longer than wood or fiberglass.

Roses will grow happily with a wide range of companions—shown here are iris, daylilies, dianthus, sedum, petunias, clematis, wisteria and several others.

A miniature white rose and the annual money plant make a stunning combination in this garden

Selecting Rose Companions

Will they grow in the same garden conditions? That's the most important question to keep asking as you put together a garden composed of roses with companion plants. Compatibility is the key to success for a garden with a diverse assortment of plants. Don't let your enthusiasm get the better of you—select your companions carefully. Before you're charmed by the ornamental features of a plant find out what its growing needs are. Does it require full sun or shade? Does it prefer dry or moist soil? Then find how the plant performs in the garden. What is its growth habit? How close can you place it to other plants? Does it have ornamental features that may or may not work with other plants? What is the plant's blooming cycle and how does this fit in with the scheme you are putting together? These are all valid questions to answer before you make an investment in rose companions.

It's obvious that if you're intending to grow roses with these companions, then they need to be full sun plants. But, you'll create shade within your garden design and that's where you can use shade plants. As your garden continues to evolve, you'll discover unique situations for unique plants—that's the fun of gardening. You know what roses need, now search for other plants with similar needs, and you'll find many.

Types of Companions

The following sections contain basic information on different plant types to help guide you through plant catalogues and nurseries as you select rose companions for your garden.

Annuals

Annuals are plants that produce their flowers and fruits in a single growing season. Once they've completed this natural function, they die. But, they will bloom all season or until the weather tells them to stop. Often a frost or extreme heat can be limiting factors on which annuals will grow well in your garden. There are annuals that are sold as cool weather annuals. These are best suited for the coolest times of the year—late autumn through early spring in the south and other warm climate regions; autumn and spring in the colder regions of our country. Deadheading, the regular removal of faded seed heads, further perpetuates blooms in all plants, especially annuals. You can save seeds for next season or simply scatter them about for a natural re-emergence.

The term annual can be a regional description in the gardening world. Often, plants that are perennial in warmer climates are grown as annuals in the north, and plants that are perennial in cooler climates are grown as annuals in the south due to the hot summers. Some annuals may also seem to be perennial because they appear year after year in the garden. What is really happening is that the plant has come back from seed dropped by its relatives last season. Annuals are easily grown from seeds. You can also buy them inexpensively in nursery packs, which contain very small plants ready to go from the nursery directly into your garden. These will give you instant gratification.

Perennials

Perennials are plants that come back to life in your garden year after year. In each growing season, they grow, flower, and create seeds. Perennials can be grown from seed or you can find good sized plants in local nurseries. I prefer perennials in at least a six-inch pot. Don't be seduced by beautiful flower displays—check the roots before buying. I only go home with plants that have well established root systems.

You can order perennials through mail order catalogs. Unless they specify differently, the plant you'll receive will be bare-rooted (dormant with no soil around the roots) and small. These are good plants for the next season, but you may want to supplement with a potted version from a local nursery.

Potted perennials can be planted at anytime, though it's always best to plant during the cool season. As they mature, perennials from your garden may be dug up and divided to make new plants. There are perennials that bloom at all times of the year, depending on where you garden. Some perennials bloom once a year, while others bloom through the entire growing season.

Biennials

A biennial is a plant that needs two growing seasons to produce flowers and fruit. Common examples are foxgloves, parsley, and forget-me-nots. Usually the main plant dies after flowering, but many biennials will

Perennials such as geraniums are great companions for roses; this is the rose 'Playgirl' with *Geranium endressii.*

continue to populate your garden by producing new plants either from the base of the original plant or from seeds dropped that season or the season before. Because of this, many biennials are mistaken as perennials.

Biennials can be grown from seed, purchased as potted plants, or ordered through catalogs. Some biennials have an interesting foliage display the first season, and the flowers are an added bonus the next. Biennials are often sold during the second season of their cycle, already blooming, or ready to bloom. I prefer first season biennials, although a foxglove in bloom easily seduces me if she has an offshoot growing from the base.

Herbaceous Plants

A plant that produces soft green stems each year and then dies to the ground at the end of the season is an herbaceous plant. Most perennials and all annuals are herbaceous. Some shrubs are also herbaceous. To maintain an herbaceous perennial or shrub you simply prune it to the ground after the above-ground part of the plant dies or looks ugly. In warmer climates, some herbaceous plants build up a woody growth instead of dying to ground level each season. These are often referred to as "sub-shrubs."

Herbs

The word herb is a shortened version of herbaceous. However, today we associate the word herb with plants that have culinary, medicinal, or aromatherapy uses. There are perennial herbs, annual herbs, shrubby herbs, and trees that are herbs. Annual herbs grow easily from seeds, while many are readily available as potted or mail order plants.

Woody Plants

A woody plant grows from old wood each season, and as the stems age, they become hard and long-lasting. Woody plants become substantial occupants of the garden. Most shrubs, roses included, are woody plants. Trees are woody plants and some perennials can become woody as well.

Shrubs

Shrubs are plants with several substantial stems growing from their base. All roses are shrubs. Shrubs can be started from seed, although it is typically a slow process for them to reach a significant size. A favorite expression often used by my clients applies here: "Will I live long enough to see it in bloom?" Mail order sources are available for some truly rare and interesting shrub specimens. This is how I prefer to buy roses. Mail order shrubs usually come bare-root, although some nurseries will ship plants in pots of various sizes from four-inch liners to six-inch pots or larger.

Shrubs are sold by local nurseries potted or balled-and-burlapped (instead of being in a pot, the root-ball is wrapped and tied tightly in burlap). Check to make sure the root systems are well developed, especially with roses. My preferred time to plant shrubs, especially roses, is in the autumn. Not only are the plants discounted at nursery centers, but also there's still a long growing season ahead of me in the fall. For southern gardeners, this is especially important since spring often turns quickly to summer.

Trees

Trees are woody plants that have either one or a couple of distinct main stems or trunks. And yep, you can grow trees from seed. As with shrubs, all good things come to those who wait, and wait, and wait. You can buy trees in all sizes and from all sources—from little mail order saplings to huge specimens with huge root balls that will require a crane to put it in place, not to mention a parade of laborers.

ROSES WITH ROSE OF SHARON

Wandering through old city neighborhoods in search of roses, I can always count on finding a red rose—most likely growing along side some sort of religious icon, usually the madonna in the bathtub, as they say in Brooklyn. Down South, the chances are that the red rose is a China, usually 'Louis Philippe' or 'Cramoisi Supérieur'. Up north, the red roses are most likely tall hybrid teas or the once-blooming climber 'Dr. Huey'. City gardens are small, often as small as three square feet, so companions are chosen carefully. On a recent journey through the old neighborhoods of Jersey City, the most popular combination I saw was an older Jackson & Perkins hybrid tea 'Red Masterpiece' with a white rose of Sharon. This makes perfect sense; both are pruned in the spring and reach for the sky with blooms all summer.

Smaller-sized trees are usually in pots, or they might be balled-and-burlapped. Both styles work for me; just be sure to choose a tree with a good, strong, well-developed root system. The word "tree" is also used as a descriptive term for the growth habit of some plants. There are annuals, herbs, and shrubs that can be trained into "tree form" or "standard," meaning they are specially groomed to grow as a single stem specimen.

Deciduous and Evergreen Plants

A deciduous plant is a plant that loses its foliage annually. Most deciduous plants drop their foliage to prepare for their dormant season, which is usually induced by cold or long periods of drought. Several deciduous plants drop their leaves after a fantastic foliar color display.

An evergreen plant is one that never loses all of its foliage, though it will lose some foliage, typically during the spring or summer. There are needle-type evergreens and broad-leaf evergreens. Many shrubs and trees are evergreen, and there are even evergreen perennials.

Vines

Vines are plants with the natural ability to climb. They either twine around other plants or structures or attach themselves with either tendrils or aerial roots. Vines can be annual, perennial, woody, or herbaceous.

Bulbs

Bulbs are a large group of plants that grow from underground plants or stems. Bulbs, corms, rhizomes, and tubers all make up the group of plants collectively known as bulbs.

Companions for Every Purpose

Companion plants can be used to fill a wide variety of functions in the garden—providing flowers, fragrance, and texture—as well as to fill a number of design needs. The following section will give you some general ideas about ways to use companion plants.

Companions for Flower Color

Companion plants are one way to extend the season by having blooms before and after the roses blossom, as well as to provide additional color as the roses bloom. Southern gardeners have a longer season to play with; cold weather sends us Yankees running indoors for the winter. But even then there are plants that can be used to add color in the garden. Besides evergreen shrubs and perennials, there are flowering shrubs such

Roses work well with trees. In this photo, the rose and its lower companions share a bed with a citrus tree.

Color and texture both work to perfection in this combination of roses, barberry, pansies, forget-me-nots, and delphinium with a gazing ball accent.

as witch hazel and winter-flowering honeysuckle. Hellebores are a welcome sight in late winter, and soon after those perennials bloom, the spring bulbs appear.

Companions for Texture

The color and texture of plant foliage play an instrumental part in the extension of color through the gardening season as well as in creating interesting partnerships during the peak of the rose blooms. Balance your garden with the contrast of textures: the soft silvers and grays of artemisia, the gray spikes of lamb's ear, the airiness of *Verbena bonariensis* and gaura. Many plants of the aster family are good sources of floral and foliage texture. Among these are santolina, artemisia, yarrow, marigolds, coneflowers, sunflowers, feverfew, and eupatorium.

Scanning the summer border, my eye is drawn through the array of leaf shapes. Green leaves are the foundation of a garden and create living architecture. Ferns do this beautifully in shaded areas, with choices such as royal fern, *Osmunda regalis*, with its tall fronds of compound leaves and elegant growth, the male fern, *Dryopteris felix-mas* with its wonderful evergreen and intricate foliage, and the Japanese painted fern, *Anthyrium nipponicum*, with its delicate colorations and lacy leaves. These plants add architectural interest to the garden. In the full sun areas of my garden I achieve the same affect with species roses.

Here is information on a collection of plants with foliage textures and colors that enhance the beauty of roses.

Chinese Fringe Flower

If you have a protected site in zone 7, or you live in a warmer climate, then you should grow 'Zhuzhou Fuchsia', a stunning variety of the Chinese fringe flower. I've only seen the flowers once in my garden, and that was because we had a mild winter that year. Small fuchsia tassel-like flowers hung close to the branches at each leaf axil in March. Even without the

blooms, this loropetalum is still beautiful. Maroon-burgundy foliage is displayed all year, matching the foliage color of many shrub and tea roses. A large growing shrub with a graceful habit, 'Zhuzhou Fuchsia' keeps its foliage during the winter and makes a great color accent in the border. I keep mine planted within sight of 'Autumn Bouquet', a fuchsia-pink shrub rose that continually produces a foliage and blooms of a similar color.

Echinops ritro 'Taplow Blue'

A wonderful contrast to the burgundy foliage of roses is *Echinops ritro* 'Taplow Blue'. This coarse-leaved perennial produces beautiful steel-blue globe shaped flowers on tall stems. Soft to touch, these flowers are long lasting and repeat through the summer. The foliage is close to the ground, so you could plant these fairly close to a shrub rose for a cool texture and color contrast.

Centaurea 'Colchester White'

Hunt for this variety of dusty miller—it's worth the search. The elegant silver-gay foliage has a texture as soft as an old fedora. In addition, the leaves are finely cut into lacy finger-like projections. I plant this annual early in the season, after the danger of frost has passed. At first it seems lost in the border, but 'Colchester White' gets better as it ages. The texture and color become stronger, and the plant is absolutely graceful, shining like a light at dusk as new long leaves continually arch from its center. I've paired mine with *Strobilanthes* 'Persian Shield' planted at the base of the lacy-leafed species rose, 'Canary Bird'.

A delightful use of dusty miller, the more

common variety of centaurea, was as an under-planting to three beautiful miniature climbing roses—'Hi Ho', 'Yellow Doll', and 'Climbing Jackie'. Every inch of the narrow bed along the wall of the house where these roses grew was filled with this silver-leafed annual, making a lovely combination.

Verbena bonariensis

The tiny crepe paper-like blooms of this

The foliage of *Rosa glauca* and the false cypress contrast in both color and form, creating a very handsome pairing.

verbena are held on wiry stems, sometimes as high as six feet, blooming in my garden from July until a severe frost. Scatter seeds around large and small roses. This tall grower doesn't have a large foliage area, so there's no threat of crowding the roses.

As if by magic, the stems suddenly appear and hang out above shorter plants, appearing very fragile. But looks can be misleading—these are rugged plants, adaptable to wind and drought conditions. During the winter or early spring, I cut down the remains and scatter the seeds that haven't already dropped.

Bronze Fennel

I love to graze the garden while I'm working if there's bronze fennel within arm's reach. The anise-flavored leaves and seeds supply me with endless energy. There are two features that make this an invaluable companion to roses—the bronze-green lacy foliage and the umbels of chartreuse flowers held high above the rest of the garden.

I grow this herb with my polyantha roses—'Mlle. Cécile Brunner', 'White Pet', and 'Yvonne Rabier'—in my birdbath garden. It's amazing to see goldfinches perch on the thin stems as they wait for their turn for the birdbath.

Companions for Fragrance

Fragrance is an important year round element of the garden. Roses are an obvious source of perfume, but fragrances can be had long before the roses have begun growing. Depending on where you garden, you can find winter fragrance in a number of plants. Witch hazel, daphne, winter jasmine, osmanthus, winter sweet, and bulbs offer many possibilities for autumn through early spring floral fragrances.

Many plants hold fragrant oils in their foliage, releasing them into the air when the humidity level is high or the foliage is fresh and emerging from new buds. Other plants release their scents when the leaves are brushed against, bruised, or crushed. Some fragrances are delightful—fruity, floral, and culinary. Some are medicinal; some are offensive.

There are annuals, herbs, perennials, and shrubs with fragrant foliage that can be used as companions to roses. The plants with the strongest foliage fragrances are those from the mint family, which are recognizable by their square stems. There is a wide selection of plants with fragrant foliage to choose from, among them calamintha, oregano, agastache, salvia, lavender, nepeta, thyme, Russian sage, basil, bee balm, germander, plectranthus, and rosemary.

When I asked friends across the country to tell me about their favorite rose companions, the one plant that appeared on everyone's list was salvia. There are three characteristics these salvias share— the flowers are borne on long spikes, hummingbirds love them, and they all have aromatic foliage. The aster family also offers an array of plants, many of them herbs and perennials, to choose from for foliage fragrances. Not all of these are as pleasant as the mint family, but they are memorable. Among the choices for good rose companions are santolina, artemesia, yarrow, marigolds, helichrysum, and feverfew.

The geranium family has both delicious

and memorable fragrances. The showy geraniums so often seen in clay pots in windowsills, as well as the wonderful scented geraniums, are a part of the pelargonium group, with large soft leaves that are irresistible to stroke and are good for filling in among roses. These are annuals in the colder zones, but are used enthusiastically by gardeners in zones nine to eleven as perennials. Caryopteris, chaste tree, Carolina allspice, boxwood, fragrant sumac, European elder, and many needle evergreens offer fragrances from either the leaves or stems. Not all of these are necessarily pleasant, but there is a definite fragrance.

Here is some detailed information on a few plants with interesting foliar fragrance that are perfectly at home in a garden with roses.

Lavender

A classic combination is arching canes of the rose 'Hebe's Lip' hanging over an edge of lavender. Fragrance is found in all parts of the lavender, especially the silver- gray foliage.

In recent years several new hybrids of lavender known as the intermedia, or lavandin hybrids, have been introduced. These have a long blooming period and are more resistant to rot. 'Provence', with tall plants and long lavender flowers is my preferred hybrid. 'Grosso' lives up to its name, producing fatter, and perhaps the tallest, spikes of violet-lavender flowers. 'Dilly Dilly' may be a bit hardier than others and grows as a compact plant with very tall spikes of purple-blue.

The key to success with lavender is good drainage. If you're growing lavender where heat and humidity are the norm for the summer, pay special attention to its location, and try to provide it with excellent drainage. If you are using it as an edger, plant with the crowns of the plants above the bed and lawn levels. In the beds, plant lavender on small hills, so water will drain away from the center of the plants. Mulch with either turkey grit or finely crushed oyster shells. This will improve drainage and add reflected heat.

Calamintha

In some gardens I work in, changes occur very quickly during the season, and it's difficult to keep up with the inventory. After pruning the hybrid teas in one garden, I kept wondering if the garden had been invaded by weeds from a batch of bad manure, since the new growth of a ground cover resembled something growing around a manure pile. So many oregano-scented leaves, slightly fuzzy, were emerging at a weed-like rate that I was preparing to pull them out. However, the placement of the tufts of green growth seemed too organized. So, I waited.

Sure enough, just as the pink hybrid tea roses 'Great Century' and 'Bride's Dream' were coming into their first flush of blooms, small airy white blossoms on delicate stems began to appear from the masses of aromatic green foliage, reaching up to about 18 inches in height. Resembling baby's breath, this mystery plant needed a name. I took time to rummage through my notes from the previous season and found I had been searching for something that would bloom white, fill in without a tall dense growth habit, and yet look full. I especially needed something for the mid- to late-season to occupy the space under the bases of the hybrid tea roses. I had added *Calamintha nepeta* 'White Cloud', and it was doing exactly what I wanted it to do. I immediately hid a small label at the base of each plant.

Agastache

When I first spotted *Agastache* 'Apricot Sunrise', it was in the tender perennial section of my local nursery. I was drawn to the apricot-orange tubular flowers beautifully set off by grayish-green foliage. I was searching for a good hummingbird plant for my garden as well as filler for around the base of my roses. I liked the colors and airy habit of this brightly colored plant, and once I touched it, I knew I had found what I was looking for. The pungent fragrance of licorice won me over. From that moment on, I was hooked on agastache.

The flowers of agastache vary from spiky, fuzzy, blue or white bottle brush-like to tubular displays of hot pink and apricot. The common thread that weaves all the varieties of this herb together is the fragrant foliage. Some of the flowers are fragrant, as well. Stroke the bottle brush-like blooms of 'Blue Fortune' for a truly delicious scent of anise.

'Blue Fortune' is the hardiest agastache, producing 4- to 5-foot tall spikes of fragrant flowers. One of my clients has a stunning display of this perennial herb planted inside the patterns of a long boxwood knot garden with the moss rose 'William Lobb' and the Bourbon rose 'Coquette des Blanches'. Spring pruning consists of cutting the dead stalks to the ground. Deadheading during the season insures a supply of fresh flowers as well as butterflies and hummingbirds.

Angelonia

I first saw this annual six years ago, in a local nursery, tagged as the "Annual Orchid". I had to try it. Sure enough, the flower had a vague resemblance to an orchid, but what was more impressive was the fragrance of bubblegum coming from the leaves. Sort of a tutti-frutti flavor, this definitely had to be in my garden.

Angelonia is perfect for the summer border, and its airy habit allows you to plant it fairly close to the base of a rose bush without crowding the rose. Since it only reaches a height of 18 to 24 inches, this annual is a perfect filler for the area around the bare lower stems of many modern rose hybrids. Angelonia also works well as a container plant. Pots of purple Angelonia make for great portable color, continually blooming through summer heat while the roses take a rest.

Artemisia × 'Powis Castle'

The power of artemisia as a medicinal herb goes back as far as Pliny in ancient Rome. For centuries medicines, teas, foods, and liqueurs have been flavored with artemisia, also known as wormwood. The infamous cordial, absinthe, was made from *Artemisia absinthium*.

This species spawned some lovely hybrids. One that I'm never without for its foliar fragrance, color, and texture is 'Powis Castle', a woody, yet delicate, silver-leaved beauty. Plant this close to roses or as an accent in the border. The lacy foliage is delightful to see mixed in with any rose color.

COMBINATIONS FOR FRAGRANCE

One of the most fragrant roses ever introduced is a Bourbon rose called 'Louise Odier'. The globular pink blooms are rich with old rose fragrance. Another extremely fragrant rose is 'Greenmantle', one of Lord Penzance's Victorian hybrids noted for a strong fragrance of green apples from its leaves.

These two roses can be key ingredients in an intimate garden of fragrance. 'Greenmantle' is tall enough to be trained to a pillar or tower. Create a square-shaped garden with this rose as the centerpiece. Surround the tower with a mix of nepeta 'Six Hills Giant' and *Santolina virens,* green lavender cotton, creating an interesting foliar and flower combination, each with a distinctive fragrance. The soft gray green of the nepeta contrasts beautifully with the dusty rose blooms of 'Louise Odier', planted in each corner of the bed.

Companions for Filler

You need to have plants that will fill in the bare spaces, especially when roses start losing their foliage during the summer. Create "skirts" for your roses with low-growing plants. Many annuals are good for this. There are also many annuals and evergreen plants that can fill in for winter color, as well. Using plants as filler also creates "living mulch" for roses. The creeping habit of something like oregano or thyme helps in keeping the roots of the roses cool, just as mulch should.

Companions for Symmetry

I've already discussed the importance of evergreen shrubs for winter color, for defining beds and garden shapes, and for creating symmetry. When adding plants to the garden, make sure you create balance and order. Don't just plop in one of this and one of that. Make some sense of your arrangement of colors, textures, and growth habits.

Creating Combinations

In this section, I'd like to share some combinations from my own garden, from the gardens I create and tend in the northeast, and from gardens I've admired in my travels. Following these vignettes is a closer look at some of my favored companions and how they work with roses. With so many choices for companions, this discussion is only intended to get you started and to inspire you to explore the many possibilities for creating combinations with roses.

■ Vignettes

■ *Rosa glauca* in August

It's August and my *Rosa glauca* has lost all it foliage. I'm not discouraged, nor am I embarrassed to announce to everyone that I have foliar issues with my roses. Spraying may have prevented this, or maybe not. This is typical of this particular species rose in a humid climate—the leaves just give up and fall off. But all is not lost. As if floating in mid-air, suspended from the plum colored canes, glow beautiful shiny orange-red hips. As I look around, there are other displays of color as well. A ruby-throated hummingbird is feeding from the indigo-blue tubular blossoms of *Salvia guaranitica* 'Black and Blue'. *Artemisia* 'Powis Castle' is bursting with fresh soft silver gray leaves. *Nicotiana* 'White Cloud' is in full bloom with long, fluted, evening-scented white flowers.

Planted in a square terracotta pot near the base of the rose is *Cestrum nocturnum*, night blooming jasmine, with its greenish-white tubular buds ready to burst into bloom at dusk. And, in the front of the border, is the bronze-tinged cream-colored foliage of *Osmanthus* 'Goshiki', a low growing variegated evergreen shrub with scalloped and spiny leaves. This shrub is important for more than just its foliage color; its texture is a noticeable element as well, adding to the wonderful August display. *Rosa glauca* can take a rest.

■ Strobilanthes in Jersey City

I was wandering through the heart of one of the oldest parts of Jersey City in search of roses, and there, in the corner pocket bed of a brick row house, was an old red climbing rose in full bloom. But what really caught my eye was the moss green ceramic planter positioned near the rose. This fourteen-inch glazed pot contained a complete foliage study: *Lamium maculatum* 'Beacon Silver' with its matte silver and green variegated foliage spilling over the edge, a generic dracena making a spiky green statement with stiff sword-like green leaves; a New Guinea

impatiens with maroon foliage, and bursting into shiny metallic purple glory was *Strobilanthes dyerianus*, or Persian shield.

Toward the end of the nineteenth century, Persian shield made a graceful step from the conservatory to the garden where it triumphed as a bedding plant, displaying its magical metallic purple foliage flecked with shades of green, pink, and silver. I use this annual whenever I can as an accent plant. It makes a beautiful complement to the softer colored roses, especially in the autumn when colors are richer.

I returned two weeks later to see how the display looked after the rose had finished. Now, without the distraction of the roses, Persian shield had all the attention, beautifully complementing the color of the new foliage growth of the rose.

■ A Garden of Evening Fragrance

On a recent February visit to New Orleans, I was astounded by the sweet fragrances drifting over the walls of the Beauregard-Keyes garden on Chartres Street. It couldn't be coming from roses because they had just been pruned and weren't blooming. The fragrance turned out to be from *Osmanthus fragrans*, an evergreen shrub growing against the wall. Known as the tea olive or sweet olive, this evergreen shrub makes a good background plant in southern gardens. It releases its evening fragrance from autumn until spring.

Plants with nighttime fragrances should be planted in locations near walkways and patios, in pots on a deck, or near a window. Where I live, the mosquitoes are thick and thirsty on summer nights. Romantic walks through the moonlit garden end up being 50-yard dashes to the screened porch. Even then, I can't resist stopping to smell the sweet fragrance of *Nicotiana alata*, flowering tobacco. And once inside the porch I can sit and enjoy the fragrant breezes and the perfume of the evening garden.

During the full moon of June, the roses

Perennials such as columbine, shrubs such as the smoke tree, and trees such as the variegated dogwood all combine well with roses.

'Madame Plantier' and 'Madame Hardy' are in full bloom and glowing from the reflected light of the moon. Trained to their respective pillars, they release their seductive perfume for anyone who ventures into the garden. These cultivars are among the earliest of the evening-scented roses. Sharing this moment with them is the extremely fragrant perennial *Valerian officinalis*, also known as garden heliotrope. The flowers of this tall perennial herb sparkle in the moonlight and sprinkle the air with the scent of fresh baby powder.

Later in the month the front garden will be filled with the powerful fragrance of the rose 'Autumn Sunset'. Described by some as fruity, its scent fills the night air greeting visitors at the front door and anyone passing by our house. Climbing 15 feet up into a blue atlas cedar, the rose sends its fragrance directly into the windows of our guest bedroom on the second floor.

Perennials with Roses

The realm of perennials is awesome as these plants provide so many variations in growth habit, hardiness, color, texture, and fragrance to choose from. Select your perennials carefully, for they could be with you for a long time. Pay attention to how they grow, giving them enough room so the relationship between the rose and the perennial is a healthy one.

With their wide range of flowering cycles, it's possible to create a four-season garden with perennials. In northern gardens, hellebores, evergreen ferns, and liriope hold their color for the winter, while in milder climates there are plants used as annuals in the north that have a longer stay further south: phormiums, grasses, and many of the wonderfully scented pelargoniums. Flower forms of perennials can be spikes, globes, airy panicles, and umbels, and together with roses they add interesting colors, textures, and fragrances to the garden. Here are a few close-up views of some perennials I've used with roses.

Early Season

■ *Salvia nemerosa* 'Lubeca'
Lubeca is an upright plant growing 18-24" that produces an early season display of long spikes of vibrant violet- blue flowers. What I find really interesting about this salvia is the reddish-purple bracts left after the flower petals have faded. Don't deadhead until this display has passed.

■ Nepeta
For the longest time nepeta was relegated to borders as an accent plant. Usually recommended in combination with the peony 'Sarah Bernhardt' and Japanese iris positioned in front of the old pink climbing rose 'Dr. W Van Fleet', *Nepeta mussinii* was grown for its "feathery" look and lavender flowers.

Today, there are numerous varieties of nepeta to choose from. An improvement on *Nepeta mussinii* is the longer blooming cultivar 'Walker's Low'. 'Souvenir d'André Chaudron' is one of tallest varieties, sometimes reaching 4 feet in height. These aromatic perennials are now popular in combination with roses.

Nepeta has aromatic foliage reminiscent of cloves and citronella. Some herbalists claim the fragrance repels bad insects. Also known as catmint, nepeta is a member of the mint family. I'm told that cats may find it interesting, but the only summer visitors to my nepeta are hummingbirds, butterflies, and bees.

■ *Campanula latifolia* 'Loddon Anna'
I recently planted this campanula near *Rosa glauca*, not really planning on what I was about to see in June. 'Loddon Anna' displays an inflorescence of small pink-tinged bell-shaped flowers on stems 5 feet tall. The

Catmint, or nepeta, is a classic rose companion, shown here with a strawberry mixed in.

Where they can be grown well, delphiniums with their tall spires make stunning perennial accents among roses.

pink-gray foliage of the rose was a perfect match for the subtle pink blush of 'Loddon Anna', especially obvious as several of the flower heads poked through the branches this species rose. This made for a wonderful June surprise.

Mid-Season

■ *Salvia nemerosa* 'Snowhill'
This is a low growing plant, mounding up to about 15 inches and spreading out to 2 feet. Plant 'Snowhill' where it will get as much sun as possible, away from the canopy of the rose

bush. Avoid crowding this perennial with taller plants. If you have a drip system set up for the roses, the water that drips out from the emitter would be enough for this salvia.

■ *Veronica spicata* 'Red Fox'
I grow this low growing perennial with Salvia 'Snowhill' as a low ground cover plant under pink hybrid tea roses. The display of 8-inch

The foxglove, usually a biennial, is another vertical flower that works beautifully with roses. In this photo, the foliage of the 'About Face' rose is a perfect match for the interior of the foxglove 'Pam's Choice.'

rose-colored spikes, along with the white flowers of 'Snowhill', creates a beautiful carpet of summer color for the front of the border.

■ Garden Phlox

Some people may be curious as to why I would recommend *Phlox paniculata*, garden phlox, with roses since so many garden phlox are susceptible to powdery mildew—the same fungus that is a problem with roses. But this shouldn't be a problem if you pick and choose your phlox carefully. There are some phlox that have proven to be fairly mildew resistant if they are grown in full sun and with good cultivation. There are three that I recommend, based on growing them with roses in a zone 7 garden, about a half-mile from the Atlantic Ocean—'Shortwood' reaches 5 feet and produces panicles of vivid pink blooms; 'David' is a pure white variety; and 'Snow White' is a harder to find white cultivar. All three will bloom from July until frost.

■ Delphinium

There's nothing more stunning to see than spires of blue delphiniums rising up from a bed of roses. The architecture and the colors of this perennial are classic combinations with roses. Hybrids available today have the capability to grow flower stalks as high as seven feet.

This look is often associated with the English border or cottage garden. Delphiniums launch a surprise attack, since they seem to suddenly appear overnight. Difficult to grow in warm humid regions, they prefer cooler locales. I often will buy them in full bloom and use them as annuals for a seasonal display.

■ Foxgloves

Foxgloves are actually biennials and are a key feature in the informal cottage garden. With their tall spikes of soft flowers emerging from a base of large leaves, they add height to the garden as well as a bit of elegance. Foxgloves can give the appearance of growing out of the rose bushes if you plant them behind shrub roses. They are also good companions for climbers and ramblers.

There are many types of foxgloves, but the most popular are the hybrids of *Digitalis purpurea*, especially the Excelsior hybrids. One in particular is 'Pam's Choice'. In my garden, the maroon throat of this white foxglove is a perfect companion for the new foliage of the new grandiflora 'About Face'.

■ Daylily

I use daylilies for fragrance, color, and foliage. Invaluable services they provide are hiding the fading foliage of spring-blooming bulbs and acting as a skirt for the naked knees of hybrid tea roses.

The fragrance of 'Hyperion' is light and lemony. I'll never part with this beauty, even though some consider this old hybrid to be ordinary in comparison to the gaudy new hybrids of daylilies coming out these days. I love the simplicity of the trumpet-shaped blooms and, of course, the lemon-scented fragrance. There is another daylily I'm eager to try, an older species *Hemerocallis citrina*. This summer-blooming species has long narrow petals with a lemon-yellow color. I'm told the blooms open only in the evening and produce a strong fragrance.

Late Season

■ *Physostegia virginiana* 'Vivid'
The parent species of this hybrid, *Physostegia virginiana* is also known as the obedient plant. However, obedience is not one of the better qualities of this native perennial, which is likely to run rampant in the garden if left unchecked. However, I forgive it for this sin because of the strong display of color that appears during the month of August from this plant and its better-behaved offspring. That's why I like to grow it with roses—for the late show of color, usually at a time when there's a lull in rose blooms.

The flowers of 'Vivid' are displayed on very straight spikes. The blooms are tubular and point straight out into the garden, welcoming every hummingbird that passes by in August. A white cultivar, 'Miss Manners', has more of a clump-forming habit and starts to bloom earlier in the summer.

■ *Helianthus* 'Lemon Queen'
I have a difficult time convincing my clients that yellow belongs in their gardens. However, I enjoy this color in my garden. Planted behind my species roses and filling in a gap below the canopy of my blue Atlas cedar, this tall yellow perennial sunflower is like a burst of refreshing sunshine in mid-summer with the vibrant display lasting until autumn.

■ Kalimeris
Tiny white pompon flowers quietly appear in the July garden, as if floating on air. The foliage is very delicate, and this can mislead you to thinking that kalimeris should be planted in tight groups. This perennial looks much better when given space, allowing one plant to have

room to show its delicate features.

Also known as the Japanese aster, this is one of the more refined looking plants from the large family of asters. Another I use frequently for summer color is the lavender-blue 'Monch' with its willowy branches floating around the bases of rose bushes. By autumn, the asters with their delicate leaves and small composite flowers spill carelessly around and through the roses.

■ *Artemisia* 'Guizhou'
Who would have thought that a plant related to mugwort could be so attractive in the garden? Artemisia 'Guizhou' is a tall growing artemisia, with ebony stems 4 feet or more in height. Unlike 'Powis Castle' and other silver-leafed varieties of artemisia, 'Guizhou' has very dark green leaves. During the summer, large creamy plumes are held erect above the black stems.

Herbs with Roses

Herbs and roses are a combination as old as gardening. In fact, many old garden roses are still grown in traditional herb gardens as medicinal and culinary herbs. The petals of the old red gallica, the apothecary's rose, was a source for rose oil, an important ingredient for most ancient medicines. A popular combination in many herb gardens is to have this rose sprawling over the chartreuse flowers of the equally ancient herb, *Alchemillia mollis*, lady's mantle. Many gardeners, including me, believe the fragrant oils in the leaves, roots, and flowers of herbs are beneficial in controlling the population of good and bad insects, especially those that feed on roses.

■ *Salvia officinalis*

Traditionally, *Salvia officinalis*, or common sage, is grown for its flavorful leaves, not the violet-blue flowers. If left to bloom, sage is a wonderful garden plant especially if planted with roses. In addition to the flowers, sage adds foliage color, texture and fragrance to the garden. There are several varieties of common sage to consider as well. Purple, tricolor, and golden sage all blend in nicely with roses when used as front border plants.

■ *Salvia rutilans*

There are a handful of salvias referred to as the fruit-scented sages. Pineapple sage, *Salvia rutilans,* is one of these with a strong pineapple fragrance when the foliage is crushed. Another of the fruit scented salvias is *Salvia dorisiana*, the grapefruit scented sage.

In gardens with long growing seasons, these fruit-scented sages are an aromatic finale to the garden season. Hummingbirds will make these gardens a favored stopping point on their way to the tropics. Borderline hardy for me, I grow the pineapple sage for the strong foliar fragrance, and the red flowers are an added bonus. To enjoy the fragrance, I make sure that I plant this within arm's reach.

■ Nasturtium

When clients return from a trip to France and they've been to Giverny in July, I can count on adding nasturtiums to their garden. The one image that stays in everyone's mind after a visit to Monet's home is the bright orange nasturtiums sprawling out from under the rambling roses onto the gravel path.

Tropaeolum majus, otherwise known as nasturtium, is a creeping annual that loves to bask in the sun or clamber up through a climbing rose. Nasturtium is a good source of flower and foliage color for the early summer border, as well as of a spicy topping for your salad.

■ Rosemary

Old rosemary plants have lots of character with their twisted and gnarled stems and, exfoliating bark. They also have a wonderful scent that makes my stomach yearn for lamb chops as soon as I smell it.

Native to dry areas, rosemary is happiest where it can bake in the sun and be free of watering systems. I use rosemary as an accent in containers. In the regions of California with a Mediterranean climate, try planting it as an evergreen companion to a bed of China or tea roses. A beautiful sight would be twisted branches of rosemary 'Tuscan Blue' weaving in and out of a yellow Noisette rose.

■ Oregano

Oregano is a big group under which all sorts of varieties fall, two of which are marjoram and "true" oregano. The "true" oregano grows more as a ground hugger, excellent for use as a ground cover under and around roses. Marjoram has a more upright and mounding habit and is best used as a fragrant edge or accent plant.

Annuals with Roses

Annuals provide the garden with a great deal of color. They are the perfect plants for filler and for foliage and flower display. Within this large group of plants you'll find very hot colors as well as soft pastels, offering something for everyone. Many annuals we grow in the north do well as winter plants in the hottest regions of our country. Other annuals we grow are actually perennials where winters are mild.

Early Season

■ Pansies

I believe in pansies. They're tough, they're beautiful, and they look great around the bases of roses during the off-season. While I was curator of roses at Brooklyn Botanic Garden, this was the first non-rose plant I let stay in the rose garden. The pruning was finished, and we had begun the monumental task of weeding. One of my volunteers, Ruth, was crawling behind a huge 'Harison's Yellow' and let out a squeal of joy. She had come across a patch of the wonderful tri-colored violas, Johnny-jump-ups, in full bloom. They had obviously blown in from the nearby compost heap, and from that moment on, Ruth guarded them as if they were her very own.

I think of Ruth each autumn as I plant the small flowered Sorbet cultivars and Crystal Bowl varieties, all descendants of *Viola tricolor*, at the bases of my French ramblers. I define the space around the roses with pansies. In zone 7, we're taking a chance with over-wintering pansies, and I find these small-flowered varieties winter best. I always make a plan to refresh them again, once the threat of a hard freeze has passed, with new spring plantings. After spring pruning of the shrub roses, I'll plant additional pansies to complement the spring bulb display as well as the newly emerging rose foliage. And of course, Johnny-jump-up is welcome anytime he appears at the garden gate.

■ Annual Phlox

Annual phlox, *Phlox drummondii*, is a decorative and easy annual to grow from seed. More adapted to cooler climates, annual phlox may fade away in the heat of the South or arid climate of the west. In the warmer climates I would recommend annual phlox as spring and autumn annuals, and in the Deep South, perhaps as a winter annual.

■ Calibrachoa/Petunia

Calibrachoa, also known as the trailing petunia, resembles a miniature cascading petunia. New cultivars of calibrachoa are being introduced each year, and the most popular series is called Million Bells. These annuals are gaining popularity both as garden plants and for containers as well, perfect for spilling around roses.

The Wave petunias and Supertunias create the same look, but have larger flowers and require more space. I recommend using these annuals as edging plants in full sun where they can spread around the bases of rose bushes and soften the edges of container gardens.

■ Larkspur

Near the end of autumn, I make it a point to go out to my curb garden and scatter seeds of larkspur for next season's display. Cold weather helps encourage seed germination. I've even scattered them on top of late winter snow.

Use larkspur to create a meadow effect, letting them fill in around tall hybrid teas, floribundas, and old garden roses. The larkspurs' pastel colors and fine foliage will soften the look of these roses. Larkspurs look especially great growing in a cottage garden or natural border.

Mid Season to Late

■ Victoria Blue Salvia

'Victoria Blue', a popular variety of *Salvia farinacea*, displays pencil-thin spikes of violet-blue flowers the entire summer. A great plant for filling in gaps in the front of a mixed border, this salvia is beautiful with any rose.

'Indigo Spires', another offspring of *Salvia farinacea*, grows tall and bushy in mild climates. I've seen this indigo-blue salvia look equally at home with yellow Noisettes, such as 'Crepescule' and 'Jaune Desprez' and the pink shrub 'Natchitoches Noisette'.

■ *Salvia guaranitica*

Blooming from early summer to frost, *Salvia guaranitica*, along with its most popular hybrids, 'Black and Blue' and 'Argentine Skies', is an invaluable addition to the rose garden. Of the three, 'Argentine Skies', with its sky blue flowers, is the hardiest. Otherwise I grow them as annuals with the hopes that maybe they'll make it through the winter. The darker *Salvia guaranitica* looks beautiful with surrounded by pink, white, and pastel colored roses. 'Argentine Skies' is magnificent when used with vibrant reds and oranges. Both are tall growing, easily reaching to 5 feet before summer's end. 'Black and Blue' is an intriguing variety with two-toned blue to near-black flowers. Shorter than *Salvia guaranitica*, its petals are an indigo blue and the calyx is so dark it appears black.

■ *Salvia uliginosa*

Salvia uliginosa is a sky-blue species that will always have a home in my garden. Tall growing with a wispy habit, *Salvia uliginosa* easily reaches 5 feet when in peak bloom by summer's end. The small flowers are pale blue and white, and there are many on each stalk. The leaves are small and textured. *Salvia uliginosa* shares a bed with the Noisette roses 'Princesse de Nassau' and 'Belle Lyonnaise' and is frequently entangled with the new red-tinged canes of the rambler 'François Juranville'.

■ *Salvia gregii*

Salvia gregii , Texas Sage, is a good heat-resistant red species that has recently spawned a collection of red summer blooming offspring, especially effective while the roses are in a rest period. A new hybrid I'm trying for the first time this year is 'Dark Dancer'. It seems to bloom a bit later in the season than other gregii hybrids, and the flowers are a rich fuchsia-red. The leaves are smooth, small, and highly aromatic, similar to common sage.

■ *Salvia coccinea*

With a common name like "bloody sage," how could you *not* plant this with your roses? *Salvia coccinea* is a perennial in the warmest of climates, which makes sense given that its origins are in the tropical regions of South America. The flowers are red, and held on spikes with generous spacing between each bloom.

Several cultivars are popular as annuals, one in particular is 'Lady in Red'. A fiery scarlet flower above pale green foliage with ample branching, this salvia quickly grows to 2-1/2 feet. Another I've used is 'Coral Nymph' (also sold as 'Cherry Blossom') with a delicate salmon-pink and white bicolor flower. I've mixed this one in with lavender 'Provence' as an underplanting for climbing roses against a south-facing wall.

■ Impatiens

The mighty impatiens—everyone grows them, even in the most sophisticated gardens. I came across a clever use of impatiens with roses in a small front garden in Brooklyn, New York. The garden spot was only big enough for one hybrid tea rose bush, in this case, 'Veteran's Honor, Opening Night'. The shrub had grown taller in search of sunlight, and the base of the rose was completely in shade. The clever gardener planted the same shade of red impatiens at the base of the rose, creating a living, as well as a color-coordinated, mulch.

While cruising my local annual grower's greenhouses two years ago, I came across two beautiful series of impatiens labeled the "Rose Parade" and "Fiesta" series. These perfect rose-like blooms have me hooked on impatiens again. Now I use them as fillers or even as the focus of the summer garden.

■ Pentas

When I asked my gardening friends from the South what annuals they would combine with roses, there was an overwhelming response in favor of pentas. I introduced pentas to my garden to attract hummingbirds, and red pentas guaranteed the arrival of these tiny winged guests. Also known as the Egyptian star flower, these annuals come in a variety of colors from hot red to soft lavender pink. They can bloom from early spring right through to late fall and reach a maximum size of four feet high by four feet wide.

■ Torenia

Used most often as shade tolerant annuals, there are now more varieties of torenia available that do well in heat and full sun. I like to have these spreading annuals fill in areas under roses for a strong autumn display of color. They're colorful in summer as well, but by the end of summer they look especially full with rich colors. Most common are the blue and purple varieties. All of the torenias have a lipped flower that children may enjoy investigating.

■ Four O'clock

To me, four o'clock, or *Mirabilis jalapa*, have a summertime fragrance. When I smell them, I remember the suntan lotion of my youth and lazy days on the beach. That's a good enough reason for me to grow this annual with my roses. Their fragrance develops in late afternoon and lasts through the night, attracting night-pollinating insects. The blooms don't open until late in the afternoon, which is the origin of the name "four o'clock".

Four o'clocks attract butterflies, moths, and hummingbirds to the garden. They are extremely useful for filling in around the naked trunks of summertime shrub roses. One word of caution, besides their invasive nature in warm climates, four o'clocks can be poisonous if eaten, so be watchful to young children around them.

■ Nicotiana

My aunt introduced me to this annual many years ago. Each June, she would plant nicotiana on either side of the 15-foot flagstone walkway leading to her front door. Nothing else was added to these foot-wide beds. Lined up like soldiers, the tall, strange looking plants with tubular flowers filled the air with a jasmine fragrance every night they were in bloom. That is a fragrant memory I will always cherish.

There are many garden cultivars of *Nicotiana alata*, but many of them are worthless since they don't have a scent. There are two I can guarantee for fragrance: 'Fragrant Cloud' and 'Lime Green'. I haven't tried the Heaven Scent varieties, but one can only hope there is a valid reason for this name. This year I'm growing an unnamed cultivar with fragrant plum red flowers in my garden. I received this from a friend in Massachusetts. When shopping for these plants, remember they're only fragrant at night, so you won't detect even the slightest bit of perfume when you're selecting them at the nursery.

There's one species I grow for its color, despite the fact that it doesn't have any fragrance—*Nicotiana langsdorfii*. The entire flower is pale, nearly translucent green, except when you look inside. The tips of the stamens are sky-blue.

■ Cuphea
Cuphea llavea is known as the bat-face flower. Get down on your hands and knees and check it out: a long green calyx ends in purple with two extended bright orange-red petals. This is the bat face. I make sure every visitor, young and old, meets the bat face flowers in my garden.

The vibrant colors are noticeable from afar, creating a hot-colored textured edge to the rose bed. Mixed into this bed is an eclectic assortment of roses: 'Mutabalis', also known as the butterfly rose, with petals of every pastel color; 'Nancy Reagan', an apricot-cream hybrid tea; and 'Moon Shadow', a new, intensely fragrant lavender hybrid tea. Rising up in the background is the French rambler 'François Juranville'. When the bat face flower and other companions are in bloom, this rambler creates a backdrop of shiny foliage. In this garden, *Cuphea llavea* blooms from April until there's a hard frost.

Cuphea ignea, cigar plant, is a taller variety I first encountered as part of a dazzling bed of bold color combinations near Houston—a Texan's attempt to bring the autumn colors of the northeast to Texas. The tubular fiery flowers of the cigar plant filled in all the spaces around the following shrub roses: 'Golden Zest', yellow; 'Dame de Coeur', red; and 'Lafter', orange.

Cuphea offers the opportunity to introduce bold colors to your garden on plants of all sizes. Dazzle the neighbors, entertain the kids, and you'll also attract hummingbirds and butterflies as they migrate south.

■ Hamelia
Speaking of hot colors, another plant I saw in Texas gardens has made its way up north as a summer annual. *Hamelia patens*, also known as the Texas firebush, is appropriately named. Scarlet-orange tubular flowers top the mounding shape of this summer annual.

I use one or two strictly as a "dash" of color. I'll add them to the garden in summer, as I find bare spots to fill. It's a stunning arrangement when Hamelia is mixed in with lacy gray leaved plants such as *Artemisia* 'Powis Castle' or *Centaurea* 'Colchester White'.

Throw in some strobilanthes and your bed will be on fire!

■ Ruellia

I first saw *Ruellia brittoniana* 'Electric Blanket', a blue-flowered dwarf variety, growing with the polyantha rose 'Marie Pavié' in the display gardens of the Antique Rose Emporium in Texas. This was during November after a long, hot, humid summer, typical of southeast Texas. 'Katie' and 'Marie Pavié' were in full bloom. 'Marie Pavié', when grown in full sun in a southern climate, can become as tall and wide as 2 to 2-1/2 feet. The pink-blushed white sweetheart roses looked beautiful with the blue flowers of 'Katie' as the backdrop. The petunia-like blooms of the ruellia completely filled the open space in the rose bed creating a groundcover of blue and green. The blue flowers were also planted as fillers around 'Duchess de Brabant' and 'Monsieur Tillier', two shrubby, pink tea roses.

In the South, ruellia is an herbaceous perennial, except for the furthest southern reaches of Florida, the Gulf coast, and the hotter areas of Arizona. In these regions this plant can become shrubby. In New Orleans, ruellia is often found around the doorsteps of older homes, earning it the nickname "Doorstep Flower".

A little bit of research made me aware of the invasive quality of *Ruellia brittoniana*, and I was hesitant to recommend it for anyone in a climate warmer than zone 7. Despite this, friends in central Florida reassured me that there were several varieties of ruellia they use as companions for roses that don't have the invasive qualities of the species or are easier to control. Recommended are *Ruellia elegans*;

'Ground Hugger', a violet-blue cultivar with a good groundcover habit; 'Electric Blanket'; 'Baby Blanket', a pink version of 'Electric Blanket'; and 'Strawberries and Cream', with purple flowers and variegated foliage. The dwarf habits of these varieties make it easier to control their spread in climates where they may become invasive. Even so, those of you gardening in the warmer climates should be cautious when using ruellia in your garden.

■ Ageratum

I'm attracted to blue flowers, but usually not ageratum. It's one of those plants you see in parking lots in New Jersey. I was surprised to find out that the luscious purple-blue mass I had spied from afar turned out to be this very same common summer annual. The property I was visiting was situated immediately behind the sand dunes of East Hampton, New York. This rose garden was behind the house, protected from the direct assault of the ocean winds, but still subject to the salty evening mists. The hybrid teas had already finished their first bloom cycle, and the only color present in this garden was *Ageratum* 'Artist Blue'. Looking like a bank of billowing violet clouds, this was the edging for the rose garden.

Twelve-foot sections were planted with small plants in the spring, after the threat of frost. In two months, the small plants had transformed into this magnificent display. At each end of the ageratum planting were small Japanese hollies, creating a solid green anchor.

Bulbs

There are many plants that begin their lives as bulbs, tubers, rhizomes, or corms. Collectively known as bulbs, there are varieties of these plants for every garden in every season. Depending on where you garden, there are bulbs that will bloom while the roses are dormant, while the roses are in their full flush of bloom, and during the summer when the roses are in a rest mode. Planting times vary for the different bulbs and the climate you are gardening in.

I plant spring-flowering bulbs right up to the base of the rose bush and throughout the canopy area. Rose pruning is finished by the time they start emerging, so there's no danger of the new bulb growth being crushed while pruning the rose. Spring bulbs create a riot of color that coexists happily with the color of the fresh spring foliage of roses. In some cases, the rose bushes are carefully disguised by the display of bulbs.

Spring

■ Narcissus
These bulbs are perennial and look best planted in groups scattered about the garden, avoiding straight lines or one bulb by itself. Mass them together among the bases of species roses—many of these bulbs will bloom as the species open. Narcissi should be planted in borders as accents to larger shrub roses, climbing roses, and old garden roses. Their colors are welcome after the dreary winter days, telling us that spring has sprung.

Here's a tip regarding the foliage after the flowers have finished: These bulbs need their foliage to build up food for next year. So, instead of tying them into tight bundles or unsightly knots, add perennials with arching leaves, such as daylilies or liriope, to help hide the slowly fading narcissus foliage.

I've selected a few narcissus from the most fragrant divisions to recommend for your garden. Every year I try new varieties, and you should too. There's always room somewhere in the garden for a bulb that does such a good job of lifting your spirits and getting you into the mood for gardening.

■ Double Narcissus—Blooming as early as April in my zone 7 gardens, these multi-petaled narcissi look like little roses on long green stems. The colors range from pure white to types with flecks of orange and apricot. Sweetly fragrant, these are two of my favorites.

■ *Albus plenus odoratus*—a very old variety, sometimes classified as a poeticus. Older gardeners may remember this as the gardenia-flowered narcissus.

o 'Bridal Crown'
A popular bulb to force indoors for mid-winter, I often use these for early spring window box displays then move the plants into the garden to naturalize. In the garden, 'Bridal Crown' blooms in April with a long-lasting fragrant display of saffron-colored center petals and a creamy white perianth.

o Tazetta Narcissus
Especially good for warm climate gardens, these multi-stemmed perennials begin blooming in April in my garden. Small flowers but many on each stem make a colorful display through the mixed border. Very fragrant, here are some I highly recommend:

- 'Avalanche'—also known as "Seventeen Sisters," this heirloom variety has been in American gardens since the colonial era. With a yellow cup and white perianth, this is an early bloomer, growing to 18 inches tall.

- 'Falconet'—a bold combination of gold and orange, this 14-inch beauty blooms in April and is also good for forcing.

  o Jonquilla Narcissus
    Fine-leafed bulbs are easy to use in the garden; the foliage disappears quickly from sight as other garden plants begin to fill in later in the season. That's the case with these narcissi, often referred to as the "chive-leafed" narcissi.

- 'Baby Moon'—one of the latest narcissi to bloom, it's always a surprise when the grass-like foliage produces long-lasting, miniature pure yellow blooms in May. I always have to resist the temptation to pull it, thinking it may be wild onion.

- 'Bell Song'—with a white perianth and a pink cup, this is a different color combination then the more common yellows and oranges of narcissi. This perennial grows to about 16 inches tall, blooming in May just in time for the first species roses.

  o Poeticus Narcissus
    These look wonderful as they naturalize year after year. They have large perianths with small cups, often tinged with orange.

- 'Pheasant's Eye'—I thought roses were confusing when it comes to finding the correct class for a name. This narcissus is sold as both a "species" and a poeticus. Its species name is *Narcissus poeticus* var. *recurvus*. A late bloomer and very fragrant, it's maybe the last narcissus to bloom , right on the doorstep of the species roses.

- 'Actea'—Large, pure white petals are the backing for a yellow cup edged in scarlet. Growing to 16 inches tall, this heirloom poeticus dates from the 1920s.

  o Triandrus Narcissus
    The distinctively separated petals of the perianth are a notable characteristic of this group of narcissi. Blooming toward the end of the season with long-lasting blossoms, the thin foliage is attractive after the flowers have faded.

- Ice Wings—a beautiful early blooming narcissus with pure white flowers.

- Thalia—Perhaps my all-time favorite narcissus, I love the pinwheel effect of the white petals. Also known as the orchid narcissus, this heirloom pure white beauty grows to about 18 inches tall.

- Tulips—If you garden in a climate with six weeks of cold weather in winter, tulips will grow without any trouble. I prefer the species types as garden plants since they naturalize best. But who can resist the showy long stemmed beauties?

  You can create a succession of bloom starting with the smallest species tulips in March continuing to the largest hybrids that bloom as late as May. Tulips are not in bloom with the modern roses, but you may be able to have some in bloom in time for the earliest old garden roses and species. Generally, use

The rose in the background sets off the strange blooms of the allium bulb in front.

tulips to bring early color into the garden and to complement the color of new rose foliage as it begins to emerge from dormant buds.

    For an interesting foliage and flower combination, I underplant *R. glauca* with a mix of 'Queen of the Night' and 'Shirley', both late-blooming tulips. The rose foliage emerges around the same time as the peak of the tulip display. Both tulips pick up on the color of the new foliage of *Rosa glauca*.

■ St. Joseph's Lily
For those gardeners who want a red bulb in spring but can't grow tulips, try this. Recommended by rosarians from the subtropical climate of New Orleans, it is the ubiquitous red amaryllis, known to some as St. Joseph's lily. This bulb has naturalized throughout New Orleans and other regions of the South. This red-flowered amaryllis family member is one of those plants that has

Lilies are lovely with roses—this is the tiger lily combined with delicate rose foliage.

survived generation after generation of neglect and deserves to be in your garden along with your collection of rustled roses.

Early Summer

■ Allium

Alliums comprise a large group of plants. Under this umbrella are chives, garlic, onions, and flowering onions. These plants will naturalize and spread year after year throughout the garden.

I use alliums in my gardens as decorative plants, for cooking, and as a method of natural pest control. I can't prove scientifically that this method of pest control works, but there has been a drop in the population of sucking insects and spider mites in my garden since I've been adding alliums on a regular basis. I'm not sure if it's due to something that is exuded underground by the fragrant bulb, or if there is a fragrance from the above ground plant that keeps the pests away. Those who recommend using alliums to ward off pests tell you to plant the bulbs as close as possible to the rose bushes. This makes for an interesting display, especially if you have the large globe types of alliums.

All sorts of architecture are suddenly introduced into the garden with flowering onions. Globes, pyramids, stars, drumsticks, snake-like forms, and pendants are the diverse shapes of the flowers. The foliage can be fine and grass-like or bold and strap-like. Some even have foliage markings that are part of their colorful display. Bloom colors range from pure white to blue to yellow. This is truly an interesting group of plants to explore and grow with roses.

My favorite was recently re-classified from an allium to a totally unpronounceable lily. Over the period of one long winter, *Allium bugaricum* became *Nectaroscordum siculum* ssp. *bulgaricum*. I still call it bulgaricum, since it's just so much easier. This is an early-summer-blooming bulb with many greenish-white bell-shaped flowers hanging from atop a long stem. Three feet up into the air, this bulb blooms right below the cherry-pink blooms of the rose 'Knockout'.

I find it easy to hide the fading stems and leaves of alliums; they blend in with the rest of the garden. The globe alliums may leave their flower heads behind all summer, but they add an extra bit of texture to the border.

■ Lilies

Lilies are wonderful plants to use with roses, especially the old garden roses. Like roses, lilies have been a part of our gardening heritage as long as there have been written documents on gardening. Medieval herbals, colonial garden records, and abandoned homesteads are all sources of roses and lilies. Carry on the tradition and plant roses with your lilies.

o Asiatic Hybrid Lilies

I use these in small groups, only because I don't find their stiff habit and blooms particularly attractive when massed in the garden. One cultivar that has naturalized in many of the older gardens I work in is 'Enchantment', a hot orange Asiatic. I've planted 'Abraham Darby' near this and have found that the colors complement each other.

o *Lilium candidum*

A lily I've always wanted to try but haven't, only because it sells out so quickly, is the madonna lily, *Lilium candidum*. In southern cemeteries these lilies come back year after year with little or no care at all. As with all lilies, the soil should be well drained. I plan on underplanting my *Rosa moschata plena* with these ancient lilies as soon as I'm able to obtain some bulbs.

o Chinese Trumpet Lilies

Chinese Trumpet Lilies are tall plants bearing magnificent trumpet-shaped flowers ranging in color from pure white to rich shades of burnt copper. The most famous of these is the Easter lily, a popular garden plant and cut flower since being introduced from Bermuda in the nineteenth century. One of my favorite trumpet lilies is 'Golden Splendor', tall and elegant, with a rich golden yellow color. Shrub roses look great backed by a mass of fragrant trumpets hanging overhead. In my garden, these lilies bloom through the month of June into early July.

o Oriental Lilies

Don't wear white in the garden when the Oriental lilies are in bloom. This is not meant to be a fashion statement, but one of practicality. With their curved-back petals and outward-facing blooms, these lilies will stain you with pollen if you brush against them in the garden. Worse than that, your nose is guaranteed to be spotted with orange pollen after a close encounter with one of these fragrant beauties. Best in cold weather gardens, these are popular lilies for fragrance and cut blooms. One that has naturalized throughout my garden is 'Whisper', the only pure white Oriental lily. When it comes into bloom, a morning ritual is to snip off the pollen-soaked stamens before guests arrive. The color of the stamens is a good match for the color of the new growth of roses.

o *Lilium lancifolium*

Many of you will know this summer bloomer by its common name, tiger lily. Some nurseries offer these as Turk's cap lilies. An accidental arrangement in my garden is the orange species *Lilium lancifolium* 'Splendens' growing up through *Rosa primula* and blooming within the canopy of the fern-like foliage of the species rose.

Mid- to Late Summer

■ Formosa Lily

A lily that is underused and suitable for all climates is *Lilium formosana*, or the Formosa lily. As the flowers develop in August, the buds gradually elongate and hang down like long bells before they open. The buds are flushed with lime green until they are ready to open, at which time there will be a noticeable maroon swirl on the outer petals of the closed bud, which then becomes a distinct outer marking on each petal of the fully opened lily. There are often up to eight flowers on each stalk. The delightful citrus scent is an added bonus. These lilies can bloom from seed during one season, so let the seed heads develop and scatter. I've planted these lilies in among the English shrub roses, and the effect was dramatic and stunning as the lilies opened up over the roses.

■ Acidanthera

In July, swords of green foliage, strap-like but not as rigid as irises, rise three feet up from the summer border marking the locations where I planted my Abyssinian gladiolus in early spring. Soon the fragrant flowers will appear, each white flower with a chocolate face and nodding blooms. Several will arise from each plant, not in massive clusters but instead in a simple display of a half dozen or so at a time, slightly higher than the foliage. The blooms don't last very long, but as one fades another opens. Each flower is delicate and extremely fragrant, especially in the evening. This display starts in mid-July and lasts until there is a frost. Acidanthera is not a stiff plant, it moves with each gentle breeze in the garden.

Roses and spirea are great companions even when the spirea isn't in bloom. In this photo, the yellow-green foliage of spirea 'Goldflame' contrasts nicely with the blooms of the 'Simplicity' rose.

■ Dahlia

Dahlias are great sources of summer color, especially when the heat has been turned on, stretching the garden season late into the autumn. The flower styles range from simple flowers to large dinner plate sized blooms with a wide range of colors available. I prefer to use varieties with burgundy-colored foliage. 'Bishop of Llandaff', 'Hot Chocolate', and 'Fascination' are three varieties with this leaf color. The foliage makes a great accent poking through the foliage of roses, and the flowers aren't so bad, either.

Shrubs

Shrubs are the bones of many gardens, providing the framework for the design. They are often also the primary source of winter color. Pay attention to their growth habits when using them as rose companions, and don't plant them too close to your rose bushes. Often, root competition can be an issue, and the shrubs will win.

Boxwood

Have you ever driven six hours with a van full of boxwood? Risking the wrath of the boxwood society, I think the clearest description, without offending too many people, of the scent of boxwood is "cat pee". I'm a cat lover—I grew up in a house full of cats, and I know this fragrance well. I have to say that I was very glad to unload my cargo at the end of the day.

Along with lavender, boxwood is probably the most popular companion plant for roses. My all time favorite boxwood is 'Graham Blandy', a columnar cultivar. After five years, my specimens of 'Graham Blandy' are approximately 8 feet tall and only a foot wide. These tight green pillars serve as a vertical element in the garden, standing alone in the winter, making strong exclamation points.

An interesting way of combining roses and boxwood is to use these two plants to create an edge to a bed. I saw this done extensively in a formal rose garden in Paris. *Buxus*

In this photo, the rose and spirea are both in full bloom, making a much more colorful show.

sempervirens 'Suffruticosa', a dwarf boxwood, is planted at the very edge of the bed to create a solid straight green line. It is kept clipped to a height of 4 inches. Behind the boxwood is planted a hybrid perpetual rose, 'George Dickson', a variety with long stems and huge globular crimson roses. Planted in a line parallel to the boxwood, the long canes of the roses are then trained along a wire suspended one foot above the ground. The result is a fragrant crimson edge of roses suspended over the green line of boxwood.

Ilex × *meserveae* 'Blue Girl'

I once had a client whose home was located on a busy city corner. The garden was separated from the sidewalk by an 8-foot high iron fence, but this fence didn't stop thieves from regularly jumping over to steal her pottery. To make her property more secure, we made a planting bed between the sidewalk and the fence, approximately four feet wide. Against the fence we planted two different climbing roses—'Social Climber' and 'Lace Cascade'—two plants of each. Both are heavily armed with hooked prickles, and they quickly grew higher than the fence. Trained in the same fashion as razor wire, we essentially created a fragrant barbed-wire fence. For added security, we planted a hedge of Ilex × meserveae 'China Girl' between the roses and the sidewalk. The pottery never walked again!

Ligustrum obtusifolium

When the rose 'American Pillar' was introduced, it was the beginning of the era of large-flowered climbing roses. This was in 1902. My client's father planted a specimen of this rose in 1920 against a south-facing wall in Bridgehampton, New York, a seaside community in eastern Long Island. As is the tradition in this area, he added *Ligustrum obtusifolium*, or border privet, to soften the wall with its dense, green, textured foliage. Over the years, the privet encroached upon 'American Pillar', but by that time the vigorous rose had already sent long canes onto and over the brick wall. Eighty-five years later, in June it appears as if the privet is in bloom with glorious pink and white flowers. A once blooming rose, 'American Pillar' leaves behind a wonderful hip display for autumn and winter decoration.

Buddleia

Buddleias bring colorful and fragrant flowers into the garden, along with foliage texture and beautiful butterflies. There are many fragrant buddleia hybrids to choose from, ranging from compact to large and aggressive growers. The Nanho series has been a popular group for compact growth, smaller foliage, and smaller blooms. 'Nanho Blue' is one of the most popular of this series.

A newer group creating a great deal of interest is the compact series from England created by Elizabeth Keep, referred to by some as the English Butterfly series. Among those to consider for use with roses are 'Peacock' (pink), 'Purple Emperor' (purple), and 'Adonis' (blue). These compact types are good for mixed borders since they don't steal too much space. Unlike their larger cousins, the leaves of the compact buddleias are narrow and dainty.

For vigor and beauty to be observed from

afar, the large-growing hybrids are ideal. Two that I use often in natural borders for accent and mid-summer color are 'Pink Delight' and 'White Profusion'. A slightly more unusual variety, 'Honeycomb', with its golden yellow flowers resembling rounded honeycombs adds an interesting color and texture to the garden as well. *Buddleia* × *weyeriana* 'Honeycomb' and my musk rose *Rosa moschata plena* share the same bed in an organized tangle. They grow independent of each other at the beginning of the season. But by summer's end, they create one airy mound of gray-green foliage bursting with fragrance. The golden-yellow blooms of the buddleia are not as noticeable or abundant as the musk rose, but they're a welcome bonus.

This is an easy combination to maintain. Of the two plants, 'Honeycomb' is more prone to winter damage. When the danger of a freeze has passed, I prune the buddleia to three feet and wait for new shoots to develop. I remove clutter from the rose bush and shorten canes to leave a specimen about six feet high by four feet wide. This disentangles the two shrubs and they once again begin their summer romance.

Vitex

During August, poking out of the same bed containing the musk rose and the 'Honeycomb' butterfly bush are the lilac-blue flowers of the chaste tree, *Vitex agnus-castus*. This shrub begins producing clusters of bloom in early July with a peak display in August and sporadic blooms until September. At the same time, the musk rose is producing fragrant white blooms. Together, they create an interesting display, each showing its flowers in large panicles. By the end of the season, my chaste tree grows to about eight feet. I'll prune it at least halfway in the spring. But until then, I leave the panicles of faded blooms intact. This is a popular spot for cardinals to sit and feed during late summer. This season, I've planted an everblooming yellow climbing rose, 'Casino', at the base of my chaste tree. My plan is to train the canes through the older branches of the shrub to create a display of yellow roses with the lilac-blue of the vitex.

Lespedeza thunbergii 'Gibraltar'

I've planted my *Lespedeza thunbergii* 'Gibraltar' in the wrong place—it's spilling onto the sidewalk that doubles as a garden path in front of my house, creating an obstacle for visitors. Last year I saw a charming specimen of this plant in bloom, and thought what a lovely perennial. I had no idea at the time that it would become this flowing shrub.

I actually thought I had lost it over the winter. This spring I pruned all the wood, which was dead, to the ground. By July, this grew into a gorgeous arching shrub five feet wide and high, and by August 'Gibraltar' was spewing crimson-purple flowers onto the sidewalk. Fortunately it's a soft plant, actually kind of pleasant to brush against.

It's exciting to have a strong color like this happen late in the season. I planted 'Gibraltar' near 'Rose de Rescht' and 'Autumn Bouquet'. Both of these shrub roses produce a noticeable bloom in the late season, sharing the border with this glorious shrub. All three are good late season pinks to blend together.

Hydrangea

Mopheads, drumsticks, snowballs, lace-caps, and cones—this is not a deli menu but instead descriptions of the various flower forms of hydrangeas. Hydrangeas are one of the most commonly used shrubs in the home landscape, from single specimen plantings to massive hedges framing houses and decorating the landscape. Hydrangeas are good shrubs to use as companions with roses. The flowers, foliage, and stems bring interesting textures and color combinations. I would recommend using vigorous growing roses for the best display when combining with any type of hydrangea.

The hybrid musk rose 'Buff Beauty' is lovely entangled with the burgeoning blooms of an oakleaf hydrangea.

feet and still growing, but very slowly.

It wasn't just the fine blue foliage that I loved, but also it seemed like the perfect mate for an old rambling rose, 'Excelsa', already on the property when I bought my house. At one time there was a split rail fence, but termites did that in, so I used a combination of an antique barn stall divider and 'Blue Ice' to serve as the new support for the rambling rose.

'Excelsa' is a once-blooming rambler. I only allow for two or three canes to grow into the cypress, and I train the others along the barn divider. Each summer, after the blooms have finished, I remove the old wood (canes that just bloomed) and replace them with new growth. This way, I prevent the rose from overwhelming my 'Blue Ice' cypress.

The combination of colors—the pink-red blooms of 'Excelsa' with the ice-blue foliage of the cypress—as well as the contrast of the blooms with the lacy foliage of the conifer is a winner and a traffic stopper.

Vines

Unlike climbing roses, vines are true climbing plants. There are many uses for them as companions to roses. A classic frame for a garden is an arbor covered in wisteria. As the pendulous blooms of wisteria drip from above, species and old garden roses are in full bloom below, with the modern roses not far behind. Climbing roses and ramblers can be discreetly hidden in amongst the foliage and stems of this vigorous climbing plant.

Annual vines such as morning glory and moonflower can decorate the gardens in the summer. One well-behaved morning glory I use is 'Chocolate', which has huge chocolate-colored blooms all summer. Passionflower vines are good mates for roses, bringing a wide assortment of colors, textures, and fragrances into the garden. Vines can be used to combine with roses on pillars and arbors to extend the season of color. Clematis is a favorite vine for this purpose.

Clematis

Over the past several years, the inventory of clematis varieties in this country has increased dramatically. No longer limited to a small number of climbing cultivars, there are now many choices in colors, blooming times, and growth habits. With proper planning you can now have a long season of clematis flowering with your roses.

Growing clematis with roses is easy if you understand when it's best to prune and how the plants grow. The growth habit and pruning requirements should be the deciding factors in matching clematis with roses.

◼ Early Season

I grew *Clematis armandii* one season in Brooklyn. We were having a mild winter, and this evergreen species burst into bloom during March. The next year we had a normal winter, and the clematis died to ground level and didn't bloom. I imagine in the warmer zones where tea and China roses grow into large shrubs, this could be a good garden mate as a background plant for those roses. The fragrant flowers are white and the foliage is a lush dark green. It is an aggressive grower, so I'd recommend *armandii* in the background or on its own arbor. Or, if you're an adventurous gardener with a huge arbor, you

may want to try planting armandii with 'Lady Banks', 'Souvenir de Mme. Leonie Viennot', or 'Fortune's Double Yellow'.

Montana types are aggressive growers suited for colder climates and should be used as background plants, not mixed in with roses. I use them to cover walls behind shrub roses. When in bloom along the top of a wall, they put on quite a show. The clematis bloom before most modern roses but would complement any of the early season species roses and European old garden roses. The flowers are small and come in many shades of pink as well as pure white. Large growing shrub roses such as 'Harison's Yellow' with its bright yellow roses or an alba variety such as 'Sauveolens' would work well with these small-flowered clematis.

If you want to try growing the montana clematis with a climbing rose, then I would recommend an aggressive rambler such as 'Paul's Himalayan Musk', 'Veilchenblau', or 'Excelsa'. These ramblers bloom after the clematis. When the roses finish blooming, remove the blooming canes and trim the clematis at the same time.

■ Early Summer
This group of clematis contains garden varieties that bloom with the roses in the beginning of the season and are capable of blooming again later in the season. Included are the large-flowered types such as 'Bee's Jubilee', 'Elsa Spath', 'Pink Cameo', 'Dr. Ruppel', and 'Henryii'.

Grow these with climbing roses, both ramblers and ever-blooming varieties. Young plants will grow very fast, wrapping themselves around the canes of the roses. As you prune the rose for new growth or continual bloom, you can prune the clematis as well.

■ Late Season

In this group of clematis are many of the small-flowered viticellas, texensis, and the non-climbing types. Many popular large-flowered climbing varieties are in this group as well, often referred to as Jackmanii types because of the large flowers they produce, similar to the ever-popular 'Jackmanii' cultivar. Some recommended cultivars are 'Jackmanii','Comtesse de Bouchard', 'Hagley Hybrid', 'Multi Blue', and 'Midnight Showers'.

Viticella types, smaller-flowered climbers derived from an Italian species *Clematis viticella*, are a part of this herbaceous group as well. Some of the popular viticellas are 'Etoile de Violette', 'Polish Spirit', 'Betty Corning', and 'Madame Julia Correvon'.

The texensis group is made up of climbing types derived from the species *Clematis texensis*. These have unique bell-shaped flowers. Of this group, some highly recommended cultivars are 'Duchess of Albany', 'Etoile Rose', 'Pagoda', and 'Lady Bird Johnson'.

Considered an invasive plant in some regions is the tenacious sweet autumn clematis, *Clematis ternifolia*. From late August through the month of September, this small-flowered, nearly evergreen species fills the night air with a sweet fragrance.

The clematis I find most adaptable to planting with shrub roses are the shrubby types, those that don't cling but scramble, sprawl, and stay close to the ground. They're also a part of this late blooming group of clematis. Try *Clematis heracleifolia davidiana* with dark blue tubular flowers, growing to about 3 feet tall; 'China Purple', which has purple tubular blooms with a rich looking dark green leaf, is a great filler in the border even without the flowers, and 'Mrs. Robert Brydon', whose blooms are pale blue to white. I've planted 'Mrs. Robert Brydon' near the front of the border where the pale flowers catch the soft light at dusk and glow like pearls in the August moonlight. Following the flowers is a long-lasting display of feathery seed heads.

Climbing Hydrangea

A very slow plant to get started, climbing hydrangea usually takes at least two seasons before you start seeing results. It establishes itself as a woody vine with interesting exfoliating bark, shiny green foliage, and in late June white fragrant flowers resembling lace hydrangeas. Climbing hydrangea is adaptable to shade and full sun. If you use it as a companion for roses, you'll need a location with as much sun as possible.

Plant a large-flowered climber, rambler, or vigorous shrub rose with climbing hydrangea. The woody vines of the climbing hydrangea provide support for the rose. One characteristic of the climbing hydrangea is that the branches not only attach themselves to a wall, but there is another layer of loose branches that create a bushy look by crossing in and out of themselves. This provides more places to sneak in rose canes. You can either weave the rose canes through the hydrangea branches, or tie the canes directly to the vine.

Schizophragma hydrangeoides

Japanese hydrangea vine, or *Schizophragma hydrangeoides,* is a very close relative of the climbing hydrangea. And like the hydrangea, this deciduous vine is a good companion for climbing roses. Very similar in habit and culture, the most popular cultivar is 'Moonlight'. One significant difference between these two vines is the growth habit. Instead of a bushy climbing habit, the Japanese hydrangea vine remains closer to the surface of the structure and has a tighter and neater look. An excellent choice for small city gardens, the silver-laced dark-green foliage is a wonderful foil for pink climbing roses.

Gloriosa superba 'Rothschildiana'

Friends in central Florida use a climbing lily, *Gloriosa superba* 'Rothschildiana', as a companion vine with their roses. Also known as the glory lily or gloriosa lily, this is a tender plant in most parts of our country, but a perennial in the Orlando area and further south.

The flowers of 'Rothschildiana' appear as if they've been blown back by the wind, with wavy petals of vivid scarlet and yellow. Tendrils grow from the tips of the leaves, giving it a very unique climbing habit. There are a handful of varieties to try, usually sold in summer bulb catalogs. Look for 'Citrina', which is orange-yellow; and *Gloriosa superba*, which is orange with yellow edges to the flower.

Golden Hops

I planted golden hops, *Humulus aureola*, next to my garage wondering if anything would come of it. Unfamiliar with its habit, I thought it could be good filler and create a colorful golden-green screen. Not much happened that first season, except for about 5 feet of gorgeous chartreuse foliage on my short fence. Next spring, as if overnight, the golden hops vine found its way to the roofline of my garage and began entwining itself around one of the main canes of 'Fairmount Pink', a rose that blooms in spring and is leafless all summer. At that moment, I loved the contrast of the yellow-green and the cerise pink of the rose.

Two months later, I'm wondering how far this monster will go, as now it has completely engulfed the rose. I checked web sites praising this vine, and I called nurseries that sell it. They all reassured me that it is indeed hardy and will become woody and grow and grow and grow. Somehow this made me think of kudzu in the south. This one's beautiful, but a potential thug, so be forewarned. I plan to be very severe when I prune this winter.

English Ivy

I came across an old planting of the red rose 'Stairway To Heaven', one of Jackson & Perkins' landmark cultivars, happily growing out of a thick under-planting of English ivy. Seventy-five years ago, I'm sure that someone planted that rose there, with the ivy as a carefree filler between fence posts. I don't like English ivy, but here it works. Completely covering the fence, the ivy is keeping the roots of the rose cool, and the rose makes the ivy look as though it has red flowers. During the winter, the fence is always green. What more could one ask?

DIRECTORY OF COMPANIONS

Ageratum
Ageratum houstonianum
MATURE PLANT SIZE: 3 feet × 2 feet
GROWTH HABIT: clump
BLOOM COLOR: blue, purple, white, pink
BLOOM SIZE: small, clusters
BLOOM TIME: summer
FRAGRANCE: no
PLANT TYPE: herbaceous annual
COLD HARDINESS: Zones 8 – 10
HOW TO USE: flower color; edging; front border

This is a fairly common garden annual in my neck of the woods. Easy to grow, durable through most weather conditions, and tolerant of ocean mist and fog, ageratum is an easy plant for difficult situations. In a garden fifty yards from the Atlantic Ocean I came across a stunning display of it being used to create a colorful edge to a rose garden.

When the plants are grown in full sun they can mound as high as 3 feet displaying small pincushion type flowers. Most popular are the blue and violet hybrids. Each season there seems to be another new designer line of this durable plant, right now the Artist series is hot. 'Artist Blue' was the variety used to edge the rose garden near the ocean.

Up north we use these as summer annuals—they're tolerant of our heat and will last until there is a killing frost. In the deep South, ageratum is best as a winter annual.

OTHER VARIETIES AVAILABLE: 'Blue Horizon'—baby blue; 3 feet; 'Artist Purple'—magenta-purple; 12 inches; 'Blue Puffs'—light violet-blue; 8 inches; 'Hawaii White'—white; 8 inches

Clown Flower
Torenia fournieri
MATURE PLANT SIZE: 12 inches × 6 inches
GROWTH HABIT: clump
BLOOM COLOR: blue, pink, and bicolor
BLOOM SIZE: 1 inch
BLOOM TIME: summer
FRAGRANCE: no
PLANT TYPE: herbaceous annual
COLD HARDINESS: Zones 8 – 11
HOW TO USE: flower color; edging; front border

We've always called them clown flowers, but *Torenia fournieri* is also known as wishbone flower due to the wishbone-like design of its stamens. Torenia is a shade-tolerant annual with an array of colors to choose from. The most popular are the blue Summer Wave series: 'Summer Wave Blue' and 'Amethyst'. The flowers are lipped like a snapdragon and bloom all summer long.

Hardy in zones 10 and 11, I suspect that torenia are better as cool weather annuals where the summers are unbearable. There are newer cultivars being introduced that are more heat tolerant.

Use torenia under roses as living mulch or to soften edges and containers. Their clown-face blooms add charming, reliable color to the garden and are fun for kids.

OTHER VARIETIES AVAILABLE: 'Summer Wave Blue'—blue bicolor; trailing; 'Pink Moon'—pink and white; 'Summer Wave Amethyst'—bicolor burgundy; 'Blue and White Clown'—blue with white center

Four O'Clocks
Mirabilis jalapa
MATURE PLANT SIZE: 3 feet × 2 feet; some dwarf, too
GROWTH HABIT: spreading
BLOOM COLOR: red, yellow, pink, stripes
BLOOM SIZE: 1 inch
BLOOM TIME: summer
FRAGRANCE: flowers, in the evening
PLANT TYPE: herbaceous annual
COLD HARDINESS: Zones 8 – 11
HOW TO USE: evening fragrance; flower color; front
to mid-border

Four o'clocks have an intoxicating evening fragrance that makes them a necessity for the evening garden. These garden antiques are annuals in northern gardens of our country, easily cultivated from seed sown directly in the garden. Sometimes, if there is a mild winter, the seeds will over-winter and sprout the following year. In the warmer zones of our country, *Mirabilis jalapa* is an herbaceous perennial that develops a tenacious taproot-like tuber. This, plus the fact that the seeds scatter freely, can make the lovely four o'clock a garden guest that may never go away.

While visiting in New Orleans I saw wonderful yellow and magenta varieties self-seeding in the gardens of the historic district. Floridians recommend using dwarf cultivars with roses. Broken Colors and Jingle are two series offered with a maximum growth of twenty inches.

OTHER VARIETIES AVAILABLE: 'Limelight'—rose; chartreuse foliage; 'Kaleidoscope'—mix of striped colors; 'Tea Time'—mix colors; Jingle Series—dwarf cultivars

Heliotrope
Heliotropium arborescens
MATURE PLANT SIZE: 2 feet × 1 foot
GROWTH HABIT: clump
BLOOM COLOR: white, purple, blue
BLOOM SIZE: small flowers; large umbels
BLOOM TIME: summer
FRAGRANCE: flowers
PLANT TYPE: herbaceous annual
COLD HARDINESS: Zones 9 – 11
HOW TO USE: flower color and fragrance; accent; edging;
front border

Heliotropium arborescens, or simply heliotrope, has been a favorite garden annual for its fragrance and soft colors. The umbels of flowers backed by dark green foliage make wonderful filler in any sunny border. With fragrance descriptions from baby powder to vanilla, how could you not have this in a garden?

As an annual, it sprawls in part shade and grows upright to 18 inches in full sun. The cultivars I use most often are 'Alba' and 'Marine', both with a vanilla fragrance, and 'Light Eyes', which has pale lavender flowers with a lighter-colored center. A popular summer garden annual up north, heliotrope is a perennial in zones 9 and warmer.

'Homestead Purple' Verbena
Verbena canadensis 'Homestead
Purple'

MATURE PLANT SIZE: 18 inches × 36 inches
GROWTH HABIT: clump
BLOOM COLOR: purple
BLOOM SIZE: small, umbel display
BLOOM TIME: summer
FRAGRANCE: no
PLANT TYPE: annual
COLD HARDINESS: Zones 8 – 10
HOW TO USE: flower color; front border; ground cover

Verbena 'Homestead Purple' is an aggressive growing perennial in the South but is a mild-mannered annual in zone 7. The rich purple flowers are borne in clusters and held high above the foliage. The plants gradually mound up to 18 inches but spread at least 3 feet in every direction.

When I first grew 'Homestead Purple' I was told it was hardy. I planted it everywhere—under roses, as fillers in open spots of the borders, and in containers. I especially loved the look of this plant cascading and reaching out from a terracotta planter. My enthusiasm was soon nipped as our first normal winter killed them all. This didn't discourage me; now I use it as an annual. A friend in Braithwaite, Louisiana, however, has successfully cultivated her 'Homestead Purple' to be a colorful ground cover plant under her roses, spilling out from under her red Bourbon rose 'Maggie' and nearly devouring her garden path.

Impatiens
Impatiens walleriana

MATURE PLANT SIZE: 3 feet × 2 feet
GROWTH HABIT: clump
BLOOM COLOR: all but blue and brown
BLOOM SIZE: 1 inch
BLOOM TIME: summer
FRAGRANCE: no
PLANT TYPE: herbaceous annual
COLD HARDINESS: 9 – 11
HOW TO USE: flower color; edging; accents; front border

Ever since Victorian times, impatiens have been one of the most popular bedding plants. Typically, they are grown as reliable shade-tolerant annuals. They tolerate more sun in cooler climates and serve as good filler at the bases of larger plants, especially roses. I find them very useful to determine if we've had a frost yet, since this is one of the first garden plants to show frost damage.

I have several situations where there are tall climbing roses trained up walls with the base of the rose in shade, the top in full sun. Impatiens are an easy solution as a source of color down at the base of the plant. My favorites are the double-flowered "rose" hybrids.

OTHER VARIETIES AVAILABLE: Impatiens Fiesta group—double flowered varieties;Impatiens Firefly series—miniature impatiens, many colors; *Impatiens glandulifera* 'Himalayan Impatiens'—white to garnet; 6 feet; *Impatiens repens* 'Creeping Impatiens'—trailing, 18-24 inches; burgundy leaves; yellow.

Johnny-Jump-Up
Viola tricolor
MATURE PLANT SIZE: 8 inches × 6 inches
GROWTH HABIT: clump
BLOOM COLOR: deep blue, white, yellow, and mixed
BLOOM SIZE: tiny to 2 inches
BLOOM TIME: cool weather
FRAGRANCE: flower
PLANT TYPE: herbaceous annual/perennial
COLD HARDINESS: Zones 4 – 8
HOW TO USE: flower color; bedding plant; winter color

The garden bursts to life when *Viola tricolor*, also known as Johnny-jump-up, appears in spring. The little flower faces and bright colors are hard to resist, especially when little effort is needed to make them grow. Pansies are hybrids of *Viola tricolor* and have evolved over the years as a useful winter and spring planting complementing the new growth of the freshly pruned roses.

Cool weather plants, pansies will put on a colorful display until the weather is consistently hot. At that time, I either shear them back to nearly ground level or pull up the scraggly plants and replace them with fresh summer annuals. In zone 7 and further south, pansies are excellent winter annuals for rose beds. I prefer the varieties with the smallest flowers—to me they look more natural and seem to have a better winter hardiness.

OTHER VARIETIES AVAILABLE: Sorbet series; Crystal Bowl series

Larkspur
Consolida ambigua
MATURE PLANT SIZE: 4 feet × 1foot
GROWTH HABIT: clump
BLOOM COLOR: blue, pink, white, purple
BLOOM SIZE: 1 inch, spikes
BLOOM TIME: summer
FRAGRANCE: no
PLANT TYPE: annual
COLD HARDINESS: Zones 3 – 7
HOW TO USE: early summer color; textured foliage

Larkspur is the annual form of delphinium and is easy to grow from seed scattered the previous autumn or in early spring. You can also allow them to self-seed by leaving the flower heads on after blooming or scattering the seeds as you cut back the finished plants in summer.

Allow larkspur to grow freely among shrub roses, to soften the look of rigid modern hybrids, or to create the look of a cottage garden with old garden roses. Larkspur grows best where the summers are cool, prolonging the blooming period.

Mealy-cup Sage
Salvia farinacea 'Victoria Blue'
MATURE PLANT SIZE: 2 feet × 2 feet
GROWTH HABIT: clump
BLOOM COLOR: blue
BLOOM SIZE: small; long spikes
BLOOM TIME: summer
FRAGRANCE: foliage, slightly
PLANT TYPE: herbaceous annual
COLD HARDINESS: Zones 8 – 11
HOW TO USE: flower color; accent; front border

Mexican Petunia
Ruellia spp.
MATURE PLANT SIZE: 12 inches to 5 feet × 12 inches to 3 feet
GROWTH HABIT: clump
BLOOM COLOR: pink, white, blue, red
BLOOM SIZE: 2 inches
BLOOM TIME: summer
FRAGRANCE: no
PLANT TYPE: herbaceous annual
COLD HARDINESS: Zones 8 – 11
HOW TO USE: flower color; foliage color; accents; front to mid-border

'Victoria Blue' is a variety of *Salvia farinacea* also known as the mealy sage or mealy-cup sage'. 'Victoria Blue' has slight hints of "mealy" gray coating on the flower stalks, a trait inherited from the parent species.

In zone 7 and colder, 'Victoria Blue' is a summer annual; in warmer zones, it's perennial. It's recommended to prune this salvia hard each season if it's grown as a perennial. 'Victoria Blue' has a color and habit that is compatible with all bush roses, especially good for softening the rigid look of hybrid teas.

Another summer blooming hybrid of *Salvia farinacea*, 'Indigo Spires', has violet-blue flowers on longer, more relaxed spires. A favorite of gardeners in New Orleans where it's used as a perennial, this plant can become large and floppy, easily attaining a height of 4 feet. If a frost doesn't prune for you, it might be a good idea to shape 'Indigo Spires' annually to keep it from crowding the garden.

OTHER VARIETIES AVAILABLE: 'Strata'—bright blue; silvery gray stems and calyx; 18 inches; 'Alba'—white; 18 inches

Named for Jean de la Ruelle, a 16th century French botanist, ruellia is grown as an annual in zones 7 and colder, while down south and in the southwest, ruellia can be used as a heat tolerant perennial. It is also known as Mexican petunia or Mexican bluebell.

The species *Ruellia brittoniana* and the varieties 'Elegans', 'Chi Chi Pink', and 'Katie' are offered in my area as annuals under the collective name of "False Petunia". The blooms of ruellia do indeed resemble small petunias, but on bushy, upright shrubs. 'Katie', a blue variety, grows to about a foot tall. 'Elegans' is bright red, reaching a height of 8 inches and is good as a low growing annual. 'Chi Chi Pink' grows to 3 feet in height with a soft pink flower with a violet-pink throat. The foliage is long and thin with a bronze tint. All of the ruellias are excellent butterfly attractors, heat-resistant and moisture-tolerant. They bloom from April through late autumn.

OTHER VARIETIES AVAILABLE: 'Chi Chi'—pink; bronze foliage; 3 feet; *Ruellia brittoniana*—lavender; 5 feet; *Ruellia elegans*—scarlet; 8 inches; *Ruellia makoyana*—purple; trailing

Million Bells
Calibrachoa spp./*Petunia* spp.
MATURE PLANT SIZE: 18 inches × 18 inches
GROWTH HABIT: clump
BLOOM COLOR: pastels
BLOOM SIZE: 1 inch
BLOOM TIME: spring/summer
FRAGRANCE: no
PLANT TYPE: herbaceous annual
COLD HARDINESS: Zones 9 – 11
HOW TO USE: flower color; filler; front border

Looking like a small-flowered petunia, calibrachoas are annuals with a spreading or cascading habit that work nicely as ground covers in front of roses or in containers, spilling over the sides.

The colors range from white to vivid fuchsia with a wide variation of colors in between. Very easy to maintain in all zones as an annual, the tubular flowers are self-cleaning and are produced all summer long. In the deep South, calibrachoa performs better as a winter annual.

Let's not forget about petunias. There are some wonderful new hybrids of this tubular flower that are similar in many ways to calibrachoa, but perhaps a bit more aggressive. Look for the Supertunia, Wave, and Surfina series.

OTHER CALIBRACHOA VARIETIES AVAILABLE: 'Terra Cotta'—yellow/terra cotta; 'Trailing Rose'—fuchsia 'White Blush'—white/soft pink; 'Trailing Blue'—violet

OTHER PETUNIA VARIETIES AVAILABL4E: 'Cherry'—hot pink, Wave series; 'Sky Blue'—azure blue; Surfina series; 'Lemon Plume'—lemon-yellow; Supertunia series; 'Priscilla'—double, dark lavender; Supertunia series

Nemesia
Nemesia spp.
MATURE PLANT SIZE: 12 inches × 12 inches
GROWTH HABIT: clump
BLOOM COLOR: a range of pastels
BLOOM SIZE: small
BLOOM TIME: cool weather
FRAGRANCE: flowers
PLANT TYPE: herbaceous annual
COLD HARDINESS: Zones 7- 8
HOW TO USE: flower color and fragrance; color for spring, autumn, and winter; front of the border

These sweetly scented cool-weather annuals tend to spread and spill, making them good candidates for the edge of a bed or for cascading over the sides of containers. The numerous varieties have soft colors, making it very easy to blend them into the garden.

Nemesia does best in spring or fall most places and is ideal as a winter annual in the warmest parts of our country. During the summer, I ignore it, shear it, or pull it out of the garden. As with pansies, these are good garden fillers as the roses are beginning to grow.

OTHER VARIETIES AVAILABLE: 'Blue Bird'—deep blue; 'Compact Innocence'—white

Nicotiana
Nicotiana spp.
MATURE PLANT SIZE: From 3 to 6 feet high, 1 to 2 feet wide
GROWTH HABIT: clump
BLOOM COLOR: white, green, pastel colors
BLOOM SIZE: up to 5 inches
BLOOM TIME: summer
FRAGRANCE: flowers, evening
PLANT TYPE: herbaceous annual
COLD HARDINESS: Zones 9 – 11
HOW TO USE: evening fragrance; flower color; plant shape; mid to rear border

Pentas
Penta lanceolata
MATURE PLANT SIZE: 2 feet × 1 foot
GROWTH HABIT: clump
BLOOM COLOR: red, white, pink, fuchsia
BLOOM SIZE: 2 inches
BLOOM TIME: summer
FRAGRANCE: no
PLANT TYPE: herbaceous annual
COLD HARDINESS: Zones 9 – 11
HOW TO USE: flower color and texture; front to mid-border

Nicotiana is a diverse annual, offering architecture, color, and a wonderful evening fragrance. Two species with notable fragrances are *Nicotiana alata* and *Nicotiana sylvestris*. Both produce white tubular flowers that are wonderfully scented at night.

The tallest, *Nicotiana sylvestris*, nearly reaches 6 feet high in the garden. This species produces a beautiful weeping candelabrum of long tubular flowers. Plant this species towards the rear of the border. *Nicotiana alata* is a moderate grower with smaller leaves, not as striking as *sylvestris*, but still fragrant.

Nicotiana langsdorfii, a third species to look for, doesn't have a fragrance. The amazing combinations of chartreuse, white, and teal blue found in the flower make it worthwhile as an unusual accent plant for the summer border.

OTHER VARIETIES AVAILABLE: 'Fragrant Cloud'—white; 'Lime Green'—green
Heaven Scent Series—mixed

In bloom all summer long, pentas brighten the border with strong colors. Annuals up north, in the South, southwest and temperate climates of the west coast, pentas can be used as herbaceous perennials or may even become small evergreen shrubs.

Pentas bloom non-stop in the heat, producing clusters of tubular flowers, perfect for the summer border. I use them near the front of the border as accents and to attract hummingbirds to the garden. In regions where they grow larger and shrubbier, I would recommend using them as middle border plants. Pink, fuchsia, and lavender varieties are especially nice with tea roses in a southern garden.

OTHER VARIETIES AVAILABLE: 'Cranberry Punch'— cranberry; 'Stars & Stripes'—scarlet with pink centers; 'Orchid Illusion'—pale lavender-pink; 'Sunrise Pink'— soft pink

Persian Shield
Strobilanthes dyerianus
MATURE PLANT SIZE: 5 feet × 3 feet
GROWTH HABIT: clump
BLOOM COLOR: pale blue
BLOOM SIZE: small, spiky
BLOOM TIME: winter
FRAGRANCE: none
PLANT TYPE: annual
COLD HARDINESS: Zones 9-11
HOW TO USE: foliage accent plant; front to mid-border

Phlox
Phlox drummondii
MATURE PLANT SIZE: 12 inches × 12 inches
GROWTH HABIT: clump
BLOOM COLOR: pastels
BLOOM SIZE: 1 inch
BLOOM TIME: cool weather
FRAGRANCE: flower
PLANT TYPE: herbaceous annual
COLD HARDINESS: Zones 8 – 11
HOW TO USE: flower color and fragrance; filler in the front border

There's no reason to wait for the flowers of strobilanthes. Some of the most spectacular color combinations to be found in the garden happen in the foliage of this plant. Also known as Persian shield, the leaves display various shades of purple flecked with pink, green, and a metallic shimmer of silver, looking especially vibrant as new foliage emerges from the square stems.

A middle border plant up north, Persian shield may grow to a height of 5 feet and, if pinched regularly, as wide as 3 feet. Persian shield thrives in full sun as well as partial shade, but some shade is good during the hottest times of the day. Too much sun will wash out the dramatic color from the foliage. In warmer climates, this plant could live through the winters but may become too woody and lose its luster.

Since the most dramatic color is in the new growth, I recommend continual pruning to encourage this. Strobilanthes is a perfect companion for pink roses and is stunning with gray and dark green foliage plants.

Annual phlox is best when used as a cool weather annual, offering a wide range of pastel colors to use as filler in the spring and fall garden. This annual is easily grown from seed sown directly in the garden, blooming on very young plants and continuing until the heat and humidity become oppressive.

Annual phlox grows in a mounding habit with the five-petaled flowers held above soft green foliage in small clusters. As the season progresses, phlox tends to spread. Some cultivars require deadheading, but there are newer cultivars that require very little maintenance to keep them in bloom. The simple flowers and delightful colors make these excellent plants to grow among roses.

OTHER VARIETIES AVAILABLE: 'Phlox of Sheep'—pastels; 21st Century Series—pastels

Red Sage
Salvia coccinea

MATURE PLANT SIZE: 3 feet × 2 feet
GROWTH HABIT: clump
BLOOM COLOR: red
BLOOM SIZE: small, spiky
BLOOM TIME: summer
FRAGRANCE: foliage
PLANT TYPE: herbaceous annual
COLD HARDINESS: Zones 8 – 11
HOW TO USE: flower color; foliage fragrance; accents;
  front border

An annual in northern gardens and a perennial for the South, this species and its hybrids are popular among Florida rosarians as companion plants for their roses. Two varieties are in my gardens: 'Coral Nymph' (also sold as 'Cherry Blossom'), with delicate salmon-pink and white blooms, and 'Lady in Red', a fiery color I use to under-plant my tea roses.

OTHER VARIETIES AVAILABLE: 'Snow White'—white;
  18 inches

Texas Fire Bush
Hamelia patens

MATURE PLANT SIZE: 4 feet × 3 feet
GROWTH HABIT: clump
BLOOM COLOR: orange-red
BLOOM SIZE: 1 inch
BLOOM TIME: summer
FRAGRANCE: no
PLANT TYPE: herbaceous annual
COLD HARDINESS: Zones 9 – 11
HOW TO USE: flower color; accent; mid-border

The Texas fire bush is a perfect choice for adding a dash of hot color into the border. Often sold as a "hummingbird magnet", hamelia is a tropical plant that requires the hottest spot in the garden for the best show of its fiery blooms. In the hottest regions of our country, this plant could be grown as an herbaceous perennial requiring enough room to show off its hot colors and add long-lasting color to the summer border. The growth habit is conducive for complementing the shapes of tea roses and other large shrubby types of roses. The color will set your garden on fire. For me, it's a low growing annual to add color when the roses are on summer siesta.

Texas Sage
Salvia gregii
MATURE PLANT SIZE: 3 feet × 3 feet
GROWTH HABIT: clump
BLOOM COLOR: red
BLOOM SIZE: small, spike display
BLOOM TIME: summer
FRAGRANCE: foliage
PLANT TYPE: herbaceous annual
COLD HARDINESS: Zones 8 – 1
HOW TO USE: flower color; foliage fragrance; accents;
   front border

Salvia gregii, also known as Texas sage, has a high tolerance for heat. The species is a late bloomer, but a collection of good summer bloomers has been produced for our gardens from this Texas species. Annuals in zone 7 and further north, these are perennials where the winters are mild.

'Wild Watermelon' grows to 2 feet producing spikes of flowers the color of the inside of a watermelon. 'Dark Dancer' has a fuchsia-red flower, produced a little bit later than the other hybrids. The leaves of this salvia are highly aromatic, similar to the culinary sage. These two hybrids and others of this group all have great colors to make a hot color garden. Be bold and use them with some of those orange-red floribunda roses such as 'Trumpeter', 'Cinnabar', or 'Europeana'.

OTHER VARIETIES AVAILABLE: 'Big Pink'—pink; 3 feet;
   'Desert Blaze'—red-orange; 3 feet; 'Furman's Red'—
   red; 3 feet; 'Raspberry Royale'—raspberry-pink; 3 feet

Andean Silver-Leaf Sage
Salvia discolor
MATURE PLANT SIZE: 3 feet × 2 feet
GROWTH HABIT: clump
BLOOM COLOR: purple-black
BLOOM SIZE: 1 inch
BLOOM TIME: summer
FRAGRANCE: foliage, slight
PLANT TYPE: herbaceous annual
COLD HARDINESS: Zones 8 – 10
HOW TO USE: foliage contrast; flower color; accent; front border

The combination of silver/green foliage and near-black flowers makes this sprawling plant a true curiosity in the garden, adding a dash of unusual colors. A low- growing annual in zone 7 gardens and colder, this salvia needs a good warm and dry site to reach a height of 3 feet.

The flowers are an added surprise, but the foliage contrast is interesting enough to use as filler among low-growing pink- and apricot-colored roses. For real fun, plant a container with this salvia and 'Viridiflora', the green rose!

Bat Face Flower
Cuphea llavea
MATURE PLANT SIZE: 12 inches to 4 feet × 2 feet to 4 feet
GROWTH HABIT: clump
BLOOM COLOR: red, purple
BLOOM SIZE: 1 inch
BLOOM TIME: summer
FRAGRANCE: no
PLANT TYPE: herbaceous annual
COLD HARDINESS: Zones 9 – 11
HOW TO USE: flower color and texture; accent; front border to mid border

There are many different types of cuphea, each offering a diverse assortment of colors and flower shapes for the garden. The most intriguing is *Cuphea llavea*, also known as the bat face flower. In New Jersey, I have to get down on my hands and knees to actually see the bat face, unless I decide to build a wall and let cuphea spill over it. In warmer climates, it could grow to a more convenient size for adults.

Besides the bat face flower, there's *Cuphea ignea*, the cigar plant or firecracker plant. The petals are fused into an orange tube tipped in white, looking like the ashen tip of a burning cigar. In zones 7 and colder, this decorative annual is good accent plant among the roses.

OTHER VARIETIES AVAILABLE: 'Variegata'—orange; yellow variegation on leaves; 'Flamingo Pink'—burgundy, white, pink; 'Purple Firecracker'—lavender; *Cuphea micropetala*— yellow/orange; also known as 'Mexican Cigar Plant'

Blue Anise Sage
Salvia guaranitica
MATURE PLANT SIZE: 6 feet × 4 feet
GROWTH HABIT: clump
BLOOM COLOR: cobalt blue
BLOOM SIZE: 1 inch; long spikes
BLOOM TIME: all summer
FRAGRANCE: foliage
PLANT TYPE: herbaceous annual
COLD HARDINESS: Zones 8 – 11
HOW TO USE: flower color; foliage fragrance; mid-border; attracts hummingbirds

---

Salvia guaranitica, or the blue anise sage, is a beautiful blue species that has produced many wonderful blue hybrids. This tall-growing species and its hybrids display fewer flowers on the spikes, making the individual blooms more noticeable. The calyx, or tube-like appendage surrounding the petals, is also a prominent feature with *Salvia guaranitica* and its hybrids. The blue anise sage blooms in mid-July with brilliant blue flowers and leaves of a mint-green color. This is a tall growing annual up north, easily attaining 5 feet in height.

Hardy in zones 8 and warmer, it's not unusual for this salvia and its hybrids to survive mild winters of zone 7 if grown in sheltered locations. Its strong upright habit makes the blue anise sage a good plant to use with vigorous shrub roses, and it creates a stunning combination with the pastel colors of tea roses and modern hybrids.

OTHER VARIETIES AVAILABLE: 'Omaha'—deep blue; gold variegation to leaf margins; 5 feet; 'Argentine Skies'—sky blue; 5 feet; 'Black and Blue'—indigo blue/cobalt blue; 2.5 feet

Bog Sage
Salvia uliginosa
MATURE PLANT SIZE: 5 feet × 3 feet
GROWTH HABIT: clump
BLOOM COLOR: sky blue
BLOOM SIZE: small; spikes
BLOOM TIME: summer
FRAGRANCE: foliage
PLANT TYPE: herbaceous annual
COLD HARDINESS: Zones 8 – 11
HOW TO USE: flower color; accent; mid-border

Salvia uliginosa's best flower display happens in the autumn. This is when the spikes bearing the sky blue flowers are long and lax, nearly out of control. In warm protected situations of zone 7, I've seen this salvia grow as a perennial, but in my garden it's an annual. Its color blends really well with hot-colored modern roses, soft pastel tea roses, and the reds of China roses. My *Salvia uliginosa* is poking through a rare yellow Noisette, 'Belle Lyonnaise', and is entangled with the new red-tinged canes of the rambler 'François Juranville'.

'Chiquita Blue' Sage
Salvia 'Chiquita Blue'

MATURE PLANT SIZE: 6 feet × 4 feet
GROWTH HABIT: clump
BLOOM COLOR: blue
BLOOM SIZE: small, long spikes
BLOOM TIME: late
FRAGRANCE: fragrance
PLANT TYPE: herbaceous annual
COLD HARDINESS: Zones 8 – 11
HOW TO USE: flower color; foliage texture; accent; rear border

It's September, and this salvia's blooms are nowhere in sight. That's okay since I'm enjoying the large soft leaves, perhaps one of the softest textures in the garden. This is a new salvia for me, although the experts say 'Chiquita Blue' will produce long spikes of blue flowers on a 6-foot plant. We'll see. Meanwhile, in anticipation of this, I've planted it near my ruby-colored shrub *Lespedeza* 'Gibraltar' and the pink shrub rose 'Autumn Bouquet'.

Dusty Miller
Centaurea gymnocarpa

MATURE PLANT SIZE: 2 feet × 2 feet
GROWTH HABIT: clump
BLOOM COLOR: mustard-yellow
BLOOM SIZE: small
BLOOM TIME: summer
FRAGRANCE: no
PLANT TYPE: herbaceous annual
COLD HARDINESS: Zones 7 – 9
HOW TO USE: foliage accent; front to mid-border

For me, the best silver-leafed annual to use as a front-of-the-border accent is a variety of dusty miller, *Centaurea gymnocarpa* 'Colchester White'. This annual looks tough enough to survive our winters, but it hasn't yet. The foliage has the same dusty texture as dusty miller but is much more silver, finely cut, and delectably soft to touch.

Because of the gray pubescent foliage, I suspect this annual may resent the humid summers of the South. There I would recommend using 'Colchester White' as a cool weather annual, instead.

An eye-catching combination in my garden is this annual planted alongside an un-named spider daylily with burnt-orange petals with the fine green foliage of 'Canary Bird', a species rose hybrid, in the background.

Mexican Sage
Salvia mexicana 'Tula'

MATURE PLANT SIZE: 6 feet × 4 feet
GROWTH HABIT: clump
BLOOM COLOR: lime-green/gentian blue
BLOOM SIZE: small, long spikes
BLOOM TIME: late
FRAGRANCE: foliage
PLANT TYPE: herbaceous annual
COLD HARDINESS: Zones 8 – 11
HOW TO USE: flower color; accent for late season; mid-border

'Tula' produces a bicolor flower of gentian-blue and lime-green on tall wispy stems. It has perhaps one of the most interesting combinations of color in one plant

Don't even try to plan where to grow this, just plant it where you can see the colors –everything else will fit in around it. I may throw in some strobilanthes and maybe an apricot rose such as 'Tuscan Sun' or 'Outrageous' – how appropriate!

Summer Snapdragon
Angelonia angustifolia

MATURE PLANT SIZE: 2 feet × 18 inches
GROWTH HABIT: clump
BLOOM COLOR: white, purple, pink, and purple/white
BLOOM SIZE: 1 inch on loose spikes
BLOOM TIME: summer
FRAGRANCE: foliage
PLANT TYPE: herbaceous annual/perennial
COLD HARDINESS: Zones 9 – 11
HOW TO USE: summer color; front and mid-border; fragrant foliage

Known as the summer snapdragon, angelonia is both a heat-tolerant and drought-tolerant annual with wonderful colors and a relaxed growth habit. Ten years ago, there were only one or two varieties in nurseries. Today, pink, plum, purple, bicolor and white cultivars are now popular additions to the summer garden. Some cultivars have the added bonus of tutti-frutti scented foliage.

Grown widely as a summer annual, in climates with mild winters this plant could be used as a winter annual. I recommend cutting back rangy plants during mid-summer to refresh the blooms and extend the season.

Angelonia has a loose habit and is great to mix in among roses. Allow the plants to weave themselves around the bare lower stems of modern hybrid roses.

OTHER VARIETIES AVAILABLE: 'Angelface Blue'—violet-blue; 'Angelface Bicolor'—white/violet; 'Angelface White'—white; 'Angel Mist Orchid'—pink

Tapien Verbena
Verbena tenuisecta Tapien Series

MATURE PLANT SIZE: 12 inches × 12 inches
GROWTH HABIT: clump
BLOOM COLOR: pastels
BLOOM SIZE: small, umbels
BLOOM TIME: summer
FRAGRANCE: no
PLANT TYPE: herbaceous annual
COLD HARDINESS: Zones 8 – 11
HOW TO USE: flower color; foliage texture; accents; front border

There are many cultivars of the Tapien series distinguishable by their finely cut foliage. The Tapien verbenas are lower growing plants, ideal for spilling over the sides of pottery or along the front edge of the garden.

Mounding to nearly a foot, these are long-blooming annuals and are tolerant of heat in our northern regions, as long as the evenings are cool and they have good drainage. However, long periods of heat will slow down the flower production and they may become afflicted with fungal diseases. During these times they can be sheared back. Once the weather cools they will begin to bloom once again. Deadheading through the season will also prolong their bloom. Besides adding beautiful colors, this verbena's lacy foliage adds texture to the garden.

Velvet Sage
Salvia leucantha

MATURE PLANT SIZE: 5 feet × 4 feet
GROWTH HABIT: clump
BLOOM COLOR: purple
BLOOM SIZE: small, long spikes
BLOOM TIME: late
FRAGRANCE: foliage
PLANT TYPE: herbaceous annual/perennial
COLD HARDINESS: Zones 8 – 1
HOW TO USE: flower color; late color accent; foliage texture; mid-border

Also known as the velvet sage, or sometimes Mexican sage, *Salvia leucantha* is a very late bloomer. Have patience, and it eventually will bloom. The long spikes of soft-textured purple flowers are a standout in the border. I would keep this one away from red roses. It blends much nicer with yellows, apricots, and pinks.

Asiatic Hybrid Lilies
Lilium × cv.
MATURE PLANT SIZE: 4 feet
GROWTH HABIT: clump
BLOOM COLOR: red, yellow, orange, pink, white
BLOOM SIZE: 6 inches; many per stem
BLOOM TIME: early summer
FRAGRANCE: flower
PLANT TYPE: bulb; herbaceous perennial
COLD HARDINESS: Zones 4 to 8
HOW TO USE: flower color; fragrance; accent; mid-border

In my Zone 7 garden, these are June lilies with upward-facing blooms. Often bearing as many as a dozen flowers on each stiff stem, Asiatic lilies are happiest in zones 7 or colder. It's best to plant Asiatic lilies in the autumn, six to eight inches deep. My favorite is the orange-red cultivar 'Enchantment'.

OTHER VARIETIES AVAILABLE: 'Fire King'—orange, spotted with purple; 5 feet; 'Citronella'—yellow, brown spots; 'Red Velvet'—red; 'Shirley'—white/rose-pink

Bearded Iris
Iris germanica
MATURE PLANT SIZE: 36 inches
GROWTH HABIT: clump
BLOOM COLOR: lavender-blue
BLOOM SIZE: 3 inches
BLOOM TIME: summer
FRAGRANCE: no
PLANT TYPE: bulb; herbaceous perennial
COLD HARDINESS: Zones 3 to 9
HOW TO USE: foliage; flower color; architecture; edging; front border; mid-border

The bearded iris is probably the most popular of all irises. Many of them bloom at the same time as most roses. The sword-like foliage is stiff and provides a good accent in the garden, especially if the leaf is variegated. Recently, new cultivars have been introduced that bloom again during the summer. Dwarf varieties make an interesting alternative for an edging to a bed.

OTHER VARIETIES AVAILABLE:'Dawn of Change'—light lavender/yellow-white; 3 feet; 'Red at Night'—velvety royal red; 3 feet; 'Breakers'—blue; re-blooms; 3 feeet; 'Champagne Elegance'—White/apricot and peach; re-blooms; 3 feet

Dahlia
Dahlia

MATURE PLANT SIZE: 12 inches to 8 feet
GROWTH HABIT: clump
BLOOM COLOR: white, red, pink, orange, and mixed
BLOOM SIZE: small to enormous; single stemmed and clustered
BLOOM TIME: summer to autumn
FRAGRANCE: no
PLANT TYPE: herbaceous bulb
COLD HARDINESS: Zones 8 to 11
HOW TO USE: flower color and texture; foliage color; accent; mid to rear border

Double-Flowered Narcissus
Narcissus

MATURE PLANT SIZE: 10-20 inches
GROWTH HABIT: clump
BLOOM COLOR: yellow, white, pink, apricot, orange, blends
BLOOM SIZE: multiple blooms per stem
BLOOM TIME: spring
FRAGRANCE: flower
PLANT TYPE: herbaceous/perennial bulb
COLD HARDINESS: Zones 3 to 8, some for Zone 9
HOW TO USE: early flower color; flower fragrance; naturalize throughout the border

Dahlias are grown from tubers or underground stems. Producing an array of styles and colors of blooms, they make great additions to the garden, especially for autumn color.

Listed as hardy from zones 8 to 11, dahlias grow best in the cooler zones as summer annuals. The tubers can be lifted after the first killing frost and saved for replanting the next season, if you so desire. The commonly available varieties may not do as well in the heat and humidity of the deep South. In hot and humid regions, you may want to search for the Mexican species that gave rise to the multitude of modern hybrids. These are more tolerant of heat.

I prefer the lower-growing types with burgundy-colored foliage to serve as color accents among the roses. One of my favorite varieties is 'Bishop of Llandaff' with burgundy foliage and stems, supporting beautiful small scarlet flowers.

OTHER VARIETIES AVAILABLE: *Dahlia merckii*—lilac; Mexican; good for warmest climates; *Dahlia coccinea*—red; Mexican; good for warmest climates; 'Fascination'—pink; 32 inches; 'Hot Chocolate'—red; 32 inches

Double-flowered narcissi resembling miniature roses or gardenias have a sweet fragrance and flowers packed with petals. They bloom early and many grow well in Zone 9 gardens.

OTHER VARIETIES AVAILABLE: *Albus plenus odoratus*—white; gardenia-like; 14 inches; very old; 'Bridal Crown'—saffron and creamy white; 16 inches; good for Zone 9; 'Obdam'—creamy white; double petals; 18 inches; 'Cheerfulness'—white with yellow in center; 16 inches; good for Zone 9

Elephant Ear
Colocasia esculenta
MATURE PLANT SIZE: 4 feet × 2 feet
GROWTH HABIT: clump
FRAGRANCE: no
PLANT TYPE: Tropical tuber
COLD HARDINESS: Zones 9 – 11
HOW TO USE: foliage color and texture; accent plant

Elephant ears are tropical plants with huge leaves displaying dramatic shapes and colors. Use them to make a bold statement in the garden.

'Illustris' is a variety I use in borders as an accent, either planted directly into the ground or in planters. I've had one for years in a cobalt blue ceramic planter that I move around when a new color combination suddenly comes into bloom. Both the planter and the irregular leaf patterns of emerald and ebony add a bold dash of color and texture to the garden. Usually placed near *Rosa glauca*, this taro's soft colors and the pinkish-gray colors of the rose's foliage make a beautiful combination.

During winter, depending on how much space I have indoors, I either store the plants on my cool porch where they continue to grow, or I'll let them go dormant and store them in the basement until spring.

OTHER VARIETIES AVAILABLE: 'Jet Black Wonder'—burgundy-black; 4 feet; 'Nancy's Revenge'—green with butter cream markings; 4 feet; 'Ruffles'—medium green; ruffled leaves; 4 feet; 'Fallax'—bright apple green; smaller leaves

Formosa Lilies
Lilium formosana
MATURE PLANT SIZE: 8 feet
GROWTH HABIT: clump
BLOOM COLOR: white, maroon stripe
BLOOM SIZE: 6 inches
BLOOM TIME: August
FRAGRANCE: flower
PLANT TYPE: bulb; herbaceous perennial
COLD HARDINESS: Zones 6 to 8
HOW TO USE: flower color; fragrance; accent; architectural; rear border

This is the last lily to come into bloom in my garden, usually not opening until the middle of August. The stems of this white trumpet-shaped lily easily grow 6 to 7 feet tall and display up to eight flowers on each stem.

Japanese Iris
Iris ensata

MATURE PLANT SIZE: 36 inches
GROWTH HABIT: clump
BLOOM COLOR: blue
BLOOM SIZE: 2 inches
BLOOM TIME: late spring – early summer
FRAGRANCE: no
PLANT TYPE: bulb; herbaceous perennial
COLD HARDINESS: Zones 4 to 9
HOW TO USE: foliage; flower color; architectural effects; mid-border

The flowers of Japanese iris have a "flattened" appearance and the leaves are stiffer than those of the Siberian iris.

OTHER VARIETIES AVAILABLE: 'White Ladies'—white; 30 inches; 'Ruby King'—dark red; 30 inches; 'Gypsy'— blue with dark veins; 30 inches; 'Variegata'—blue; white edged foliage; 30 inches

Louisiana Iris
Iris spp.

MATURE PLANT SIZE: 4 feet
GROWTH HABIT: clump
BLOOM COLOR: white, red, yellow, blue
BLOOM SIZE: 8 inches
BLOOM TIME: mid-spring to early summer
FRAGRANCE: no
PLANT TYPE: bulb; herbaceous perennial
COLD HARDINESS: Zones 6 to 9
HOW TO USE: flower color; foliage; architecture; mid border

Louisiana iris grows tall, with large, somewhat flat flowers and long ribbon-like foliage. Many colorful hybrids have been created from iris native to the Gulf coast area. I grow several of these in my garden.

OTHER VARIETIES AVAILABLE: 'Eolian'—ruffled blue with yellow; 42 inches; 'Frank Chowning'—currant-red with yellow; 3 feet; 'Margaret Hunter'—ruffled, light violet; 36 inches; 'Professor Jim'—mid-red with red-violet veins with yellow; 42 inches

Oriental Lilies
Lilium
MATURE PLANT SIZE: 6 feet
GROWTH HABIT: clump
BLOOM COLOR: white, pink, yellow, blends
BLOOM SIZE: 6 inches
BLOOM TIME: July/August
FRAGRANCE: flower
PLANT TYPE: bulb, herbaceous perennial
COLD HARDINESS: Zones 4 – 8
HOW TO USE: flower color and fragrance; foliage texture; accent; architectural; rear border

July is the month for Oriental lilies in my garden. As the roses begin to fade 'Casablanca', a pure white Oriental lily, becomes the main attraction. The long and wide foliage of this tall lily gives an interesting texture to the border long after the flowers have finished. Like the other lilies, they grow best when planted in the autumn in well-drained soil.

OTHER VARIETIES AVAILABLE: 'Rubrum'—pink/white; 5 feet; very old; 'Black Beauty'—raspberry/pink; 5 feet; 'Stargazer'—raspberry/white; 5 feet

Ornamental Onion
Allium spp.
MATURE PLANT SIZE: 12 inches to 36 inches
GROWTH HABIT: clump
BLOOM COLOR: white, pink, purple, green
BLOOM SIZE: clusters from 2 inches to 6 inches
BLOOM TIME: late spring to early summer
FRAGRANCE: no
PLANT TYPE: herbaceous bulb
COLD HARDINESS: Zones 4 to 9
HOW TO USE: flower color and texture; foliage color and texture; naturalize; throughout the border

Alliums have diverse growth habits, blooming periods, colors, and shapes. Most are ideal for zones 4 – 7, although some do well in zones 8 and 9.

Many alliums bloom at the same time as roses. I use *Allium bulgaricum* (*Nectaroscordum siculum* ssp. *bulgaricum*) as a companion for shrub roses. In the autumn, my bed of polyantha roses is accompanied by the white flowers of garlic chives.

OTHER VARIETIES AVAILABLE: *Allium bulgaricum*—clusters of pendant, greenish-white flowers; 36 inches; June; 'Gladiator'—rose-purple globe, 6 inches across; 4' stalks; June; 'Mt. Everest'—white globe, 6 inches; 3'; May; *Allium schubertii*—rose-purple star-like blooms; 16 inches; May; *Allium tuberosome*—Garlic Chives; white; 8 inches; August; *Allium porrum*—Leeks; white; 3'; cool curving stems; summer

Abyssinian Gladiolus
Acidanthera murieliae

MATURE PLANT SIZE: 3 feet × 1 foot
GROWTH HABIT: clump
BLOOM COLOR: white, brown face
BLOOM SIZE: 2 inches
BLOOM TIME: late summer
FRAGRANCE: flower
PLANT TYPE: tender bulb (corm)
COLD HARDINESS: Zones 8 – 10
HOW TO USE: fragrant flower; foliage shapes

Also known as Abyssinian gladiolus, *Acidanthera murieliae* produces a fragrant star-shaped white flower with a chocolate face. Several stems bearing multiple nodding blooms arise from each plant, not in massive clusters, but instead in a simple display of a half dozen or so at a time held slightly higher than the foliage. This display starts in mid-July and lasts until frost.

Acidanthera grows from corms that need to be planted each spring or late winter after danger of a freeze has passed. The corms should be lifted before winter and stored the way you would store a dahlia tuber. Or, simply plant new ones next spring. If there's been a mild winter in New Orleans and other regions of the Gulf coast, the corms will survive outdoors during the winter

Chinese Trumpet Lilies
Lilium regale

MATURE PLANT SIZE: 6 feet
GROWTH HABIT: clump
BLOOM COLOR: white, yellow, copper, pink
BLOOM SIZE: 6 inches
BLOOM TIME: mid-June/July
FRAGRANCE: flower
PLANT TYPE: bulb; herbaceous perennial
COLD HARDINESS: Zones 5 –8
HOW TO USE: Flower color; fragrance; accent; vertical element; rear border

The tall and fragrant Chinese trumpet lilies come into bloom in my garden as the roses are in peak bloom, usually from mid-June thru July. They look great with the large trumpet-shaped blooms hanging over shrub roses or backed by the masses of blooms from a climbing rose. Trumpet lilies are more tolerant of southern heat and humidity than other lilies and should be planted in the autumn, deep in well-drained soil.

OTHER VARIETIES AVAILABLE: 'Copper King'—copper, amber; 6 feet; 'Golden Sunburst'—clear yellow; 6 feet; 'Regal Lily'—white, burgundy; 6 feet; 'Silver Sunburst'—white, hints of yellow

Heirloom Lily Species
Lilium spp.

MATURE PLANT SIZE: 6 feet
GROWTH HABIT: clump
BLOOM COLOR: orange, red, white, yellow
BLOOM SIZE: large; many blooms per stem
BLOOM TIME: summer
FRAGRANCE: flowers
PLANT TYPE: bulb; herbaceous perennial
COLD HARDINESS: Zones 3 to 8
HOW TO USE: flower color; flower fragrance; mid to rear border

These are mid- summer blooming heirlooms, which are beautiful with roses. Many are tall and full of small, reflexed flowers just when you need color.

OTHER VARIETIES AVAILABLE: *Lilium lancifolium* 'Splendens'—orange, brown spots; 6 feet; *Lilium speciosum album*—white; 6 feet; *Lilium speciosum rubrum*—crimson/white margins, magenta spots; 6 feet; *Lilium citronella*—citronella yellow, spots; 6 feet

Jonquil Narcissus
Narcissus

MATURE PLANT SIZE: 10 to 16 inches
GROWTH HABIT: clump
BLOOM COLOR: white, yellow, peach, orange
BLOOM SIZE: small
BLOOM TIME: spring
FRAGRANCE: flower
PLANT TYPE: herbaceous/perennial bulb
COLD HARDINESS: Zones 4 to 9
HOW TO USE: flower color; flower fragrance; naturalize throughout the border

Jonquils are often referred to as "chive-leaved" due to their thin foliage. They like heat and are good for southern gardens. They have a sweet fragrance and are later blooming.

OTHER VARIETIES AVAILABLE: 'Baby Moon'—pale canary-yellow; 7 inches; 'Bell Song'—white/pink; 16 inches; 'Sweetness'—golden yellow; 14 inches; especially good for warm zones; 'Suzy'—canary-yellow/red-orange; 16 inches

Kaufmanniana Tulip
Tulipa kaufmanniana

MATURE PLANT SIZE: 8 inches
GROWTH HABIT: clump
BLOOM COLOR: cream-white with a yellow/orange center
BLOOM SIZE: mid-sized
BLOOM TIME: early spring
FRAGRANCE: flower
PLANT TYPE: herbaceous perennial/bulb
COLD HARDINESS: Zones 3 to 8
HOW TO USE: flower color; foliage color; naturalize; throughout the border

This species and its numerous varieties are collectively known as Kaufmanniana hybrids. They are short tulips with interesting foliage patterns. During the day the blooms open flat, at night they close up tight. Often called peacock tulips, these are excellent for naturalizing. These perennial tulips bloom in early spring.

OTHER VARIETIES AVAILABLE: 'Heart's Delight'—outer petals carmine, inner pale rose; 8 inches; 'Johann Strauss'—red and pale yellow; 8 inches; 'Elise'—cream-yellow, blends of pink; 10 inches; 'Red Riding Hood'—carmine red; 12 inches

Lily Flowering Tulips
Tulipa

MATURE PLANT SIZE: 16 to 24 inches
GROWTH HABIT: clump
BLOOM COLOR: all colors
BLOOM SIZE: large; long elegant stems
BLOOM TIME: late spring
FRAGRANCE: flower
PLANT TYPE: herbaceous bulb
COLD HARDINESS: Zones 3 to 8
HOW TO USE: strong late spring display of flower color; cut flowers; mass plantings

These hybrids have a fluted shape, making a dramatic statement in groups displayed between roses as the rose foliage is becoming green and lush. Their bloom time is late season, in may for Zone 7.

One of my favorite cultivars of this tulip division is 'Marilyn' with bright white petals flamed with red. Growing up to 22 inches tall, I plant 'Marilyn' at the base of everblooming climbing roses.

OTHER VARIETIES AVAILABLE: 'Elegant Lady'—pale cream edge in rose; 24 inches; 'Elegans Alba'—cream colored; twisted petals; 16 inches; 'Elegans Rubra'—blood red, long pointed petals; 16 inches; 'China Pink'—medium pink with a white heart; 20 inches

Madonna Lily
Lilium candidum

MATURE PLANT SIZE: 5 feet
GROWTH HABIT: clump
BLOOM COLOR: white
BLOOM SIZE: 3 inches; multiple blooms per stem
BLOOM TIME: April to June
FRAGRANCE: flower
PLANT TYPE: bulb; herbaceous perennial
COLD HARDINESS: Zones 6 – 9
HOW TO USE: flower color; fragrance; accent; mid-border

Lilium candidum, the 'Madonna Lily', is one of the first lilies to bloom in the garden. This fragrant white lily is very old, dating back to ancient Greece. Historically they're a natural for a bed with old garden roses. They have clusters of clear white, fragrant trumpet-shaped blooms borne on 5-foot spikes. They bloom as early as April in the South and in June up north. These lilies need to be planted at the end of the summer, with only an inch of soil covering the bulb.

Parrot Tulips
Tulipa

MATURE PLANT SIZE: 18 to 22 inches
GROWTH HABIT: clump
BLOOM COLOR: all colors
BLOOM SIZE: large; fringed and scalloped petals
BLOOM TIME: late spring
FRAGRANCE: flowers
PLANT TYPE: herbaceous bulb
COLD HARDINESS: Zones 4 to 7
HOW TO USE: strong late spring display of flower color; cut flowers; mass plantings

These varieties have fringed and scalloped petals, some with very subtle color blends. They make a beautiful display of early texture in the spring garden, blooming in May.

OTHER VARIETIES AVAILABLE: 'Black Parrot'—velvety purple-black; 20 inches; 'Orange Favorite'—deep orange, shaded with rose and green; 20 inches; 'Apricot Parrot'—soft apricot, blends of pink, yellow, green; 20 inches; 'Rococo'- cardinal red, blends of purple and green; 14 inches

Poeticus Narcissus
Narcissus

MATURE PLANT SIZE: 12 to 16 inches
GROWTH HABIT: clump
BLOOM COLOR: white, yellow
BLOOM SIZE: small; usually one bloom per stem
BLOOM TIME: late spring
FRAGRANCE: flower
PLANT TYPE: herbaceous/perennial bulb
COLD HARDINESS: Zones 3 – 8
HOW TO USE: flower color; flower fragrance; naturalize throughout the border

Poeticus narcissi are late blooming with a rich perfume. These are wonderful companions for old garden roses and one of the best groups for naturalizing. They have large perianths and small cups.

OTHER VARIETIES AVAILABLE: 'Pheasant's Eye'—white/yellow; recurved petals; 14 inches; 'Actea'—white/yellow; 16 inches; 'Milan'—hite/yellow/crimson; 18 inches; 'Green Pearl'—white with green eye; 18 inches

Siberian Iris
Iris sibirica

MATURE PLANT SIZE: 4 feet
GROWTH HABIT: clump
BLOOM COLOR: purple, white, yellow; blue
BLOOM SIZE: 2 inches
BLOOM TIME: late spring
FRAGRANCE: no
PLANT TYPE: bulb; herbaceous perennial
COLD HARDINESS: Zones 3 to 9
HOW TO USE: flower color; foliage; architectural; mid border

Siberian iris bloom in early spring. These are good iris for Southern gardens as well as colder climates. They tolerate to heat as long as they receive ample moisture. The foliage is grass-like and light green.

OTHER VARIETIES AVAILABLE: 'White Swirl'—white; 30 inches; 'Caesar's Brother—purple; 4 feet; 'Butter & Sugar'—white/yellow; 28 inches; 'Baby Sister'—sky blue; 14 inches

Single Late Tulips
Tulipa

MATURE PLANT SIZE: 20 inches to 36 inches
GROWTH HABIT: clump
BLOOM COLOR: all colors
BLOOM SIZE: large; long stems
BLOOM TIME: late spring
FRAGRANCE: flowers
PLANT TYPE: herbaceous bulb
COLD HARDINESS: Zones 3 to 8
HOW TO USE: strong late spring display of flower color; cut flowers; mass plantings

---

These varieties are tall and elegant. Their flowers stay fresh for a long period of time and share the garden with species roses and a few of the earliest old garden roses. Single late tulips bloom in May.

OTHER VARIETIES AVAILABLE: 'Blushing Beauty'—aureolin-yellow, rose; 30 inches; 'Queen of the Night'—velvety-maroon; 24 inches; 'Shirley'—yellow to ivory with flecks of purple; 22 inches; 'Catherina'—cream-white; 24 inches

St. Joseph's Lily
Hippeastrum × *johnsoni*

MATURE PLANT SIZE: 2 feet
GROWTH HABIT: clump
BLOOM COLOR: red with a white stripe
BLOOM SIZE: 6 inches
BLOOM TIME: early
FRAGRANCE: flower
PLANT TYPE: bulb
COLD HARDINESS: Zones 7 to 11
HOW TO USE: flower color and fragrance; foliage shape; edging

---

Related to the amaryllis we grow as potted winter plants, the St. Joseph's lily is often referred to as the "old red amaryllis" by gardeners on the Gulf coast. The large, red trumpet-like flowers appear in late March and early April, just as the tea roses are coming into their full glory. With a habit that won't over-shadow the roses, the lily-like flowers are borne on stalks reaching up to about 2 feet in height, with three to four flowers per stalk. When not in bloom, the strap-like leaves stay green and healthy looking all year. St. Joseph's lily is not an aggressive grower, but each year it produces new offsets from the base of the plant.

In New Orleans, experts recommend planting the large bulbs in rose beds from September through January in clumps of seven to nine bulbs with the neck of the bulbs sticking out of the ground.

OTHER VARIETIES AVAILABLE: *Zephyranthes candida*—White Rain Lily; zones 7 – 11l *Crinum* 'Ellen Bosanquet'—wine red; summer; 3 feet; 8 – 11l *Lycoris squamigera*—Surprise Lily; pink; summer; 3 feet; 5 – 8 *Rhodophiala bifida*—Oxblood Lily; red; summer; 18 inches; 7 – 10

Tazetta Narcissus
Narcissus

MATURE PLANT SIZE: 10 to 18 inches
GROWTH HABIT: clump
BLOOM COLOR: white, yellow, orange
BLOOM SIZE: small, multiple blooms per stem
BLOOM TIME: spring
FRAGRANCE: flower
PLANT TYPE: herbaceous/perennial bulb
COLD HARDINESS: Zones 5 to 9
HOW TO USE: early flower color; flower fragrance; naturalize throughout the border

Tazetta narcissi are strongly scented with clustered blooms. They're especially recommended for Southern gardens and other warm climates.

OTHER VARIETIES AVAILABLE: 'Avalanche'—15 to 20 small blooms per stem; yellow/white; 18 inches; 'Falconet'—yellow/orange; 14 inches; 'Geranium'—cream-white/orange; 16 inches; 'Cragford'—white/orange; 18 inches

Triandrus Narcissus
Narcissus

MATURE PLANT SIZE: 10 to 16 inches
GROWTH HABIT: clump
BLOOM COLOR: white, yellow
BLOOM SIZE: small; many per stem
BLOOM TIME: spring
FRAGRANCE: flower
PLANT TYPE: herbaceous/perennial bulb
COLD HARDINESS: Zones 4 to 9
HOW TO USE: early flower color; flower fragrance; naturalize throughout the border

Triandrus daffodils are fragrant; mid-season bloomers. The petals of the perianths are distinctly separated. Some varieties have reflexed petals and nodding blooms. Many of these are ideal for warm climate gardens.

OTHER VARIETIES AVAILABLE: 'Ice Wings'—white; nodding blooms; 12 inches; 'Thalia'—white; 18 inches; 'Petrel'—white; 14 inches; 'Hawera'—yellow; 8 inches

Turkestan Tulip
Tulipa turkestanica
MATURE PLANT SIZE: 12 inches
GROWTH HABIT: clump
BLOOM COLOR: cream-white with a yellow/orange center
BLOOM SIZE: 1 inch, displayed in clusters
BLOOM TIME: early spring
FRAGRANCE: flowers
PLANT TYPE: herbaceous perennial/bulb
COLD HARDINESS: Zones 4 to 8
HOW TO USE: flower color; early color accent; naturalize; throughout the border

The Turkestan tulip is a Victorian favorite with clusters of creamy-white star-like blooms produced in clusters of up to a dozen flowers per stem.

Like roses, the species tulips include some of the oldest known varieties, some dating back over five hundred years. Real antiques, they're great naturalized among old garden roses and species roses and are true perennials. Bloom times among the various species range from March to May.

OTHER VARIETIES AVAILABLE: *Tulipa acuminate*—long narrow, wavy petals; scarlet/ yellow; 18 inches; *Tulipa sylvestris*—yellow; fragrant; 12 inches; *Tulipa* 'Lady Jane'—white/rose red; 10 inches; *Tulipa bakery* ' Lilac Wonder'—lilac-pink; 8 inches; *Tulipa clusiana* 'Cynthia'—red/yellow; 10 inches

Viridiflora Tulips
Tulipa
MATURE PLANT SIZE: 16 to 24 inches
GROWTH HABIT: clump
BLOOM COLOR: green, blending with all colors
BLOOM SIZE: large; long stems
BLOOM TIME: late spring
FRAGRANCE: flowers
PLANT TYPE: herbaceous bulb
COLD HARDINESS: Zones 3 to 7
HOW TO USE: flower color; early color accent; naturalize; throughout the border

Unusual yet beautiful, these tulips have rare color combinations. A broad green stripe on the outer petals is the signature of green tulips. The colors are long lasting in the garden. Green tulips bloom in May.

OTHER VARIETIES AVAILABLE: 'Greenland'—rose and soft green stripes; 20 inches; 'Green Wave'—mauve-pink; scalloped petals; 20 inches; 'Spring Green'—ivory and green; 20 inches; 'Artist'—salmon, rose, blends of purple; 16 inches

Bronze Fennel
Foeniculum vulgare 'Rubrum'

MATURE PLANT SIZE: 6 feet × 2 feet
GROWTH HABIT: clump
BLOOM COLOR: chartreuse/yellow
BLOOM SIZE: 6 inch umbel
BLOOM TIME: summer
FRAGRANCE: foliage
PLANT TYPE: perennial herb
COLD HARDINESS: Zones 6 – 9
HOW TO USE: flower color and texture; foliage texture; architectural; mid-border

Foeniculum vulgare 'Rubrum', also known as bronze fennel, is a versatile plant for the garden. Tasty leaves, flowers, and seeds attract birds, butterflies, and hungry gardeners. The lacy foliage adds color and texture to the bed as well.

A perennial herb that seeds itself freely, bronze fennel doesn't take up much space hovering over the rest of the garden. Up to 6 feet tall, the umbels of chartreuse flowers tie in with all colors of roses.

An important reason for growing bronze fennel in the garden is to attract beneficial insects. Beneficial predators, such as the Syrphid fly and the parasitic wasp, *Aphelinus abdominalis*, find shelter and nectar among the umbels of plants like bronze fennel. When they aren't feeding on nectar, they rid the garden of aphids.

Germander
Teucrium chamaedrys

MATURE PLANT SIZE: 15 inches × 12 inches
GROWTH HABIT: clump
BLOOM COLOR: pink
BLOOM SIZE: small
BLOOM TIME: spring
FRAGRANCE: foliage
PLANT TYPE: evergreen herb
COLD HARDINESS: Zones 4 – 8

Germander, *Teucrium chamaedrys*, is frequently used to create low hedges and edging for rose gardens. I've used it as a substitute for lavender to give a garden a darker colored edge. One garden that I worked in had several rose beds surrounded by light colored French marble. As an edge to these beds, the green glossy leaves of this evergreen herb created a strong defining line between the rose beds and the patio. When germander gets out of hand, you can prune it as hard as you like.

Lavender
Lavandula spp.

MATURE PLANT SIZE: 18 inches to 3 feet × 18 inches to 3 feet
GROWTH HABIT: clump
BLOOM COLOR: lavender, white, and pink
BLOOM SIZE: small, on spikes
BLOOM TIME: summer
FRAGRANCE: flowers and foliage
PLANT TYPE: perennial evergreen herb
COLD HARDINESS: Zones 5 – 9
HOW TO USE: flower color and fragrance; foliage fragrance; edging; accents; winter interest

There are two varieties of lavender I highly recommend with roses—'Hidcote' and 'Provence'. *Lavandula angustifolia* 'Hidcote' is the traditional variety used in most European gardens as an edging for rose beds. This variety has a dark-violet flower in early summer. *Lavandula × intermedia* 'Provence' is a bigger plant with a lighter-colored flower, a longer blooming season, and higher tolerance to humid and damp conditions.

Lavender needs protection from winter winds. The hybrids are supposedly cold hardy to zone 5, but every spring I replace all of those damaged or killed in my zone 7 garden as a result of the northeast winds of late winter and early spring.

Compulsive pruners insist on shearing back their lavender in the autumn, but it's best to hold off until you see growth in the spring.

OTHER VARIETIES AVAILABLE: *Lavandula angustifolia* 'Munstead'—lavender; 15 inches; late spring; *Lavandula angustifolia* 'Nana Compacta'—violet; 18 inches; early summer; *Lavandula intermedia* × 'Grosso'—violet; 24 inches; summer; *Lavandula intermedia* × 'Dilly Dilly'—violet; 14 inches; summer

Nasturtium
Tropaeolum majus

MATURE PLANT SIZE: 8 inches × 6 feet
GROWTH HABIT: spreading
BLOOM COLOR: red, orange, yellow
BLOOM SIZE: 2 inches
BLOOM TIME: summer
FRAGRANCE: no
PLANT TYPE: herb
COLD HARDINESS: Zones 8 – 11
HOW TO USE: flower color; front border; climbing plant

Tropaeolum majus, otherwise known as nasturtium, is a fast-creeping annual that loves to bask in the sun but doesn't enjoy prolonged exposure to evening heat and humidity. Down south, these are best used as early spring plants. In my neck of the woods the blooms start fading by mid-July; up in coastal New England, they're pretty much a summer plant. I've had success growing these in Cape Cod, spilling out into a pathway from behind lavender 'Provence'.

Plants started indoors will give you earlier color, but these annuals are easy to start from seed directly sown in the garden. Soak the seeds overnight. Try planting them at the base of pillars with early blooming shrub roses such as 'Mme. Legras de St. Germain' for a colorful display after the roses have faded. Or, let them scramble up into the arms of 'Mermaid' for a hot display of passionate color!

OTHER VARIETIES AVAILABLE: 'Crimson Beauty'—deep velvety-red; 'Empress of India'—orange-scarlet; blue-gray foliage; 'Aurea'—salmon; chartreuse foliage; Double Gleam hybrids

Oregano
Origanum vulgare

MATURE PLANT SIZE: 3 feet × 3 feet
GROWTH HABIT: clump
BLOOM COLOR: pink/white, spike
BLOOM SIZE: small
BLOOM TIME: summer
FRAGRANCE: foliage
PLANT TYPE: evergreen herb
COLD HARDINESS: Zones 4 – 9
HOW TO USE: foliage texture and fragrance; ground cover;
    accent; front border

Pineapple Sage
Salvia rutilans

MATURE PLANT SIZE: 4 feet × 2 feet
GROWTH HABIT: clump
BLOOM COLOR: red
BLOOM SIZE: small, long spikes
BLOOM TIME: late
FRAGRANCE: foliage
PLANT TYPE: herb
COLD HARDINESS: Zones 7 – 10
HOW TO USE: foliage fragrance and texture; flower color;
    mid border

This is the true oregano, the one that is used most often to flavor sauces, soups, and Italian dishes. A spreading ground cover plant, oregano can grow as high as 3 feet in the garden.

Oregano is a good plant for places with full sun, such as in front of roses. As the plant grows and fills in, it essentially becomes a fragrant living mulch.

Marjoram is a form of oregano, more upright and just as fragrant and tasty. Gardeners in California use this and other varieties of oregano as fragrant ground covers in among the roses. 'Kent Beauty', a trailing variety that grows like a prostrate shrub, is popular in southern California. The stems of this shrub bear silver-veined leaves and pinkish-purple flower bracts that hang like paper lanterns during the summer months.

OTHER VARIETIES AVAILABLE: *Origanum majorana*— 'Sweet Marjoram'; 30 inches; zone 5 – 9; *Origanum onites* 'Aureum'—'Gold Marjoram'; *Origanum vulgare* 'Compactum'—dwarf oregano; 6 inches; zone 5 – 9; *Origanum vulgare* 'Dark Leaf'—'Greek Oregano'; red foliage

Salvia rutilans is commonly known as pineapple sage, a name it earned from the strong pineapple scent of its foliage.

The flowers of the pineapple sage are scarlet, and the leaves are fuzzy, pale green and pointed. The plant grows to about 4 feet in height before the frost knocks it down. If there's an early frost, I'll never see the flowers. This is always a strong possibility since the pineapple sage is one of the last salvias to come into bloom – starting often as late as October.

Plant pineapple sage within arm's reach so you can pinch the foliage to smell its fragrance. The color is vivid, so avoid red roses, instead mixing it with pinks and whites.

OTHER VARIETIES AVAILABLE: *Salvia dorisiana*, grapefruit-scented sage—4 feet; bright pink; *Salvia elegans* 'Honey Melon'—2 feet; red

Rosemary
Rosmarinus officinalis
MATURE PLANT SIZE: 2 – 8 feet × 2 – 6 feet
GROWTH HABIT: clump; spreading
BLOOM COLOR: blue
BLOOM SIZE: small
BLOOM TIME: spring to summer
FRAGRANCE: foliage
PLANT TYPE: evergreen herb
COLD HARDINESS: Zones 7 – 10
HOW TO USE: foliage texture and fragrance; bark texture; flower color; architecture; accents; front, mid, and rear border

Rosemary adds a strong fragrance as well as plant architecture to the garden. If you are in the right climate, with dry, warm days and cool evenings, then rosemary is a great plant to use as edging, a background hedge, or as an accent.

I've had great success in pairing rosemary with tea roses in a walled garden in central Virginia. Rosemary is also great as a potted plant to move around the garden as an accent.

Rosemary is borderline hardy in my region. If you have a nice sheltered spot in full sun, some varieties will make it through a zone 7 winter. Too much snow or too much rain spells instant death for this Mediterranean plant.

OTHER VARIETIES AVAILABLE: 'Albiflorus'—white flowered form of the species; *Rosmarinus officinalis prostratus*— 'Cascading Rosemary'; zones 8 –10; 'Hill Hardy'— 5 feet; blue; shrubby; zones 6—10; 'Tuscan Blue'— 6 feet; blue; lots of character

Sage
Salvia officinalis
MATURE PLANT SIZE: 1.5 feet × 1.5 feet
GROWTH HABIT: clump
BLOOM COLOR: blue
BLOOM SIZE: small; spiked
BLOOM TIME: late
FRAGRANCE: foliage
PLANT TYPE: perennial evergreen herb
COLD HARDINESS: Zones 6 – 10
HOW TO USE: foliage fragrance and texture; edging; front border

Common sage, *Salvia officinalis*, is the herb used in cooking. It is also a good garden plant with its aromatic foliage right at home filling in around the base of roses or serving as a front-of-the-border plant.

Salvia officinalis and its varieties grow best in cooler climates, and need a well-drained site. They grow to 1¹/₂ feet high and spread to 2¹/₂ feet. Common sage is the hardiest of the group, and the varieties need some winter protection to survive cold winters. Like most hairy-leafed plants, they don't do as well in hot humid climates.

OTHER VARIETIES AVAILABLE: 'Tri-color'—red, white, green foliage; 24 inches; 'Purple'—purple foliage; 24 inches; 'Aurea'—yellow variegations; 18 inches; 'Berggarten'— silver foliage; 20 inches

Society Garlic
Tulbaghia violacea

MATURE PLANT SIZE: 1 foot × 6 inches
GROWTH HABIT: clump
BLOOM COLOR: lavender-pink
BLOOM SIZE: small, cluster
BLOOM TIME: summer
FRAGRANCE: leaves and flower
PLANT TYPE: bulb
COLD HARDINESS: Zones 9 – 11
HOW TO USE: flower color; foliage texture and color; edging; accent; front border

Valerian
Valeriana officinalis

MATURE PLANT SIZE: 6 feet × 3 feet
GROWTH HABIT: clump
BLOOM COLOR: white
BLOOM SIZE: small; large umbel
BLOOM TIME: early summer
FRAGRANCE: flower
PLANT TYPE: perennial herb
COLD HARDINESS: 3 – 10
HOW TO USE: flower fragrance, texture, and color; texture; vertical element; mid to rear border

Society garlic, *Tulbaghia violacea*, is not a garlic but instead a member of the amaryllis family. Society garlic hails from South Africa where it is known as wild garlic.

Use society garlic to edge beds in southern gardens where this plant is hardy and evergreen. Some gardeners use it as a substitute for liriope, which can become invasive in warmer climates. The foot-high, thin, strap-like leaves have a strong scent of garlic when crushed; the leaves can be used to flavor soups and sauces. During the summer, clusters of lavender-pink blooms are produced. I use this as an annual accent at the front of the border.

OTHER VARIETIES AVAILABLE: *Tulbaghia violacea* 'Variegata'—white edged leaves; 12 inches; *Tulbaghia fragrans*—also known as "pink agapanthus"; sweetly scented; 24 inches; *Tulbaghia fragrans* 'Alba'—creamy white; 12 inches

Valerian officinalis, also known as garden heliotrope or true valerian, is a perennial herb. If grown from small seedlings, the first year there will only be a large mound of green leaves. Starting from the second season and continuing year after year, tall trusses of fragrant blooms are produced at the time of the peak of the rose bloom. The tiny white blossoms are displayed in umbels high above the rest of the garden; mine grow 5 to 6 feet tall.

Hardy from zones 3 to 10, this self-sowing perennial can become a garden weed. If you don't have a great deal of space, keep an eye on it. Often during the season, I prune away lower leaves to keep them from crowding out other plants. As the flowers finish blooming, cut back the plant, out of sight.

Agastache
Agastache spp.

MATURE PLANT SIZE: 18 inches to 6 feet × 2 feet
GROWTH HABIT: upright
BLOOM COLOR: blue, white, purple, apricot, pink, raspberry, violet
BLOOM SIZE: small, large spikes
BLOOM TIME: summer
FRAGRANCE: foliage
PLANT TYPE: herbaceous perennial/herb/annual
COLD HARDINESS: Zones 6 –11
HOW TO USE: flower color; fragrant foliage; front and middle of border

Calamint
Calamintha nepeta 'White Cloud'

MATURE PLANT SIZE: 18 inches × 18 inches
GROWTH HABIT: clump
BLOOM COLOR: white
BLOOM SIZE: tiny
BLOOM TIME: summer
FRAGRANCE: foliage
PLANT TYPE: herbaceous perennial/herb
COLD HARDINESS: Zones 4 – 7
HOW TO USE: fragrant foliage; light texture; front border

Agastache foeniculum is one of many agastaches that make good companions for roses. Also known as anise hyssop due to the anise-like fragrance found in the foliage, this species and all other agastaches are members of the mint family, but unlike mint, agastache is well behaved in the garden. All of the agastaches have fragrant foliage.

Hardy from zones 6 to 9, many agastache tend to behave more like annuals in colder areas of zones 6 and 7. 'Blue Fortune', the most shrub-like of this group, is cold hardy, making a reliable display of color during the summer, especially good with the bourbon rose 'Coquette des Blanches'. 'Apricot Sunrise' is low growing and the most tender for me, good for filling in around the bases of roses.

OTHER VARIETIES AVAILABLE: *Agastache rugosa* 'Alabaster'—white; 3 feet; ' Black Adder'—smoky violet-blue; 3 feet; 'Firebird '– raspberry; 3 feet; 'Golden Jubilee'– long purple spikes; yellow-green foliage; 2 feet

Also known as savory calamint, *Calamintha nepeta* is an aromatic perennial from the mint family often included in herb gardens for the strong and pleasant fragrance in its foliage. 'White Cloud' is one of several varieties that is a good companion to roses, especially hybrid teas. Low-growing and good as an under-planting in the front of a border, 'White Cloud' produces thin stalks of airy white blooms all summer. In the garden, I often plant this with pink hybrid teas.

Calamintha grows best in cooler zones, and rotting may occur if the site is too wet and humid. One shearing during the season is advisable, and once a frost has hit, cut the plants back to ground level. There are several other varieties to try near the edge of a border, all requiring good drainage.

OTHER VARIETIES AVAILABLE: *Calamintha nepeta grandiflora*—large rosy-pink flowers; 24 inches; *Calamintha nepeta grandiflora* 'Variegata'—large rosy-pink flowers; leaves are flecked with pink; 24 inches; *Calamintha nepeta* spp. *Nepeta*—airy plumes of pale blue flowers; noted oregano-like foliage fragrance; 15 inches

Delphinium
Delphinium elatum

MATURE PLANT SIZE: 7 feet × 2 feet
GROWTH HABIT: clump
BLOOM COLOR: white/ blue/pink
BLOOM SIZE: long spikes
BLOOM TIME: early summer
FRAGRANCE: no
PLANT TYPE: herbaceous perennial/biennial
COLD HARDINESS: Zones 3 – 7
HOW TO USE: flower color; vertical element; rear border

Spires of delphinium blooms can reach as high as seven feet, an astounding sight to behold. The plants are not as noticeable when they aren't blooming. Plant them behind mounding shrub roses so they appear to grow from the mound of green created by the rose. Delphiniums also look good when they are grown with climbing roses. As the blooms fade, cut them back, out of sight. Some varieties may re-bloom.

Delphiniums are difficult to grow as perennials in warm climates. They prefer cooler weather and less humidity, preferably in zone 6 and cooler. Today, there are new cultivars being introduced under the series name of "Millennium Hybrids" with a higher tolerance to heat and humidity. These are worth looking exploring.

OTHER VARIETIES AVAILABLE: 'Blue Lace'—light blue; Millennium; 'Green Twist'—white tinged with green; Millennium; 'Purple Passion'—deep purple; Millennium; 'Blue Bird'—blue/white

Foxglove
Digitalis purpurea

MATURE PLANT SIZE: 6 feet
GROWTH HABIT: clump
BLOOM COLOR: white, pastels
BLOOM SIZE: 1 inch, long spikes
BLOOM TIME: late spring – early summer
FRAGRANCE: no
PLANT TYPE: biennial
COLD HARDINESS: Zones 3 – 8
HOW TO USE: flower color and texture; vertical element; mid to rear border

Foxgloves add a soft and colorful vertical element to the garden, often blooming at the same time as the peak flush of the roses. There are many types of foxglove to explore; the most popular are the hybrids of *Digitalis purpurea*.

The tall spikes of soft, bell-shaped blooms complement any type of rose. When the blooms are done, remove the faded flower spike. Some varieties will bloom a second time during the summer after deadheading, but this bloom is never as grand as the spring display.

By summer's end, it's likely that new plants will have formed at the base. Autumn is the best time to plant new foxgloves. Use one-year-old seedlings for next spring's display. Plant them at least two feet from any rose bush

OTHER VARIETIES AVAILABLE: 'Excelsior'—mixed pastel colors; 6 feet; 'Alba'—white; 'Apricot'—creamy pastel pink; 'Foxy'—larger flowers, shorter plants, pastels; 2 feet

Garden Phlox
Phlox paniculata
MATURE PLANT SIZE: 6 feet × 2 feet
GROWTH HABIT: clump
BLOOM COLOR: pink, white, and lavender
BLOOM SIZE: large panicles
BLOOM TIME: summer to autumn
FRAGRANCE: flowers
PLANT TYPE: herbaceous perennial
COLD HARDINESS: Zones 3-8
HOW TO USE: flower color; vertical element; rear border

Globe Thistle
Echinops ritro 'Taplow Blue'
MATURE PLANT SIZE: 4 feet × 3 feet
GROWTH HABIT: clump
BLOOM COLOR: blue
BLOOM SIZE: 2 inches globe
BLOOM TIME: summer
FRAGRANCE: no
PLANT TYPE: herbaceous perennial
COLD HARDINESS: Zones 3 – 7
HOW TO USE: flower color and texture; mid-border

There are three cultivars of *Phlox paniculata* that I would recommend with roses. 'Shortwood' has vivid pink flowers that are slightly fragrant, moreso at night. 'David' and 'Snow White' are both white cultivars. These grow to 5 feet tall, and form large clumps as they age. The clumps can be lifted in the autumn and divided to make more plants.

Blooming from late June and continuing until frost in zone 7, these phlox prefer that faded blooms be removed to encourage new blossoms and a healthier plant. It's crucial that they are watered regularly, and like roses, the foliage should not get wet. During winter, scatter wood ashes from the fireplace in the garden bed, and after spring pruning, mulch the beds with a fine layer of chicken manure.

These cultivars have proven to be highly disease resistant in my gardens. However, as a safety precaution, during spring thin out growth to allow only four to six canes for improved air circulation.

OTHER VARIETIES AVAILABLE: *Phlox carolina* 'Miss Lingard'—white; early summer; 3 feet

Echinops, or globe thistle, produces globes of blue flowers that resemble round pincushions. The texture and the steel blue color make this an interesting plant, easy to use in the border as a textural accent.

'Taplow Blue' is one variety that I've had for years, blooming on and off through the summer within the shade of the lacy foliage of *Rosa hugonis*. This variety has performed the best for me of all the globe thistles.

Echinops have the same requirements as roses—full sun and good drainage. I like the surprise effect they create with the appearance of their steel-blue flowers, usually coming into bloom at mid-summer and lasting right through to frost. The color mixes well with all rose colors and foliage plants. The texture is especially interesting when you combine 'Taplow Blue' with the feathery foliage of species roses.

OTHER VARIETIES AVAILABLE: 'Blue Glow'—intense steel blue; 4 feet; late; 'Veitch's Blue'—dark steel blue; 3 feet; summer; 'Arctic Glow'—white; mahogany stems; 32 inches; summer

Kalimeris
Kalimeris pinnatifida
MATURE PLANT SIZE: 3 feet × 2 feet
GROWTH HABIT: clump
BLOOM COLOR: white
BLOOM SIZE: 1 inch
BLOOM TIME: summer
FRAGRANCE: no
PLANT TYPE: herbaceous perennial
COLD HARDINESS: Zones 5 – 8
HOW TO USE: flower color; foliage texture; mid border

Kalimeris is a tiny aster-like plant that creates an airy feel to the border with its finely cut foliage and pompon-like small white flowers.

Blooming from mid-summer through autumn, kalimeris is an easy perennial to grow. Plant it as an isolated specimen, rather than in groups, for the best display of its delicate features. I use this to dress up any rose bush that is looking naked during the summer months.

Nepeta
Nepeta spp.
MATURE PLANT SIZE: from 18 inches to 3 feet × 2 feet
GROWTH HABIT: clump
BLOOM COLOR: blue, white, and salmon
BLOOM SIZE: small, on spikes
BLOOM TIME: summer
FRAGRANCE: foliage
PLANT TYPE: herbaceous perennial
COLD HARDINESS Zones: 3 – 8
HOW TO USE: flower color; fragrant foliage

When *Nepeta faassenii* 'Walker's Low' bursts into bloom, it's quite a sight. Long stems of violet-blue blooms fill the plant, reaching as high as 2 feet, often spilling into walkways and over edging. This cultivar seems to be the most popular as a companion for roses, especially as an under-planting for climbing roses. The plants grow so thickly that they become living mulch, keeping the roots of the roses cool by shading them from the hot summer sun.

For the middle of the border I recommend 'Souvenir d'André Chaudorn', a tall, blue-flowered cultivar reaching to at least 3 feet. This is a perfect perennial to surround a tower or pillar of roses.

Hardy from zones 3 to 8, nepeta performs best when grown in well-drained soil. 'Souvenir d'André Chaudron' gets cut back in my garden by mid-summer, and with 'Walker's Low', a shearing is also necessary during mid-summer.

OTHER VARIETIES AVAILABLE: *Nepeta faassenii* 'Blue Wonder'—lavender-blue; compact growth, 15 inches; *Nepeta faassenii* 'Six Hills Giant'—violet-blue, large flowers; 3 feet; *Nepeta faassenii* ' Snowflake'— 15 inches, white, zone 3 - 8; *Nepeta grandiflora* 'Dawn to Dusk'—salmon; 3 feet

Obedient Plant
Physostegia virginiana 'Vivid'
MATURE PLANT SIZE: 30 inches × 30 inches
GROWTH HABIT: clump
BLOOM COLOR: orchid-pink
BLOOM SIZE: small blooms, tall spikes
BLOOM TIME: late summer
FRAGRANCE: no
PLANT TYPE: herbaceous perennial
COLD HARDINESS: Zones 2 – 9
HOW TO USE: flower color; texture of blooms; mid-border

The parent species of this hybrid, *Physostegia virginiana*, is also known as the obedient plant. However, obedience is not one of the characteristics of this native perennial. *Physostegia virginiana* is likely to run rampant in the garden if left unchecked. However, I forgive it for this sin because of the strong display of color during the month of August.

'Vivid' is an orchid-pink hybrid of this species, and well behaved, growing to nearly 3 feet in the garden with absolutely straight spikes of tubular blooms. Tolerant of some shade, 'Vivid' is a solid mass of bloom when grown in full sun, excellent for the middle of the border and mixing with tall growing roses.

Every couple of seasons, lift and divide the clumps to prevent this perennial from becoming too aggressive.

OTHER VARIETIES AVAILABLE: 'Miss Manners'—white; 24 inches; mid-summer to fall; 'Red Beauty'—3 feet; rose-lavender; summer; 'Variegata'—4 feet; lilac-pink; variegated foliage; late; 'Rosea'—3 feet; pink; summer

Perennial Sunflower
Helianthus × 'Lemon Queen'
MATURE PLANT SIZE: 7 feet × 3 feet
GROWTH HABIT: clump
BLOOM COLOR: lemon yellow
BLOOM SIZE: 2 inches
BLOOM TIME: summer
FRAGRANCE: no
PLANT TYPE: herbaceous perennial
COLD HARDINESS: Zones 5 – 9
HOW TO USE: flower color; background, rear of border

'Lemon Queen' is a tall growing perennial that produces bright lemon-yellow flowers from July through September. A member of the group known as perennial sunflowers, it provides welcome color during the heat of summer.

Perfect for the rear of the border, as a backdrop, or as a display of its own, I use it behind species roses, in a partially shaded area, where it provides good texture and strong color from behind *Rosa hugonis*. Hardy from zone 5 to 9, this perennial is tolerant of neglect. As the flowers fade, the seed heads become a favorite feeding station for migratory birds.

OTHER VARIETIES AVAILABLE: 'Loddon Gold'—double yellow; late summer to frost; 4 feet; 'Gold Lace'—yellow-gold; autumn; 5 feet; *Helianthus hirsutus*—pale yellow; July –August; 6 feet; *Helianthus salicifolius*—bright yellow; autumn; 12 feet

'Powis Castle' Artemisia
Artemisia 'Powis Castle'

MATURE PLANT SIZE: 3 feet × 3 feet
GROWTH HABIT: clump
BLOOM COLOR: yellow
BLOOM SIZE: small
BLOOM TIME: late
FRAGRANCE: foliage
PLANT TYPE: herbaceous perennial/sub-shrub/annual
COLD HARDINESS: Zones 6 – 9
HOW TO USE: foliage texture; accent in front of middle border

Purple-top Verbena
Verbena bonariensis

MATURE PLANT SIZE: 5 feet × 2 feet
GROWTH HABIT: clump
BLOOM COLOR: purple
BLOOM SIZE: small; loose umbel
BLOOM TIME: summer
FRAGRANCE: no
PLANT TYPE: herbaceous perennial
COLD HARDINESS: Zones 7 – 10
HOW TO USE: airy texture; flower color; mid to rear border

Perhaps the best of the feathery-leaved artemisias, 'Powis Castle' creates a stunning display in the garden. Plant it with other perennials and roses, and their colors will all seem to jump out at you.

Sometimes offered as an annual in zones 7 and colder, this is a perennial for me if planted in full sun with the best drainage possible. Avoid the urge to prune 'Powis Castle' during the winter, even though the ragged foliage is ugly. Wait until spring when you see signs of growth.

In my zone 7 garden, this artemisia can be used either as a front border accent or a good middle border clump. Adaptable to hot humid summers, this perennial really prefers drier climates, such as California, where it can reach to about 3 feet high and often twice as wide.

OTHER VARIETIES AVAILABLE: 'Huntington Gardens'—18 inches; *Artemisia abrotanum*—3 feet; *Artemisia schmidtiana* 'Silver Mound'—10 inches; *Artemisia frigida*—2 feet

This is the only verbena that I would recommend as a reliable perennial in zone 7. I'm not sure if it really is perennial or just a good re-seeding annual. This tall-growing verbena, named for the city of Buenos Aires, re-seeds itself fairly aggressively. For that reason, I have some every year in the garden in places I never intended them to grow. But, that's okay with me. I love the tall stems, reaching up to six feet, topped with tiny, purple blooms. Also called the purple-top verbena, this South American native fills in the air spaces around and above roses without taking up very much of their garden space.

Verbena bonariensis does best in full sun, growing in soil with good drainage.

'Big Blue' Liriope
Liriope muscari 'Big Blue'
MATURE PLANT SIZE: 18 inches × 18 inches
GROWTH HABIT: clump
BLOOM COLOR: violet
BLOOM SIZE: small, spiked
BLOOM TIME: late summer
FRAGRANCE: no
PLANT TYPE: evergreen perennial
COLD HARDINESS: Zones 6-10
HOW TO USE: evergreen edge; accent; foliage texture; flower color

Also known as big blue lily-turf, this evergreen perennial grows to 18 inches high with thin, dark-green strap-like leaves in a beautiful fountain-like habit. In late August, spikes of lavender-blue flowers emerge. After the flowers fade, dark black berries form and persist through the winter. Growing initially in a clump formation, liriope is a spreading perennial that tolerates full sun to shade.

Tolerant of heat, humidity, and cold, liriope is hardy to zone 6. In warmer climates this perennial is an aggressive grower. In zone 7, 'Big Blue' is ideal for edging beds, for planting under roses, and for planting with spring bulbs to hide their fading foliage. The variegated form, *Liriope muscari* 'Variegata', makes a dramatic alternative.

OTHER VARIETIES AVAILABLE: 'Majestic'—deep lilac; 15 inches; 'Royal Purple'—deep purple; 15 inches; 'Variegata'— violet; 12 inches; green/yellow leaf; 'Monroe White'—white; 15 inches

'Guizho' Artemisia
Artemisia lactiflora 'Guizho'
MATURE PLANT SIZE: 6 feet × 3 feet
GROWTH HABIT: upright; tall
BLOOM COLOR: white
BLOOM SIZE: small; sprays
BLOOM TIME: summer
FRAGRANCE: none
PLANT TYPE: herbaceous perennial
COLD HARDINESS: Zones 3 – 9
HOW TO USE: tall texture from the airy blooms; stem color; rear border

Artemisia lactiflora 'Guizhou' is a tall growing artemisia producing long-lasting sprays of tiny white flowers held high above the garden on ebony stems that stand straight and erect.

Hardy from zones 3 to 9, this artemisia doesn't have the soft gray foliage associated with other artemisia and is therefore more tolerant of humid conditions.

'Guizhou' would be best used as a background plant where the ebony stems can be included as part of the color display. At the end of the season, cut this perennial to the ground.

OTHER VARIETIES AVAILABLE: *Artemisia chinensis* 'Rosenschleir'—pastel pink; black stems; 5 feet; summer

'Hyperion' Daylily
Hemerocallis × 'Hyperion'

MATURE PLANT SIZE: 40 inches × 3 feet
GROWTH HABIT: clump
BLOOM COLOR: lemon yellow
BLOOM SIZE: large
BLOOM TIME: mid-season
FRAGRANCE: flower
PLANT TYPE: herbaceous perennial
COLD HARDINESS: Zones 3 – 9
HOW TO USE: flower color and fragrance; foliage shape; hide bulb foliage; front to mid-border

Daylilies are popular all over the country. Like roses, there are hundreds to choose from, from very simple to seemingly overproduced gaudy varieties. I feel those that look best with roses are the daylilies with simple flower shapes.

Daylilies are hardy from zones 3 to 9. Some go dormant, disappearing completely each winter, while others are evergreen. The evergreen varieties are hardy from zone 7 southward. Many gardeners in Florida and other warm climates prefer the evergreen varieties to the dormant types.

'Hyperion', a dormant type, is one of the older hybrids still available today. This is the daylily with clear lemon yellow trumpets and a pure citrus fragrance you often see in old gardens. 'Hyperion' blooms for me from June through the entire month of July.

OTHER VARIETIES AVAILABLE: 'September Gold'—deep gold; 32 inches; late; 'Autumn Prince—light yellow; 48 inches; late; *Hemerocallis fluva*—orange; 48 inches; early; *Hemerocallis citrina*—lemon-yellow; 36 inches; mid-season; night bloomer

Milky Bellflower
Campanula lactiflora 'Loddon Anna'

MATURE PLANT SIZE: 5 feet × 2 feet
GROWTH HABIT: clump
BLOOM COLOR: blush pink
BLOOM SIZE: 1 inch, in loose panicles
BLOOM TIME: early summer
FRAGRANCE: no
PLANT TYPE: herbaceous perennial
COLD HARDINESS: Zones 5-7
HOW TO USE: flower color; mid border

Campanulas are commonly known as bellflowers, and many have been longtime favorites in the garden. The growth habits and flower shapes are diverse, from tall plants with bell-like flowers to creeping varieties covered in little star-like blooms. The colors are generally blue, white, and pink with a few newer cultivars of reddish-pink. I prefer to use varieties from *Campanula lactiflora* with roses.

'Loddon Anna' is a cultivar derived from *Campanula lactiflora*, a tall-growing species known as the milky bellflower. 'Loddon Anna' is also tall-growing and displays many pale pink flowers in a loose panicle during late spring and early summer. Happiest in partial shade, this is a delightful plant to have growing in the company of many of the old garden roses, especially those with an upright arching habit. I've had great luck with this perennial as a companion to *Rosa glauca*.

OTHER VARIETIES AVAILABLE: *C. lactiflora* 'Prichard's Variety'—blue; 36 inches

'Snowhill' Salvia
Salvia nemerosa 'Snowhill'
MATURE PLANT SIZE: 18 inches × 18 inches
GROWTH HABIT: clump
BLOOM COLOR: white
BLOOM SIZE: small; spikes
BLOOM TIME: summer
FRAGRANCE: no
PLANT TYPE: herbaceous perennial
COLD HARDINESS: Zones 4 – 7
HOW TO USE: flower color; front border

'Snowhill' is one of many perennial hybrids created from the species *Salvia nemerosa*. This is a summer bloomer, and its continual bloom is aided by regular deadheading of the spikes of white flowers.

A low growing perennial, 'Snowhill' looks best near the front of the border and in areas with excellent drainage. Plant near the base of hybrid tea roses and this low growing perennial with soft gray-green foliage becomes "living" mulch for the rose.

Hardy in zones 4 to 7, the nemerosa hybrids grow better as perennials in gardens in colder climates. Good drainage is absolutely essential for their survival. Prune to ground level in the spring.

OTHER VARIETIES AVAILABLE: 'Lubeca'—violet; 18 inches; summer; 'Carradonna'—blue-purple; purple stems; 30 inches; early; 'Plumosa'—dusty rose-purple; 18 inches; early; 'Blue Hill'—blue; 24 inches; summer

'Valerie Finnis' Artemisia
Artemisia 'Valerie Finnis'
MATURE PLANT SIZE: 3.5 feet × 3 feet
GROWTH HABIT: spreader
BLOOM COLOR: yellow
BLOOM SIZE: small
BLOOM TIME: summer
FRAGRANCE: foliage
PLANT TYPE: herbaceous perennial
COLD HARDINESS: Zones 4 – 9
HOW TO USE: foliage color and texture; accent plant; mid border

Artemisia 'Valerie Finnis' is a deciduous perennial with strong silver-gray coloring and wide leaves. This artemisia withstands more moisture and heat than other gray varieties. Unlike its species parent *Artemisia ludoviciana*, 'Valerie Finnis' is not invasive and is very well-behaved, especially in colder zones.

Growing to a height of $3^1/_2$ feet, 'Valerie Finnis' proved to be the perfect filler around pink hybrid tea roses I planted at the base of a bluestone wall in a bed facing the ocean in southern Maine. Pruned to the ground each autumn to accommodate the rose cones needed to protect the hybrid teas during winter, 'Valerie Finnis' came back up from the roots, even after the roughest and coldest winters.

OTHER VARIETIES AVAILABLE: 'Silver King'—3 feet; 'Silver Queen'- 30 inches; tiny white flowers

'Annabelle' Hydrangea
Hydrangea arborescens 'Annabelle'

MATURE PLANT SIZE: 5 feet × 6 feet
GROWTH HABIT: clump
BLOOM COLOR: green to white
BLOOM SIZE: 1 foot wide
BLOOM TIME: summer
FRAGRANCE: no
PLANT TYPE: deciduous/herbaceous shrub
COLD HARDINESS: Zones 3 to 9
HOW TO USE: flower color and texture; mid to rear border; accent plant

Boxwood
Buxus spp.

MATURE PLANT SIZE: 4 inches to 15 feet
GROWTH HABIT: bushy; upright shrub
BLOOM COLOR: white
BLOOM SIZE: tiny
BLOOM TIME: early
FRAGRANCE: flowers
PLANT TYPE: evergreen shrub
COLD HARDINESS: Zones 4 – 10
HOW TO USE: foliage; accent; edging; hedge; architectural; winter accent; all areas of the border

This deciduous shrub produces large snowball flowers each summer on new growth. The blooms start out as greenish-white domes with a distinct puckered texture. By summer they turn to pure white balls measuring up to a foot wide, and then fade to a pale lime-green before turning brown.

'Annabelle' is a "smooth hydrangea", so named because the pubescent leaves are soft and smooth. A mature plant grows to 5 feet high by 6 feet wide. Hardy from zones 3 to 9, this hydrangea makes an impressive summer display, especially when grouped with large shrub roses or climbers. Of the summer blooming hydrangeas, 'Annabelle' and other arborescens cultivars are good choices for areas where there are damaging winter and early spring winds. Prune 'Annabelle' anywhere from ground level to 12 inches high either at the end of the season or in late winter.

OTHER VARIETIES AVAILABLE: 'Hayes Starburst'—double white; 6 feet; 'White Dome'—white lacecap; 4 feet; 'Samantha'—white; foliage has silver underside; 5 feet

There are many types of boxwood with varying growth habits from tall and columnar growth to short and spreading. There are many variations in leaf size and color, as well. All boxwoods serve a good architectural purpose in the garden, either as edging, hedges, or strategically placed accent marks. Boxwoods have small leaves, making them ideal as background plants for roses as well as good subjects for sculpting.

I recommend 'Suffruticosa' for elegant-looking hedging or as an edging. 'Graham Blandy', with a columnar habit, is a good choice for adding a green vertical element to the garden. I use this variety along with 'Elegantissima', a variegated shrub variety with a cream and green variegation, to liven up the winter garden.

OTHER VARIETIES AVAILABLE: *Buxus macrophylla* 'Compacta'—dark green; 1 foot; *Buxus sempervirens* 'Suffruticosa'—3 feet; *Buxus sempervirens* 'Elegantissima'—3 feet; variegated; *Buxus sempervirens* 'Graham Blandy'—15 feet × 2 feet

Butterfly Bush
Buddleia davidii
MATURE PLANT SIZE: 15 feet × 10 feet
GROWTH HABIT: arching
BLOOM COLOR: lavender
BLOOM SIZE: small, long panicles
BLOOM TIME: summer
FRAGRANCE: flowers
PLANT TYPE: deciduous shrub
COLD HARDINESS: Zones 5 – 9
HOW TO USE: flower fragrance, color, and texture; foliage texture; accent; mid to rear border

There are many cultivars of *Buddleia davidii* to choose from for use as companions for roses. All bring interesting flowers, foliage, fragrance, and butterflies to the garden.

Hardy from zones 5 to 9, buddleias are pruned in the spring to fit the design of your garden. If you have a small space, there are plenty of compact hybrids to choose from. If you are creating a large sweeping border, then there are large shrubs to choose from as well.

OTHER VARIETIES AVAILABLE: 'Pink Delight'—pink; 8 feet; 'White Profusion'—white; 8 feet; 'Nanho Blue'—blue; 5 feet; 'Peacock'—pink; 5 feet; 'Honeycomb'—yellow; 10 feet

Chaste Tree
Vitex agnus-castus
MATURE PLANT SIZE: 20 feet × 20 feet
GROWTH HABIT: clump
BLOOM COLOR: blue
BLOOM SIZE: small; panicles
BLOOM TIME: summer
FRAGRANCE: flowers, foliage
PLANT TYPE: shrub/tree
COLD HARDINESS: Zones 6 – 9
HOW TO USE: flower color and texture; foliage texture; seed heads; accent; rear border

Chaste tree can become more tree-like in warmer zones, but in my garden I prune it to maintain a flowering shrub form. Reaching a maximum height of 8 feet and a width of 4, this is a good companion for larger shrub roses and climbers.

I maintain this shape by pruning each spring to about 3 feet to keep it in scale with the rest of the bed. I've recently added a yellow climbing rose, 'Casino', to train through the older stems of the shrub.

OTHER VARIETIES AVAILABLE: 'Abbeville Blue'—violet-blue; 8 feet; 'Alba'—white; 8 feet; 'Shoal Creek'—blue-violet; 8 feet; *Vitex rotundifolia*—blue; silver leaves; 2 feet—good as a groundcover

'China Girl' Holly
Ilex × *messerve* 'China Girl'

MATURE PLANT SIZE: 10 feet × 10 feet
GROWTH HABIT: clump
BLOOM COLOR: white
BLOOM SIZE: small
BLOOM TIME: spring
FRAGRANCE: no
PLANT TYPE: evergreen shrub
COLD HARDINESS: Zones 6- 8
HOW TO USE: hedge; foliage; fruit; winter accent

The Messerve hybrids are a group of large-leaved hollies with a dark greenish-blue leaf, a noticeable purple stem, and a good berry display. The Messerve hybrids tolerate regular shearing and also have attractive natural shapes, some growing as high as 15 feet. As with all hollies, you need male and female plants in close proximity in order for the female to produce a good berry display. One male can take care of several females.

OTHER VARIETIES AVAILABLE: 'Dragon Lady'—20 feet × 6 feet; bronzy-green; zone 5 – 8; 'China Boy'—10 feet × 8 feet; green; 'Golden Girl'—yellow fruits; 'Blue Girl'— 10 feet × 8 feet

Chinese Fringe Flower
Loropetalum chinense var. *rubrum*

MATURE PLANT SIZE: 10 feet × 5 feet
GROWTH HABIT: arching
BLOOM COLOR: fuchsia
BLOOM SIZE: small
BLOOM TIME: early
FRAGRANCE: flower
PLANT TYPE: evergreen/deciduous shrub
COLD HARDINESS: Zones 7 – 9
HOW TO USE: foliage color; flower color and fragrance; accent; mid-border

The maroon-burgundy foliage won me over when I first saw the 'Zhuzhou Fuchsia' variety of the Chinese fringe flower at a local nursery. More intense in the younger foliage, the rich burgundy stays with this shrub year-round if the winters aren't too cold.

Hardy to zone 7 with protection, this is a good "ever-burgundy" shrub to have in a border. The color ties in nicely with the color of the new growth of tea, China, bourbon, and modern shrub roses as well. 'Zhuzhou Fuchsia' has a graceful habit that doesn't seem to need any pruning to improve it.

Forsythia
Forsythia spp.
MATURE PLANT SIZE: 10 feet × 12 feet
GROWTH HABIT: arching
BLOOM COLOR: yellow
BLOOM SIZE: small
BLOOM TIME: early spring
FRAGRANCE: flower
PLANT TYPE: deciduous shrub
COLD HARDINESS: Zones 5-8
HOW TO USE: edging; hedge; flower color

Forsythia is the flower that means spring to so many of us. For rosarians in the northeast, this is the plant that signals the beginning of rose-pruning season.

In the garden, forsythia requires proper pruning to look like a garden plant. Too many people shear it into balls and tight hedges, usually just after all the fresh new growth has established itself. This results in a very strange flowering pattern the next season. Instead of shearing, forsythia should be thinned of older wood, accenting its arching habit.

Hardy to zone 5, and tolerant of the heat of zone 8, forsythias can be damaged by late winter or early spring freezes. Dramatic early spring displays can be created as a backdrop to a rose garden. The weeping variety, *Forsythia suspensa*, is good for planting to spill down a wall or an embankment. My way of using forsythia with roses is to create a living edge with the branches as described in the section on edging.

OTHER VARIETIES AVAILABLE: *Forsythia suspensa*—
10 feet; yellow; long trailing branches

Night Blooming Jasmine
Cestrum nocturnum
MATURE PLANT SIZE: 6 feet × 6 feet
GROWTH HABIT: arching
BLOOM COLOR: white; chartreuse
BLOOM SIZE: 2 inches tubular
BLOOM TIME: mid-summer to frost
FRAGRANCE: flowers, in the evening
PLANT TYPE: tropical shrub
COLD HARDINESS: Zones 9 – 11
HOW TO USE: evening flower fragrance; texture

Night-blooming jasmine, *Cestrum nocturnum*, is not a true jasmine but a tropical shrub grown for its evening fragrance. Cestrum grows quickly from a small plant to about 3 feet high by 3 feet wide when kept in a 12-inch pot. Regular watering and plenty of sunshine guarantee blooms from mid-summer until frost.

A hardy garden plant in zone 9 and warmer, this is popular as a potted plant in colder climates. When there's a danger of a freeze, I bring my plants indoors and keep them in a cool and well-lit porch, growing them as houseplants. I've also stored them dormant in the basement by withholding water till spring.

OTHER VARIETIES AVAILABLE: *Brugmansia* —many wonderful colors on a tall shrub; fluted flowers; good for containers in northern gardens; *Daphne* × *transatlantica* 'Jim's Pride'—white; everblooming; 4 feet × 5 feet; zones 5- 8

Princess Flower
Tibouchina urvilleana
MATURE PLANT SIZE: 5 feet × 4 feet
GROWTH HABIT: clump
BLOOM COLOR: violet-blue
BLOOM SIZE: 2 inches
BLOOM TIME: summer
FRAGRANCE: no
PLANT TYPE: shrub
COLD HARDINESS: Zones 8 – 11
HOW TO USE: flower color; foliage texture; accent; mid to rear border

There are two forms of tibouchina currently offered for gardeners in my region, both annuals. *Tibouchina grandiflora* has large leaves, producing 18-inch panicles of small purple flowers from late in the summer until frost. *Tibouchina urvilleana* looks very similar in habit, except that the leaves are smaller and the purple flowers are borne singly through the entire summer. The foliage has a distinct orange rim, and as the leaves age, they attain more of a bronze-green color.

Down south, the princess flower has been a more familiar sight in gardens. It's grown as an herbaceous perennial in the Gulf region, while in the warmest climates, it's a shrub. In one garden I know of south of New Orleans, the princess flower towers over a large shrub of 'Mrs. B.R. Cant', a dusky pink tea rose.

OTHER VARIETIES AVAILABLE: *Tibouchina grandiflora*— violet-purple; panicles of blooms; 8 feet

Privet
Ligustrum obtusifolium
MATURE PLANT SIZE: 12 feet × 15 feet
GROWTH HABIT: clump
BLOOM COLOR: white
BLOOM SIZE: small
BLOOM TIME: early summer
FRAGRANCE: flower
PLANT TYPE: deciduous shrub
COLD HARDINESS: Zones 4 – 7
HOW TO USE: hedge

Considered extremely ordinary, this deciduous shrub is used as a boundary marker on every property where I work. Privet is often trained into arches, marking the entrance to a garden and offering climbing roses shelter from the wind. In some cases, the hedges are nearly twelve feet high, often growing this tall very close to the ocean. Tolerant of salt and wind, this is an ideal hedging plant for zones 4 to 7, except that it is an invasive exotic in zones 6 and 7, escaping into the wild and crowding out valuable native plants.

The leaves are dark green, small, and dense, making it an ideal shrub for a background hedge, a bed divider, and for topiary. Privet responds very well to regular shearing; indeed, it must be clipped several times a season to keep its shape. It can be maintained at different heights depending on your needs and your willingness to spend lots of time with the hedge-clippers. Its flowers have an odor most people find unpleasant.

OTHER VARIETIES AVAILABLE: *Ligustrum* × *vicaryi*—'Golden Privet'; zone 4 – 9; *Ligustrum japonicum*—'Japanese Privet'; evergreen; zone 7 – 10

Sweet Box
Sarcococca hookeriana var. *humilis*
MATURE PLANT SIZE: 1 foot × 2 feet
GROWTH HABIT: clump
BLOOM COLOR: white
BLOOM SIZE: small
BLOOM TIME: early
FRAGRANCE: strong and sweet
PLANT TYPE: evergreen shrub
COLD HARDINESS: Zones 5 – 8
HOW TO USE: flower fragrance; foliage; texture; edging; winter accent

---

Sweet box, *Sarcococca hookeriana* var. *humilis*, is a low-growing evergreen shrub ideal for shade and part-shade conditions. Once it's established, sweet box spreads slowly by stolons (underground stems) filling in nicely around taller shrubs or along a garden edge. The glossy foliage is dark green and very attractive. An added bonus is the sweet early spring fragrance from the tiny white flowers hidden behind the foliage.

Growing only to about 12 inches in height, and spreading at least that wide, sweet box is hardy from zones 5 to 8. In warmer climates it would do better with more shade than sun.

This is an excellent choice for edging a bed, especially with a bed of perennials and roses that may arch out over the edge and create some shade.

OTHER VARIETIES AVAILABLE: *Euonymous japonicus* 'Silver Princess'—dark green foliage, white edge; 3 feet × 2 feet; zone 6—9; *Gardenia jasminoides;* 'Radicans'—double white; 3 feet × 4 feet; used by Florida rosarians; zone 8 – 10; *Leucothoe fontanesiana* 'Scarletta'—white; foliage scarlet/green/burgundy; 2 feet; zone 5 – 8; *Rhaphiolepis umbellata* 'Georgia Petite'—light pink; 2.5 feet × 3 feet; zone 7b – 10

Bush Clover
Lespedeza thunbergii 'Gibraltar'

MATURE PLANT SIZE: 6 feet × 6 feet
GROWTH HABIT: arching
BLOOM COLOR: pink, white; purple; purple/white
BLOOM SIZE: small
BLOOM TIME: late
FRAGRANCE: no
PLANT TYPE: deciduous/herbaceous shrub
COLD HARDINESS: Zones 5 – 8
HOW TO USE: flower color and texture; foliage texture; accent; mid border

Named for the Spanish governor of Florida who financed some of André Michaux' nineteenth century plant explorations, *Lespedeza thunbergii* is a deciduous shrub also known as bush clover, introduced into our gardens in 1837.

'Gibraltar' is a hybrid that begins to bloom in late summer displaying crimson-purple flowers. Growing to over 6 feet high and wide, this is an airy-looking shrub with wiry stems and very fine foliage. The habit is arching, making it an ideal candidate for the middle of the border or for spilling over an embankment. Hardy from zones 5 to 8, in zones 7 and colder 'Gibraltar' dies to the ground each winter. Since it blooms on new growth, that's okay. If the plant doesn't die back, then it should be pruned hard in the spring.

OTHER VARIETIES AVAILABLE: 'Avalanche'—white; 5 feet; 'Edo-Shibori'—purple/white; 5 feet; 'Spring Grove'—purple; 5 feet; 'Pink Fountain'—pink; 5 feet

Camellia
Camellia oleifera hybrids

MATURE PLANT SIZE: 5 – 7 feet × 5' – 7 feet
GROWTH HABIT: clump
BLOOM COLOR: white, pink, striped, red
BLOOM SIZE: 3.5 inches
BLOOM TIME: spring; fall
FRAGRANCE: no
PLANT TYPE: evergreen shrub
COLD HARDINESS: Zones 6 – 9
HOW TO USE: flower color; foliage accent; architecture; winter accent; mid to rear border

My focus here is on the newer cold-hardy camellias, cultivars created from crossing *Camellia oleifera*, the tea-oil camellia, with other camellia species. Known as the Ackerman hybrids, these have bloomed and proven hardy in my zone 7 gardens for several years.

Slow-growing, averaging 5 to 6 feet in height, there are autumn- and spring-blooming varieties to choose from. Beautiful glossy foliage covers these shrubs year round. Late-fall-bloomers risk losing their flowers to an early freeze, and white flowers usually become messy after a frost. These camellias should be planted in spring.

Camellias are useful as evergreen anchors in the garden, extending the season of bloom and providing green for the winter.

OTHER VARIETIES AVAILABLE: *Camellia oleifera* 'Lu Shan Snow'—white; 6 feet; fall; *Camellia* × 'April Blush'—pink; 5 feet; spring; *Camellia* × 'Winter's Star'—reddish-purple; 7 feet; fall; *Camellia* × 'Blood of China'—salmon-red; spring

Fragrant Wintersweet
Chimonanthus praecox 'Luteus'

MATURE PLANT SIZE: 15 feet × 12 feet
GROWTH HABIT: arching
BLOOM COLOR: pale yellow
BLOOM SIZE: 1 inch
BLOOM TIME: winter
FRAGRANCE: flower
PLANT TYPE: deciduous shrub
COLD HARDINESS: Zones 6 – 9
HOW TO USE: flower fragrance; winter architecture

Fragrant wintersweet, *Chimonanthus praecox* 'Luteus', is a winter-flowering deciduous shrub with intensely scented flowers. The spicy-sweet fragrance is produced from small, transparent, cupped flowers borne close to the arching stems.

Hardy from zones 7 to 9 (6 with protection), wintersweet begins blooming in December in milder climates and as late as February in zone 7. It may take a while for enough wood to develop to start producing flowers, but it's worth the wait.

'Luteus' produces many light yellow flowers along arching stems reaching 8 feet high by 6 feet wide. A sudden hard freeze while the flowers are in bloom will end the blooming cycle.

'Goshiki' Holly Osmanthus
Osmanthus heterophyllus 'Goshiki'

MATURE PLANT SIZE: 4 feet × 5 feet
GROWTH HABIT: clump
BLOOM COLOR: white
BLOOM SIZE: small
BLOOM TIME: autumn
FRAGRANCE: flower
PLANT TYPE: evergreen shrub
COLD HARDINESS: Zones 7 – 9
HOW TO USE: foliage; accent; flower fragrance; winter accent; mid-border

The name 'Goshiki' means "five colors" in Japanese, and that's a pretty accurate description of the foliage of this evergreen shrub. The spiny leaves range in color from cream, pink, and white, to various shades of green

Hardy from zone 7 to 9, possibly in 6 with protection, this shrub attains a height of 4 feet and a width of 5 feet. I have mine towards the front of the border as a colorful evergreen "dot". Every autumn I'm on my hands and knees sniffing and searching for blooms.

OTHER VARIETIES AVAILABLE: 'Gulftide'—10 feet; glossy green; 'Variegata'—5 feet; green edged in cream

'Limelight' Hydrangea
Hydrangea paniculata 'Limelight'
MATURE PLANT SIZE: 6 feet × 8 feet
GROWTH HABIT: clump
BLOOM COLOR: white/green/pink
BLOOM SIZE: 6 to 12 inches
BLOOM TIME: summer
FRAGRANCE: no
PLANT TYPE: deciduous shrub
COLD HARDINESS: Zones 4 to 7
HOW TO USE: flower color; accent plant

'Nigra' Hydrangea
Hydrangea macrophylla 'Nigra'
MATURE PLANT SIZE: 6 feet × 6 feet
GROWTH HABIT: clump
BLOOM COLOR: pink/blue
BLOOM SIZE: 6 inches
BLOOM TIME: summer
FRAGRANCE: no
PLANT TYPE: deciduous shrub
COLD HARDINESS: Zones 6 to 9
HOW TO USE: stem color; flower color; accent plant

Hydrangea paniculata is a late-blooming deciduous shrub, usually coming into its full display by the middle of August and lasting well into autumn with huge pyramidal heads of flowers. 'Limelight' is a new cultivar; a late bloomer producing masses of glowing lime-green flowers that eventually fade to pink.

There are many varieties of *Hydrangea paniculata* available. Two white varieties, 'Tardiva' and 'Grandiflora', are longtime favorites often found in old gardens and cemeteries. All are hardy from zones 3 to zone 8 and adaptable to all weather conditions, especially good for seaside gardens.

'Limelight' and all other cultivars bloom on new growth. Prune these shrubs in late winter as severely as you need to make them fit your design.

OTHER VARIETIES AVAILABLE: 'Pink Diamond'—white, turns pink; 8 feet; 'Tardiva'—white; 10 feet; latest bloomer; 'The Swan'—white, 6 feet; 'Kyushu'—white; 10 feet

'Nigra' is a Japanese mop-head variety, a hortensia type of macrophylla. Introduced to England over a century ago, 'Nigra' has only recently gained notoriety in our country as an interesting garden plant. What sets this hydrangea apart from the others is its shiny ebony stems. Even without blooms, this stem color makes 'Nigra' a worthwhile plant to have in the garden. It grows 6 feet high by 6 feet wide.

Like other macrophylla types, the flower color of 'Nigra' is easily affected by soil acidity. Acid soil turns the flowers blue and neutral to slightly alkaline soils create pink flowers. Hardy from zones 6 to 9, all macrophylla hydrangeas need protection from winter and early spring winds.

OTHER VARIETIES AVAILABLE: 'Blue Wave'—blue lacecap; 6 feet; 'Tokyo Delight'—white lacecap; 4 feet; 'Pia'—pink mophead; 3 feet; 'Sister Therese'—white; 4 feet

Blue Atlas Cedar
Cedrus atlantica 'Glauca'

MATURE PLANT SIZE: 60 feet × 15 feet
GROWTH HABIT: single trunk
PLANT TYPE: evergreen conifer
COLD HARDINESS: Zones 6 – 9
HOW TO USE: foliage color and texture; architectural; support for climbing roses; winter accent

My blue Atlas cedar is the focal point of my front garden. It's not just the tree with its beautiful blue foliage that draws attention, but also the sunset-colored rose that has found its way to nearly the top of this conifer, now close to 20 feet. Every June, people stop to compliment me on my blooming tree, as 'Autumn Sunset' comes into its first flush of bloom displaying the colorful and fragrant blossoms spilling from the wispy blue branches.

This was an accidental pairing, but this tree is the perfect living trellis. The branches are spaced far enough apart so that the rose doesn't bunch together at one level. This irregular arrangement of branches gives this tree character and beauty, as well as a place to launch a rose skyward.

Pear and Apple
Pyrus communis/Malus × *domestica*

MATURE PLANT SIZE: 30 feet × 30 feet
GROWTH HABIT: single trunk
BLOOM COLOR: white, blush, and pink
BLOOM SIZE: 1 inch
BLOOM TIME: spring
FRAGRANCE: flower
PLANT TYPE: deciduous trees
COLD HARDINESS: Zones 5 –8
HOW TO USE: flower color and fragrance; fruit color texture; architectural accents; mid to rear border

I grow two pears, 'Bartlett' and 'Turnbull', an Asiatic pear. I use them espaliered, or trained to the wall, as architecture for the walled garden or background to a garden bed

To save space and add a pattern to the garden, I often use espaliered apples in two ways: as a Belgian fence, trained in diamond patterns against a wall or free standing, and as single cordons, or single trunks. I plan on using the cordons as living pillars for old garden roses.

Tea Olive
Osmanthus fragrans

MATURE PLANT SIZE: 25 feet × 25 feet
GROWTH HABIT: clump
BLOOM COLOR: white
BLOOM SIZE: small
BLOOM TIME: early spring and autumn
FRAGRANCE: flower
PLANT TYPE: evergreen shrub/tree
COLD HARDINESS: Zones 7-10
HOW TO USE: evening fragrance; foliage; architecture; winter accent; rear border

Osmanthus fragrans, also known as tea olive and sweet olive, is a traditional evergreen plant of old Southern gardens. A strong and sweet fragrance permeates the evening air as this shrub comes into bloom from autumn to spring.

Hardy in zones 8 to 10, marginally hardy in 7, this is a slow-growing shrub, reaching to at least 25 feet in height. I've seen it growing in courtyard gardens down south, tightly pruned to stay in scale with the space.

OTHER VARIETIES AVAILABLE: *Osmanthus × fortunei*—white; autumn bloom; 15—20 feet × 20 feet

Weeping European Larch
Larix decidua 'Pendula'

MATURE PLANT SIZE: 5 feet × 7 feet
GROWTH HABIT: weeping
PLANT TYPE: deciduous conifer
COLD HARDINESS: Zones 4 – 7
HOW TO USE: architectural accent

The weeping European larch, *Larix decidua* 'Pendula', is the focal point of a section of our winter garden behind the house, even though it drops all its needles in the autumn. It's the curve of the trunk and the way the branches hang down to the garden that make this plant interesting and worth including among my roses.

There's a single trunk curving up to a peak of 5 feet, then curving down to ground level. During the spring, small green buttons appear as the new needles begin to grow. In summer and autumn the tree is coated with soft, glaucous-green needles that eventually turn a soft autumnal gold. Petting is allowed.

'Blue Ice' Arizona Cypress
Cupressus arizonica 'Blue Ice'
MATURE PLANT SIZE: 35 feet × 8 feet
GROWTH HABIT: single trunk
PLANT TYPE: evergreen tree
COLD HARDINESS: Zones 7 – 9
HOW TO USE: foliage color and texture; support rambling roses; winter accent

---

This blue cypress is a cultivar of our native Arizona cypress, introduced from New Zealand in the 1960s. Also known as the blue ice cypress, this tree has a somewhat columnar shape, growing much taller than wide. The airiness and the icy blue foliage attracted my attention when I first saw it growing in the Brooklyn Botanic Garden. I planted mine near the corner of my house, where it gets full sun all day in the summer, while during the winter, as the sun is lower in the sky, it receives early morning sun and late afternoon sun.

Not as large as the native species, it should reach about 10 feet tall in New Jersey according to the nursery professionals in my area. Six years after planting, my specimen is approximately 15 feet high and 5 feet wide, and still growing. Drought tolerant, which is good, because mine is growing in very sandy soil, this tree also has the added feature of a rich, mahogany-colored bark. Its hardiness range is from zones 7 to 9.

I use this tree as a living trellis. I've allowed 'Excelsa', an old red rambling rose, to grow up and into the branches of this tree producing an amazing show of color each July.

'Natchez' Crape Myrtle
Lagerstroemia indica 'Natchez'
MATURE PLANT SIZE: 20 feet × 12 feet
GROWTH HABIT: single trunk; clump
BLOOM COLOR: white
BLOOM SIZE: 2 inches
BLOOM TIME: summer
FRAGRANCE: no
PLANT TYPE: deciduous tree/shrub
COLD HARDINESS: Zones 6 – 9
HOW TO USE: flower color, late season; bark texture and color; seed pods for winter; architectural; mid to rear border

---

Crape myrtles are late-season flowering trees, tolerant of heat. Some of the varieties show a strong bark color and texture. One of the best for this purpose is 'Natchez', a tall-growing white cultivar with a strong cinnamon color to its bark.

My 'Natchez' creates a mound of white in the latter part of the summer, with the display lasts well into the autumn. After the flowers fade, a display of hard fruit remains through most of the winter.

Crape myrtles are becoming more popular in zone 6 and the colder regions of zone 7. Until recently they were considered only for southern landscapes. Today, more cultivars are being used in the north, extending the gardening season into winter. There are also dwarf habit cultivars good for small gardens. The colors range from pure white to hot fuchsia.

OTHER VARIETIES AVAILABLE: 'Chickasaw'—pink-lavender; 4 feet; 'Tonto'—fuchsia; 10 feet; 'Victor'—crimson; 5 feet; 'Sarah's Favorite'—white; 20 feet

Anemone Clematis
Clematis montana
MATURE PLANT SIZE: 25 feet
GROWTH HABIT: climber
BLOOM COLOR: white
BLOOM SIZE: 2 inches
BLOOM TIME: early summer
FRAGRANCE: no
PLANT TYPE: deciduous vine
COLD HARDINESS: Zones 7 – 9
HOW TO USE: wall cover; flower color

This is one of the early blooming species of the clematis group. Early blooming and aggressive, these are a natural for covering walls and lattice panels. Prune this species and its varieties after blooming. This makes them ideal companions with once-blooming ramblers and shrub roses. Annual pruning is not necessary, prune only when the vine is out of control.

OTHER VARIETIES AVAILABLE: 'Rubens'—pink; 7 – 9; 'Odorata'—pale pink, fragrant; *Clematis spoonerii*— white; 7 – 9; Tetra Rose—mauve-pink; fragrant; bronze leaves

Chocolate Vine
Akebia quinata
MATURE PLANT SIZE: 40 feet
GROWTH HABIT: twining
BLOOM COLOR: white; chocolate
BLOOM SIZE: small
BLOOM TIME: early spring
FRAGRANCE: flower
PLANT TYPE: evergreen/deciduous vine
COLD HARDINESS: 5 – 8
HOW TO USE: foliage texture; cover structures; flower fragrance

Akebia quinata, also known as the chocolate vine, is a vigorous twining vine that may or may not be deciduous, depending on its exposure to the elements. Its Latin name refers to the clusters of five leaflets produced along the vine.

Akebia is a fast-growing vine, which once established can reach up to 40 feet. The twining stems need some sort of support, which can be as thin as a fishing line or as thick as a pergola or arbor. The growth can be controlled by pruning as severely as you need, after blooming in spring. Hardy from zones 5 to 8, this vine blooms as the new leaves emerge in spring. The small clusters of chocolate-purple grape-like clusters are fragrant. The new foliage has a purple tinge and eventually attains a bluish-green cast.

This vine creates a soft green backdrop for climbing roses and helps to soften surfaces in the garden.

Climbing Hydrangea
Hydrangea anomala petiolaris

MATURE PLANT SIZE: 80 feet
GROWTH HABIT: clinging
BLOOM COLOR: white
BLOOM SIZE: 10 inches
BLOOM TIME: summer
FRAGRANCE: flower
PLANT TYPE: deciduous vine
COLD HARDINESS: Zones 4 – 8
HOW TO USE: wall cover; texture; support for climbing roses

There are two plants with the common name climbing hydrangea. One is a native to the southeast, *Deucumaria barbara*, also known as wood vamp. I haven't grown this, but it does sound interesting. The other, with which I am very familiar, is *Hydrangea anomala petiolaris*, known simply as climbing hydrangea and best in zones 4 through 7. In warmer climates, it would be advisable to provide more shade.

Climbing hydrangea is a woody vine that attaches itself to structures by way of root-like holdfasts. It creates several layers thick of leafy branches. Roses can be tied to and trained through the loosely arranged branches, giving the rose a place to call home.

Blooming from June through July, the lacy, flat-topped white flowers may go unnoticed. They have a sweet fragrance.

Japanese Hydrangea Vine
Schizophragma hydrangeoides 'Moonlight'

MATURE PLANT SIZE: 60 feet
GROWTH HABIT: clinging
BLOOM COLOR: white
BLOOM SIZE: 10 inches
BLOOM TIME: summer
FRAGRANCE: no
PLANT TYPE: deciduous vine
COLD HARDINESS: Zones 6 – 9
HOW TO USE: wall cover; texture; support for climbing roses

Japanese hydrangea vine, *Schizophragma hydrangeoides*, is very similar in appearance and habit to the climbing hydrangea. This is a clinging deciduous vine that remains close to the surface of the structure. Less vigorous than the climbing hydrangea, this woody vine blooms in July and can reach heights of 40 to 60 feet.

'Moonlight' is a popular cultivar with serrated heart-shaped leaves. The blue-green color is lightly frosted with silver and produces lacy, flat-topped flowers in late June. There is a new hybrid called 'Roseum' recently introduced to our gardens. The flowers are flushed with pink and the foliage is dark green.

Moonflower Vine
Ipomea alba
MATURE PLANT SIZE: 12 feet
GROWTH HABIT: twining
BLOOM COLOR: white
BLOOM SIZE: 4 inches
BLOOM TIME: late summer
FRAGRANCE: flower
PLANT TYPE: annual vine
HOW TO USE: flower fragrance, evening; fruit texture

Sweet Autumn Clematis
Clematis ternifolia
MATURE PLANT SIZE: 30 feet
GROWTH HABIT: climber
BLOOM COLOR: white
BLOOM SIZE: 1 inch
BLOOM TIME: late summer
FRAGRANCE: flowers
PLANT TYPE: herbaceous vine
COLD HARDINESS: Zones 5 – 9
HOW TO USE: flower fragrance and color

Moonflower, *Ipomea alba*, is an annual vine closely related to morning glory and sweet potato vine. Quickly growing to 10 or 12 feet, this tender vine produces huge, white, very fragrant blooms that only open in the evening. The flowers start to appear later in the summer, after the vine has sent out a substantial amount of growth, twining around any structure or plant in its way. Just before opening, the flower is tightly wrapped in a spiral, turban-like bud.

You will smell the blooms before you see them; the fragrance is intoxicating. By morning, the flowers close up and take a rest. Interesting seedpods form by the end of autumn. The seeds can be saved indoors, or in some gardens they may self-sow. To grow this vine from seed, nick the hard seed case and soak the seeds overnight before planting.

OTHER VARIETIES AVAILABLE: 'Chiaki'– morning glory; blue outer rim, pink throat; 15 feet; 'Chocolate'— morning glory; creamy chocolate color; variegated; 10 feet; 'Heavenly Blue'—morning glory; sky blue; 20 feet; 'Cypress Vine'—tubular red flowers; feathery foliage; 12 feet

A garden thug in some regions, sweet autumn clematis fills the air with fragrance from late August through the month of September. I never planted this in my garden; it just appeared. I keep a good eye out for unwanted growth and prune and pull all summer long. I've left it on my once-blooming 'Fairmount Pink Rambler', the rambler growing up my garage roof. This rose is always naked by summer's end, so why not let someone else have the glory?

'Bee's Jubilee' Clematis
Clematis × 'Bee's Jubilee'

MATURE PLANT SIZE: 8 feet
GROWTH HABIT: climber
BLOOM COLOR: mauve-pink
BLOOM SIZE: 8 inches
BLOOM TIME: summer
FRAGRANCE: no
PLANT TYPE: deciduous vine
COLD HARDINESS: Zones 4 – 9
HOW TO USE: flower color; wall cover

'Bee's Jubilee' belongs to the group of clematis that blooms in the early summer with the capability to bloom again later in the season. After the danger of a freeze has passed, prune to a swelling leaf bud, about one quarter to halfway down the stem. To encourage more blooms later in the season, cut back the faded blooms and their stems to the next leaf bud. If at anytime there is too much clematis, just prune it. Grow this with once-blooming and everblooming roses.

OTHER VARIETIES AVAILABLE: 'Henryii'—white; 'Dr. Ruppel'—rosy-pink; 'Elsa Spath'—blue; 'Niobe'—red

Gloriosa Lily
Gloriosa superba 'Rothschildiana'

MATURE PLANT SIZE: 6 feet
GROWTH HABIT: climbing
BLOOM COLOR: scarlet/yellow
BLOOM SIZE: 4 inches
BLOOM TIME: summer to autumn
FRAGRANCE: no
PLANT TYPE: vine
COLD HARDINESS: Zones 8-10
HOW TO USE: flower color and texture

In Lakeland, Florida, the gloriosa lily is a popular vine with climbing roses, adding color to structures during the summer months until late autumn. An herbaceous perennial vine, the gloriosa lily dies to the ground each winter then starts again from underground tubers. This cycle of growth works well with the pruning needs of climbing roses.

I'm told that with winter mulching, this vine will grow in zone 7. It needs to grow on a support such as a pillar or arbor, and I'm planning to try it with some of my pillar roses. The gloriosa lily doesn't create a dense foliar texture, so it could easily be trained with climbers on pillars and arbors without looking weedy and cluttered.

A strong warning from my southern friends is to wash your hands after handling the tuber of this climber, since it's highly poisonous if ingested.

OTHER VARIETIES AVAILABLE: 'Citrina' (*lutea*)—orange-yellow; *Gloriosa superba*—orange/yellow

Italian Clematis
Clematis viticella

MATURE PLANT SIZE: 16 feet
GROWTH HABIT: climber
BLOOM COLOR: blue-violet
BLOOM SIZE: 2 inches
BLOOM TIME: summer
FRAGRANCE: no
PLANT TYPE: herbaceous vine
COLD HARDINESS: Zones 3 – 9
HOW TO USE: flower color, texture

The viticella clematis belong to the group of late-season clematis. The time to prune is in early spring, at the same time you prune shrub roses. For this reason, I recommend growing these with shrub roses, old and new, as well as with climbing roses. Prune very hard each spring, Simply cut back last year's wood as far as you need, to a visible swelling bud.

OTHER VARIETIES AVAILABLE: 'Abundance'—wine red, nearly flat; 'Betty Corning'—pale pink-mauve; slight fragrance; 'Madame Julia Correvon'— claret-red; 'Polish Spirit'—dark purple; wide open

'Mrs. Robert Brydon' Bush Clematis
Clematis heracleifolia
'Mrs. Robert Brydon'

MATURE PLANT SIZE: 8 feet
GROWTH HABIT: spreading
BLOOM COLOR: blue/white
BLOOM SIZE: 1 inch
BLOOM TIME: late summer
FRAGRANCE: flowers
PLANT TYPE: herbaceous shrub
COLD HARDINESS: Zones 4 – 9
HOW TO USE: flower color and texture; mid border

One of the groups of shrub-like clematis includes the hybrids of the species *Clematis heracleifolia*, also known as the tube clematis. The species has small tubular flowers, a trait passed on to the hybrids. There are a handful of *heracleifolia* hybrids available, all good for spilling around roses, especially the once-blooming types. They provide color when the gallicas and other European old garden roses are not blooming. They also work well around modern shrub roses.

OTHER VARIETIES AVAILABLE: *Clematis heracleifolia*—blue; fragrant; *Clematis heracleifolia* 'China Purple'—purple; fragrant; *Clematis recta* —white; fragrant; tall grower; *Clematis recta purpurea*—white; fragrant; purple-bronze foliage; 3 feet

'Ramona' Clematis
Clematis × 'Ramona'

MATURE PLANT SIZE: 10 feet
GROWTH HABIT: climber
BLOOM COLOR: lavender-blue
BLOOM SIZE: 8 inches
BLOOM TIME: summer
FRAGRANCE: no
PLANT TYPE: herbaceous vine
COLD HARDINESS: Zones 4 – 9
HOW TO USE: flower color; texture

'Ramona' is one of the many large-flowered late-blooming clematis. Prune these as hard as you need to in the early spring, cutting back to a noticeable swelling bud. Grow these large-flowered clematis with everblooming shrubs and climbers.

OTHER VARIETIES AVAILABLE: 'Jackmanii'—purple; 'Comtesse de Bouchard'—mauve-pink; 'Hagley Hybrid'—shell pink; 'John Huxtable'—white

Scarlet Clematis
Clematis texensis

MATURE PLANT SIZE: 7 feet
GROWTH HABIT: climber
BLOOM COLOR: scarlet
BLOOM SIZE: 1.5 inches
BLOOM TIME: summer
FRAGRANCE: no
PLANT TYPE: herbaceous vine
COLD HARDINESS: Zones 4 – 9
HOW TO USE: flower color and texture

The 'Scarlet Clematis' is native to Texas and is a late-blooming clematis. Prune this vine and its cultivars as hard as you need to each spring before the vine breaks dormancy. Prune to a noticeable swelling bud. Grow these bell-shaped clematis with everblooming roses.

OTHER VARIETIES AVAILABLE: 'Duchess of Albany'—pink; 'Etoile Rose'—cherry-pink with lighter pink margin; 'Lady Bird Johnson'—dusky-red; 'Pagoda'—white with mauve-pink

PRUNING ROSES

Once-Blooming Roses

Species

- After bloom, remove a few older canes to make room for new growth; do not remove too much or you may lose your hip display.
- In winter, after the hips have rotted or have been eaten by birds, thin out one-third of the oldest wood to give the shrub a clean look.

Gallica

- After bloom, remove old wood to make room for new growth.
- Do not prune too much of 'Complicata' during the season to preserve the hip display.
- During winter, shorten all canes to various lengths to eliminate crossing and rubbing; trim back all side shoots to three or four bud eyes.

Damask

- After bloom, remove old wood to make room for new growth.
- During winter, shorten all canes to various lengths to eliminate crossing and rubbing; trim back all side shoots to three or four bud eyes.

Alba

- After bloom, remove old wood to make room for new growth.
- During winter, shorten all canes to various lengths to eliminate crossing and rubbing; trim back all side shoots to three or four bud eyes.

Centifolia

- After bloom, remove old wood to make room for new growth.
- During winter, shorten all canes to various lengths to eliminate crossing and rubbing; trim back all side shoots to three or four bud eyes.

Moss

- After bloom, remove old wood to make room for new growth.
- Some old blooms may need to be shaken off or trimmed.
- During winter, shorten all canes to various lengths to eliminate crossing and rubbing; trim back all side shoots to three or four bud eyes.

Hybrid China and Hybrid Bourbon

- After bloom, remove old wood to make room for new growth.
- Some old blooms may need to be shaken off or trimmed.
- During winter, shorten all canes to various lengths to eliminate crossing and rubbing; trim back all side shoots to three or four bud eyes.
- Re-train to pillars or structures in winter.

Ramblers

- After bloom, remove old wood (canes that bore blooms) unless the rose is a hip producer. Then save the old blooming wood for a hip display.
- In late winter, remove deadwood and clutter along with faded hips.
- Re-train to structures after pruning or during winter

Ever-Blooming Roses

Rugosa

- *Rosa rugosa* and hybrids can be pruned at any time.
- *Rosa rugosa* can be pruned to the ground annually, either at the end of autumn or after the first flush of bloom.
- *Rosa rugosa* hybrids should be thinned of older wood at any time of the year, to make room for new growth; remove old wood and crossing branches; trim to desired height in spring.
- If you are growing these roses for hips, do not prune after blooming; instead thin out during winter after the hips have rotted or fallen.

Rosa moschata

- Prune *Rosa moschata* and its varieties in late winter or spring, after danger of frost has passed.
- Remove crossing branches and some old wood to create room for growth.
- Trim to desired height.

China

- Between peaks of bloom, thin out old and dead wood to keep a nice shape.
- Trim to keep rose in scale with garden.
- In cold climates, wait until danger of frost has passed, then remove dead wood.

Tea

- Between peaks of bloom, thin out old wood and dead wood.
- Trim to keep rose in scale with garden.

- In cold climates, wait until danger of frost has passed, then remove dead wood.

Noisette

- Between peaks of bloom, thin out old and dead wood to keep a nice shape.
- Trim to keep rose in scale with garden.
- In cold climates, wait until danger of frost has passed, then remove dead wood.

Bourbon

- At the end of winter or when dormant, prune to shape, removing twiggy growth, crossing branches, and dead wood.
- Remove old wood during the season to make room for new growth.
- Knock off faded blooms during season
- Shorten blooming shoots to strong bud eyes during the season

Portland

- In early spring, shorten all twiggy growth; remove clutter and dead wood.
- Deadhead during the season to promote re-bloom by shortening blooming shoots to strong bud eyes.

Moss

- After bloom, remove old wood to make room for new growth.
- Some old blooms may need to be shaken off or trimmed.
- Shorten blooming stems to strong bud eyes
- During winter, shorten all canes to various lengths to eliminate crossing and rubbing; trim back all side shoots to three or four bud eyes.

Hybrid Perpetual

- In early spring, shorten all lateral growths to three or four bud eyes, trim a few inches off all long canes, remove dead wood and twiggy growth, and remove clutter.
- During the growing season, deadhead faded blooms, remove old growth to make room for new, and trim to fit design.
- During the season, shorten all blooming shoots to two or three bud eyes

Hybrid Tea

- At the end of winter, remove dead wood, one-third of old wood, and shorten remaining canes by half.
- During the growing season, deadhead faded blooms and remove old wood to make room for new growth.
- When deadheading, make your pruning cut above a leaf with five leaflets

Floribunda

- At the end of the dormancy period, remove winter damage, remove one-third of old wood, and shorten remaining canes to random lengths.
- During the growing season, deadhead faded blooms and remove old wood to make room for new growth.

Grandiflora

- At the end of the dormancy period, remove winter damage, remove one third of old wood, and shorten remaining canes to random lengths.

- During the season, deadhead faded blooms and remove old wood to make room for new growth.

Shrub

- At the end of the dormancy period, remove winter damage, remove one third of old wood, and shorten remaining canes to random lengths.
- During the season, deadhead faded blooms and remove old wood to make room for new growth.

Miniature and Polyantha

- At the end of the dormancy period, remove winter damage, remove one third of old wood, and shorten remaining canes by half.
- During the season, deadhead faded blooms and remove old wood to make room for new growth.

Large-Flowered Climber

- During dormant period, shorten all branches that are shorter than arm's length to three or four bud eyes, trim tips of all long branches, remove clutter and dead wood, and remove one-third of old wood to make room for new growth.
- During growing season, deadhead faded blooms and shorten all canes in the same manner as spring pruning, remove old wood to make room for new growth, and remove clutter.

BIBLIOGRAPHY

Ackerman, William L. *Growing Camellias in Cold Climates*. Noble House, 2002

Armitage, Allan M. *Herbaceous Perennial Plants*. Stipes Publishing. 1997. 2nd ed.

Armitage, Allan M. *Armitage's Manual of Annuals, Biennials, and Half-Hardy Perennials*. Timber Press. 2001

Batdorf, Lynn R. *Boxwood Handbook: A Practical Guide to Knowing and Growing Boxwood*. The American Boxwood Society. 1997

Bryan, John. *Bulbs*, Volumes 1 and 2. Timber Press. 1989

Bush-Brown, James and Louise, editors. *America's Garden Book*, 1996 – revised edition edited by Howard Irwin

Dirr, Michael A . *Manual of Woody Landscape Plants*. 1998, 5th ed. Stipes Publishing, Champaign, Illinois

Evison, Raymond J. *Making the Most of Clematis*. Floraprint, 2nd ed. 1992

Gardner, Jo Ann. *Herbs in Bloom*. Timber Press. 1998

Heath, Brent and Becky. *Daffodils for American Gardens*. Elliott & Clark. 1995

Lowery, Gregg. *Vintage Gardens Nursery Catalog, 2003*. 2nd edition.

Ogden, Scott. *Garden Bulbs for the South*. Taylor. 1994

Scanniello, Stephen. *A Year of Roses*. Holt. 1997

Scanniello, Stephen and Tania Bayard. *Climbing Roses*. Prentice Hall. 1994

Seidenberg, Charlotte. *The New Orleans Garden*. University Press of Mississippi. 1993

Toomey, Mary, and Everett Leeds and Charles Chesshire. *An Illustrated Encyclopedia of Clematis*. Timber Press. 2001

Zuk, Judith, editor. *The American Horticultural Society A-Z of Garden Plants*. Dorling Kindersley. 1997

INDEX

PHOTO CREDITS

MEET THE AUTHOR

Stephen Scanniello is a popular author, lecturer, and garden design consultant. He has written three books on roses—*Roses of America, Climbing Roses,* and *A Year of Roses.* The latter received the American Horticultural Society's Annual Book Award in 1998. He has also served as the guest editor for the Brooklyn Botanic Garden Handbook, *Easy Care Roses* and continues to write for major publications, including gardening columns for the *New York Times.* He is known for combining the technical expertise of a knowledgeable rosarian with an approachable style that communicates to even the most novice gardener.

Scanniello is credited with transforming Brooklyn Botanic Garden's Cranford Rose Garden into an internationally acclaimed rose garden. After leaving the Cranford in 1999, Stephen is devoting his full attention to maintaining and designing private gardens for his clients from Maine to Texas. He continues to lecture, write, and serve as a judge for the international rose trials in Europe, Argentina, and the United States.

Stephen is one of the founding members of the Heritage Rose Foundation and is currently serving as President. He is also a member of the American Rose Society, the Manhattan Rose Society, and the Dallas Area Historical Rose Society.

Stephen lives and gardens in Jersey City and Barnegat, New Jersey.